No. 1863
$24.95

TIME GATE:
HURTLING BACKWARD
THROUGH HISTORY

CHARLES R. PELLEGRINO

TAB BOOKS Inc.
Blue Ridge Summit, PA 17214

FIRST EDITION

FIRST PRINTING

Copyright © 1985 by TAB BOOKS Inc.
Printed in the United States of America

Library of Congress Cataloging in Publication Data

Pellegrino, Charles R.
Time gate.

Bibliography: p.
Includes index.
1. Historical geology.   I. Title.
QE28.3.P45   1985   575   84-23955
ISBN 0-8306-1863-5 (pbk.)
ISBN 0-8306-1863-X

The photograph of the Earth used to create the front cover photograph is courtesy of
NASA Aerospace Education Services Project
Lewis Research Center
21000 Brookpark Center
Cleveland, OH 44135

Contents

Earth Abideth Not

A foreword by Isaac Asimov

The pessimistic biblical book of Ecclesiastes finds almost everything to be void and empty of meaning ("vanity," in other words). It says in its opening: ". . . vanity of vanities; all is vanity. What profit hath a man of all his labour which he taketh under the sun? One generation passeth away, and another generation cometh: but the earth abideth for ever."

With all due respect to biblical authority, this is wrong. It might be that everything is pointless and empty of meaning, and that human beings get nothing in return for all the labor involved in living. That is a matter for discussion and opinion. And it is certainly true, and beyond dispute, that one generation passes and another comes.

It is *not* true, however, that the Earth "abideth for ever." The implication is that it is eternal and changeless—the mere scenery props, the backdrop against which the drama of humanity is played—but it isn't.

Even in biblical terms, it isn't. The first book of the Bible, Genesis, describes its creation by God and the last book of the Bible, Revelation, describes its destruction by God. Between these two fanciful descriptions, written by ancients who were, of course, innocent of the findings of modern science, is a time gap of about five thousand years. It is estimated, after all, that the Creation, as described in the Bible, must have taken place about 4000 and 5000 B.C., while the end is visualized in Revelation as coming not long after that book was written—about A.D. 100.

Modern science has a much grander vision, however. Earth formed about 4,600,000,000 years ago through the collision of innumerable pieces of matter, collecting out of a vast cloud of dust and gas that condensed into a central star and innumerable whirling planets and other small bodies on the outskirts. Earth will come to an end, perhaps 6,000,000,000 years from now, in the furnace of the Sun as it expands into a red giant. Earth's entire lifetime will be some ten billion years, or two million times as long as the biblical writers had imagined.

If one limits oneself to the impoverished time scale of the Bible, then the Earth would seem to be changeless. There are earthquakes and volcanic eruptions but these are pinpricks, comparatively. They pass and "the Earth abideth," so that we can use, as a favorite cliche' for great age, "old as the hills." That is not bad, for the hills are far older than the history of civilization.

Yet suppose we don't take the history of civilization as a basis for comparison. Civilization has existed on Earth for a mere fleeting instant, for little more than a millionth of the planet's existence. If the entire existence of the Earth, so far, were squeezed into a year, civilization has only existed during the last half-minute of that year.

Let us imagine ourselves, instead, sweeping our eyes over the history of the Earth, from end to end, in the fashion that we allow our eyes to sweep over the history of civilization. Naturally, we would have to move through time two million times as fast in the first case as in the second.

Speed up time in that fashion and there is nothing changeless about the Earth. It heaves and shifts like a living thing. Continents break up, move about, reunite, break up again. The sea retreats and advances. Islands thrust above the sea and shorelines sink. Vast mountain ranges are heaved up and worn down. Enormous glaciers advance from the poles and retreat again. It is an ever-changing vista full of drama and excitement.

But in that fast-moving perspective, the works of humanity—and humanity itself—are obscured and lost. That is certainly a loss, for it is not hard to argue that what we have done to the Earth (whether for good or for evil) in the brief moment of our existence is perhaps the most amazing thing that has ever been seen on this planet. What's more, it might be something—as far as we have any way of knowing so far—that has never taken place on any other planet in the entire vast universe.

Charles Pellegrino found a solution to this dilemma in which a slow perspective shows us human change against a changeless Earth, while a fast perspective shows us a changing Earth with all human works lost.

Pellegrino moves backward in increasing steps—first one year, then two years, then four—doubling each time. We begin by watching the works of humanity slowly peel away, then more rapidly, and then, faster and faster, the Earth begins to change, and the very stars in the sky begin to drift and then to race.

And at every step, Pellegrino pauses to discuss the nature of the changes and the latest findings with reference to them. In so doing, he gives us a charming overview of human history, of evolutionary development, of biology, of geology, of astronomy, and of everything else he has chosen to touch.

I have myself written well over three hundred books now, on all sorts of subjects, so I have small cause to envy any other writer, but I envy Pellegrino this book. I wish I had written it.

My consolation is the knowledge that, had I written it, I would not have done anywhere near the beautiful job he has done, and that, in any case, reading it has been for me almost as much fun as writing it would have been.

Acknowledgments

Many colleagues gave generously of their time to provide helpful information, criticisms of individual chapters and manuscripts prepared for this book, assistance in the laboratory, identification of specimens, and so forth. I am grateful to Joshua Stoff, of the Cradle of Aviation Museum, New York, for ferreting out many of the little-known historical details appearing in early chapters, especially those relating to rocketry and the German atomic bomb. I found an additional repository of historical trivia in Helen McMahon Douglass, to whom I am also indebted for bringing Tige into the world. Besides being my wife, my number-one field and lab assistant, and one hell of a good editor, Tige is *neat fun*. She has to be. Who else would marry a fellow who loves spiders and old bones and thinks of the dinner table as a dandy place to discuss how things rot?

I thank Bori Olla, of the Sandy Hook Marine Laboratory, for planting the seed that started all my questions about energy conservation in evolution. Stewart Wilk and Mike Fahay, also of Sandy Hook, provided information about bluefin tuna and European eel migrations. I am glad to acknowledge Merv Loper, of Victoria University, New Zealand, for untold hours of conversation, and for putting me on the right track when it came down to developing a practical method for measuring, within square millimeters, the surface areas of such complex shapes as crabs and crystal clusters.

I thank Andy Frost, also of Victoria University, for fascinating discussions about the biology and geology of Antarctica. Dave Lane (Victoria University) got me to ask some good questions about worms. Isaac Asimov was "a natural resource," Bob Craw was an enigma, and Don Peterson was there (with eel patties, of course).

Gerard R. Case taught me almost everything there is to know about field work on fossils. George Skurla, Tom Kelly, Fred Haise, Bob Watkins, Manning Dandridge, Al Munier, Herman Schonenberg (Grumman Aerospace Corporation), and Jesco von Puttkamer (NASA's Washington Headquarters) let me have a peek at the future.

Alan Beu, Grahame Stevens, and Sir Charles Flemming (all of the New Zealand Geological Survey) kept me up to date on Miocine New Zealand. This book has benefited from countless conversations with Frank Andrews (of the New Zealand National Observatory), Edward I. Coher (Southampton Center, Long Island University), and Clair E. Folsome (University of Hawaii), who also offered critical advice on the text. Ellen Druffel (Woods Hole Oceanographic Institution) spotted and corrected errors in my discussion of carbon-14 and the "Little Ice Age."

Niles Eldredge (American Museum of Natural History) advised me on my fossil crab work, which formed the basis for many of the views discussed herein. P. Wygodzinsky, Alice Gray (both of the American Museum of Natural History), Edward I. Coher, and August Schmitt assisted with the identification of insects in amber. Donald Baird (Princeton University) reviewed chapters dealing with technological evolution, and the manuscript has also profited from our conversations about dinosaurs and mesosuars (and I thank Harvy and Michael Siegel for finding the mesosuars).

Luis and Walter Alvarez (Lawrence Berkley Laboratory) and Stephen Jay Gould (Harvard University) participated in a lengthy and rewarding correspondence regarding asteroids and dinosaurs. Sidney W. Fox (University of Miami) provided microspheres, and a nifty name for a new feature. Frank Bristow (NASA/JPL) provided a much-appreciated *Voyager*-Saturn link to New Zealand.

Bartholomew Nagy (University of Arizona) caused me to do some rethinking about the role of comets and carbonaceous meteorites in the origin of life, just when I thought I knew what I was talking about. Francis Crick (the Salk Institute) pointed the way toward new questions about planetary origins and genesis, and offered helpful ideas on some of the answers I came up with (particularly the "Genesis and Galactic Blight" scenario).

Carl Sagan (Cornell University) offered his views on the embronic universe, organic cosmo chemistry, and carbonaceous meteorites. Ed Harrison (University of Massachusetts) changed the way I looked at the universe, as did Jesse Stoff (my coauthor on *Darwin's Universe*), who predicted the existence of ice worlds with underground oceans almost a decade before *Voyager-1* arrived at Jupiter. He also was the first person, to my knowledge, to make the connection between sulfide oases on the bottom of the Pacific Ocean and a possible route for the origin of E.T.s in worlds without suns.

Stephen King gave encouragement when it was needed most ("From one literary slut to another," Steve, thanks). For the same reason, special thanks go to Niles Eldredge and Edward I. Coher. I am also thankful for the patience and guidance of Russ Galen (Scott Meredith Literary Agency).

Thanks to two members of the fine team of TAB: Steven Bolt, who edited this book, and Douglas Robson, who designed the cover. And thank you to Mrs. Meredith M. Collins, president of Brown Brothers, Sterling, PA, the supplier of many of the photographs used in this book.

Of course, none of the above are to be tried by fire or hung by their toenails at moonrise for any heresies that remain.

Special thanks—very special thanks—are due to Mrs. Dobie, Barbara and Dennis Harris, Agnes Saunders, Ed McGunnigle, Mr. and Mrs. John Pellegrino; and to Tige, my little everything (and if you think that's corny, well, tough noogies).

Dedication: To my grade school teachers at P.S. 23, Flushing, who never let me go along on class field trips to the American Museum of Natural History for fear that I might "touch something." They were absolutely right.

They are the men and women in this world who had a vision or a dream or an inspiration. They saw that in some way our world, which is largely unintelligible and greatly chaotic, could be made a little more orderly and a little more beautiful . . . They were scorned, hit over the head and knocked down, but they were never destroyed. They always had the guts and the strength to get up on their feet and continue their work. At the end of their lives, they accomplished some modest part of what they had set out to do . . .

Irving Stone

Hey-ho, let's go!   The Ramones

Introduction

One of the finest teachers I have ever known once leafed through a scientific publication so loaded with 10-syllable words and run-on sentences that he could not possibly explain what the author was going on about—*and he was the author*. The lesson has not been forgotten. "Write it in English," he told me. "Avoid the pretense and write it in English. It is, after all, a perfectly respectable language."

Following this piece of advice, I have endeavored to make this book accessible to both the practicing scientist and the intelligent public. I hope it is also, as they say, "down under," a good read for all.

Writing an up-to-date history of life when most of the subject areas involved are under active and sometimes violent debate, when it seems from time to time that biology has become a spreading intolerance of new ideas rivaled only by modern fundamentalism—well, enough to say that it has been both exciting and exhausting. Most of all it has been rip-roaring fun; that is what science is supposed to be.

Charles R. Pellegrino
New York
April 1983

1 Thoughts for a Countdown

The first thing every child learns is that he is not the entire universe.

Robert Silverberg

With a bit of a mind flip
You're into the time slip
And nothing can ever be the same

Riff Raff and Columbia

Let's talk, you and I. Let's talk about time.

As you read this, I can call attention to the year in which you live . . . to the day of the week . . . to the hour. Now, think upon this: what are your plans for the next few hours? For tomorrow evening? You can probably recall with reasonable detail what you were doing about a year ago today. Were you living in the same building? Were you working for your present employer? In how many ways have your experiences during the past year shaped your expectations of where you might or might not be living and what you might or might not be doing a year from now?

Get the picture?

Your mind is a time machine, of sorts. Of the countless million forebearers whose DNA runs in your veins, you are among the very first to live outside the present. Man is the only species known to arrange the events of his life into deliberate, constant intervals of time. But this goes beyond the simple measure of years and hours. Out of experience of cause and effect, we learn to anticipate the future in moderate detail.

It is likely that human beings have been doing this for more than a quarter of a million years. We are exceptional in this long habit; one of its earliest consequences must have been an awareness that death was not merely something that happened to everybody else. Hand in hand with this knowledge went the realization that the stream of time neither begins with one's own birth nor ends with one's own death. Instead, it runs away from us in opposite directions—past and future.

An almost uncanny obsession to peer as far as possible in both directions is mirrored in such disparate writings as the Bible, Charles Darwin's *Origin of Species,* and Arthur C. Clarke's *Fountains of Paradise.* In *Time Gate,* we shall only explore one direction: whence we came. It is only fair to warn you, before you read any farther, that this is a story with no ending. But it does have a definite beginning.

The time is 1984 and the place is Manhattan. Except for the Empire State Building, and perhaps two or three others, all the skyscrapers are missing 13th floors (following King Kong's example, I shall make no effort to avoid evil numbers).

Now, step back four years to 1980, and look carefully at the New York City skyline. Battery Park City, located near the center of the picture and standing prominently against the World Trade Center Twin Towers, was then barely under construction.

If you now double your four-year step backward, bringing you to the year 1972, the changes become even more pronounced. The Empire State Building, soon to be eclipsed by the Twin Towers, still reigns as the world's tallest building. There are other noticeable changes; rectilinear shapes are missing from the skyline.

Manhattan, indeed the world and the universe in which it is embedded, will continue to change as this book progresses. At the beginning of Chapter 2, we will double the eight-year step backward (from 1980 to 1972) and move to 1956—and from there to 1924. In succeeding chapters—doubling the step again and again—New York City will give way to a pre-Columbian forest, and then to a kilometer-high blanket of ice as historic time converges with geologic time, and geologic time converges with cosmic time and the evolution of organisms.

What follows is a—well, a history of the universe, backwards.

New York City happens to be a very good indicator of time

measured within the experience of human lives. Its ever-changing skyline becomes unfamiliar in the space of only a dozen years. By contrast, the Moon's Taurus-Littrow Valley, visited by Eugene A. Cernan and Harrison H. Schmitt in December, 1972, has changed hardly at all over a dozen *million* years.

Charles Robert Darwin. Photo by Brown Brothers.

The Battery and the lower Manhattan sky-line are seen from New York Harbor in the years 1984, 1980, and 1972. Photos by C.R. Pellegrino.

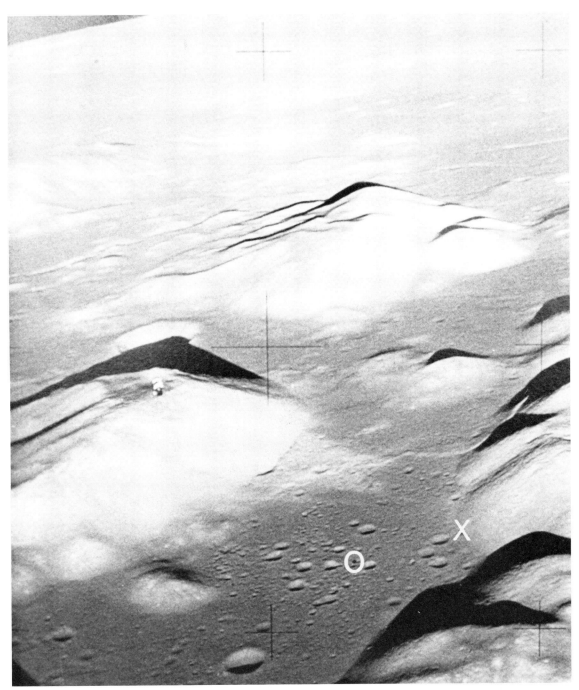

The valley of Taurus-Littrow is viewed here from an altitude of 16 kilometers (10 miles). Seen in transit against the South Massif (in left center of photo) is the Apollo 17 command module. The white circle in the middle of the valley marks the Apollo 17 landing site. The white cross at the base of the valley's North Massif (right center) marks the position of Split Rock. Courtesy of NASA's Johnson Space Center, Houston, Texas.

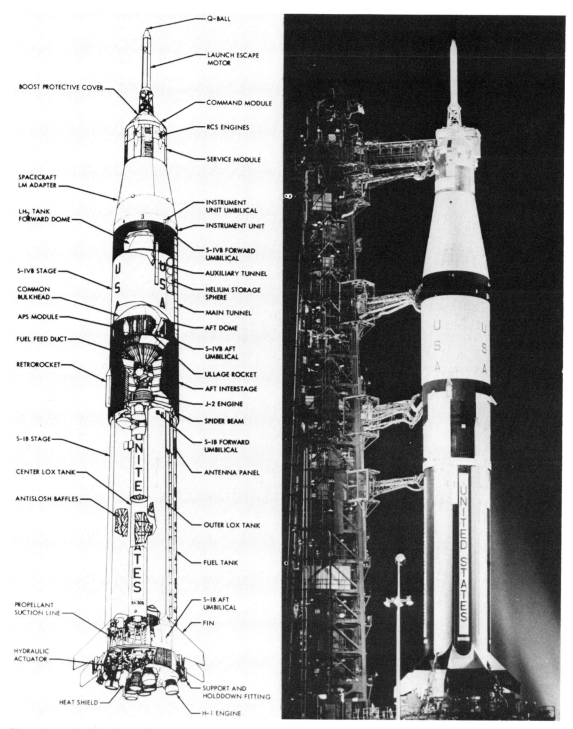

The cutaway drawing shows the structure of the Apollo 7 launch vehicle and space craft. The space vehicle is shown on Launch Pad 34 at the Kennedy Space Center, Florida. Photo by NASA/Brown Brothers.

6

Astronaut Russell L. Schweickart, lunar module pilot, took this view of Astronaut David R. Scott's extravehicular activity on the fourth day of the Apollo 9 Earth-orbital mission. Scott is standing in the open hatch of the Command Module. Apollo 9 Commander James A. McDivitt was inside the Lunar Module "Spider." The land area in the center of the picture is the Mississippi River valley. Photo by NASA/ Brown Brothers.

The valley measures approximately 6 kilometers (4 miles) across. It is a lava-drowned fissure that was born of the same violent event that dug the Serenitatis Basin, which is seen at the top of Eugene Cernan's high-altitude photo (taken from 16 kilometers up) of the *Apollo 17* landing site. The multiringed depression was excavated by a flying mountain—an asteroid—impacting with a force equivalent to 100 times its weight in nitroglycerine. Deeply hammered into the Moon's crust, the basin provided an exit for dark mare basalt.

Potassium-argon isotope dating of rocks from the valley tells

us the basalt was last molten about 3.7 billion years ago. The Serenitatis Basin ran full with the Moon's issue and became the great lava "sea" of Serenitatis. The overflow spilled into the valley, lapped at its up-thrust massifs, and then froze solid. Taurus-Littrow has remained geologically quiescent ever since.

A sprinkling of house-sized boulders—some originating as the ejecta of distant craters, others streaking down direct from space—has pitted the lava field. On the valley floor, "Split Rock" lies in five pieces. The 8-meter-wide (26 feet) boulder once perched high on the northern massif. Dislodged, probably by the shock of a nearby meteorite impact, it rolled down the mountain and came apart as it ground to a halt. At that time, dinosaurs had not yet appeared on Earth.

Except for a slow weathering away by micrometeorites, a dusting of lunar soil, and the sudden appearance of a lunar rover in 1972, Split Rock has lain undisturbed and unchanged for over 200 million years.

Toward the horizon, about 200 meters (180 yards) away, lies a

The last lunar rover to be driven on the moon's surface is seen parked near Split Rock in the Taurus-Littrow Valley. The boulder appears to have tumbled down the valley's North Massif, cracking in five places as it came to rest (hence the name, Split Rock). This happened shortly before the first dinosaurs appeared on Earth. The rock has lain undisturbed ever since. Courtesy of NASA's Johnson Space Center, Houston, Texas.

Apollo 16 at the Descartes landing site on April 23, 1972. Photo by NASA/Brown Brothers.

crater that predates the arrival of Split Rock. It could accommodate a football field. Its rim has been softened by erosion.

Never assailed by wind and rain, the craters—ranging from mammoth to medium to minuscule and dotting every square centimeter of the surface—are the weathering force that has left Taurus-Littrow unmarked by a single jagged peak. Even small, marble-sized meteorites (many thousands of times more common than, for example, table-sized meteorites), arriving on occasion like grapeshot from space, splash thousands of lunar particles to all points of the compass. Impacting on the soil, the particles excavate additional craters.

Seen in terms of geologic time, the valley has been pelted by a torrential downpour that stretches over 3.7 billion years, pulverizing and breaking and stirring the surface until it has come to resemble a dusting of fresh snow (this blanket of fine-grained material is called a *regolith*). Indeed, the dark grey Moon dust was described by astronauts as having a consistency somewhere between fresh snow and talcum powder. *Apollo 15* commander David Scott commented that it "mantles virtually every physical feature of the lunar surface. Our boots sink gently into it as we walk; we leave sharply chiseled footprints."

Cratering events range down to the microscopic. Particles of

In space, even a snowflake can have teeth. Shown here is a microscopic view of a rock brought to Earth by Apollo 11 astronauts. Traveling through a virtual vacuum at several tens of kilometers per second, a micro-meteorite splattered down on the Moon's surface, scarring this rock with a crater so small (diameter = 2 microns, or 2/1000ths of a millimeter) that it can be seen only in the realm of distances measured by electron microscopes. Photograph by Merv Loper and C.R. Pellegrino.

cosmic dust, impacting at 10 to 20 kilometers (6 to 13 miles) per second, have dug craters visible only in the realm of distances measurable by electron microscopes. Save for these cratering events, the lunar surface is changeless.*

The Earth, of course, is different. Whole continents are adrift; their peaks and valleys are quickened by life, wind, and echoes. Fed by the seething hell that dwells within the Earth, convective spasms are nudging the Australian Plate northward at 7.5 centimeters (3 inches) a year, and will inevitably send the continent crunching directly into Southeast Asia.

Having stepped backward from 1984 to 1972, seafloor spreading, seen in reverse, has already brought London approximately 25 centimeters (10 inches) closer to New York. In our next step backward, assuming that spreading rates are constant (apparently not the case, at least over spans of millions of years), this distance will double.

Having to swim 2.1 centimeters farther with every passing year might not seem very dramatic for European anguillid eels (*Anguilla anguilla*). At this moment, adults and larvae are successfully conquering the space between Europe and the Sargasso Sea near Bermuda. Two centimeters a year does not seem dramatic until you multiply this distance across thousands of generations of eels. Adult eels, leaving their European streams and heading west, must pass over the Mid-Atlantic Ridge; there two gigantic slabs of the Earth's crust are being pushed apart. On the American side of the spreading center, where the distance between the mainland and the Sargasso Sea remains essentially unchanged, lives a related species, *Anguilla rostrata*.

Both American and European eels migrate to and spawn in the Sargasso Sea. After mating at a depth of some 460 meters (1508 feet), the adults die. Eggs float to the surface and hatch, and then larvae commence the return trip.

A major difference between the two species lies in the time required for migration. It takes a year for the returning American young, a journey of several months for Sargasso-bound American adults, about a full year for European adults to reach the spawning grounds, and three years for their offspring to complete the return trip. Not surprisingly their life cycles differ. For example, they mate at different times. There are also anatomical differences; an example is the more muscular aspect of European females.

---

*We know now that astronauts working on the Moon were struck by dust-sized meteorites. On the surface of one helmet were found two microcraters. Neither dent was deep enough to cause harm, but small cratering events are a serious concern in space. Traveling through a vacuum at 20 km per second, even a snowflake can sting.

When the Atlantic Ocean was hundreds of kilometers narrower, American and European eels probably were a single, interbreeding species with a common spawning center. One of the earliest consequences of gradually increasing the migration time on one side of the ocean would have been to throw breeding times into disharmony, leading to segregation, on a behavorial level, of the eastern and western populations.

Similarly, recent tagging results for the Atlantic bluefin tuna (*Thunnis thynnus*) suggest that we might be reading a closing chapter on the geographic division and differentiation of a species. As with European and Atlantic eels, there are two groups of bluefin tuna. Both migrate in clockwise circles. The western group moves into the Straits of Florida during the spring, is found off Long Island, New York during much of the summer, and is believed to follow the Gulf Stream northeast into deep Atlantic waters during the fall. The eastern group (also known as the Mediterranean group) is found off the coast of Norway in summer and appears to sweep south into the waters of southern Spain with the onset of winter.

The two migratory paths apparently overlap near the Mid-Atlantic Ridge, and occasional springtime recovery of tagged Mediterranean-group fish off the Florida coast suggests a winter intermix of the two groups. Again, in a younger, narrower Atlantic Ocean, the two must have been a single, interbreeding species.

Despite certain anatomical differences, they actually might still be a single species because we could probably cross fertilize western sperm with eastern eggs (or vice versa) and produce offspring that would in turn be capable of producing viable offspring. But the eastern and western groups spawn at different times: a behavioral barrier as powerful as any physical barrier we might imagine. Each group has its own guarded and separate gene pool that paves the way for a growing dimorphism. In order for speciation to carry on, the requirement that two groups in the wild *do not* interbreed overrides any question about whether or not they *can*.

That a significantly narrower Atlantic Ocean once permitted bluefins to follow an unbroken migratory path—a single circle— seems to be a reasonable conclusion. Projecting into the future, if New York continues to inch away from London, winter encounters between the two groups will become fewer and fewer until at last the two circles separate altogether.

In the following chapters, the positions of continents will be viewed from above the Earth's poles. During the first few steps backward in time, land masses will appear to remain stationary. As our recession from the present gains momentum, the crust's wrenchings and tearings and crunchings will become visible— slowly at first, then bursting everywhere at once. Although the

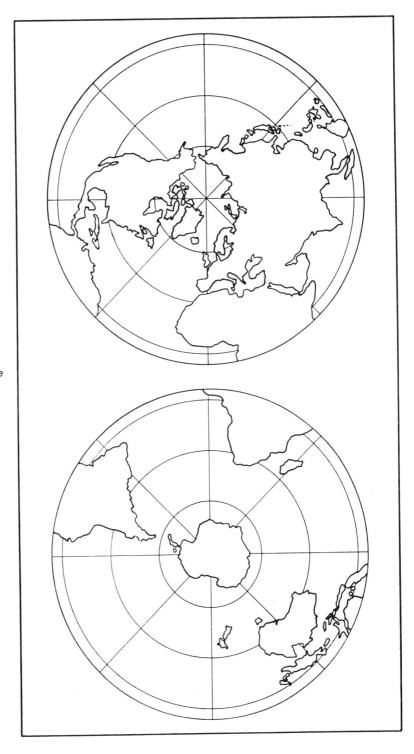

The continents, seen from above the North and South Poles, in 1972.

shapes of continents have varied considerably through geologic time, modern shapes are used where possible for the ease of reference.

Another good indicator of time is the changing pattern of stars in the sky. Not even the constellations are immutable.

The Big Dipper is, among other things, the traveler's guide to the North Star, and is prominent in the star lore of every continent. To the Britons it was known as the Plough. To the Vikings it was the Great Chariot of Odin.

Curiously, the seven-starred figure has been known to almost all others—including Aristotle, the pharaohs, and the Iroquois and the Algonquians in North America—as the Great Bear (from which we derive its Latin name, Ursa Major). The curious part is that, even when connected to nearby stars, the constellation cannot by any stretch of the imagination be made to resemble a bear (perhaps a running squirrel but not a bear).

Nope, no bears here.

Fine. Then why the name? A joke of history? Perhaps a coincidence that makes us ask a lot of silly questions? Or because the positions of stars in the Dipper are slowly shifting, the name might have been given at a time when the constellation more closely resembled a bear than it does today.

If we are considering historic time—back to when the first written references to the Great Bear are known (about 350 B.C.)—

The stars of the Big Dipper.

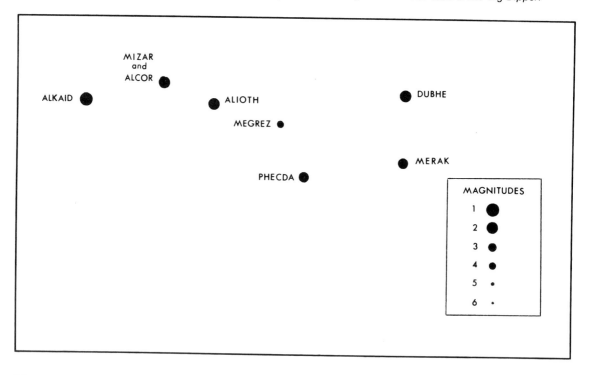

An Indian settlement on the southern tip of Manhattan Island upon the arrival of Henry Hudson. Photo by Brown Brothers from the Museum of the City of New York.

the change has been too slight and the explanation does not stand. But surely the Great Bear was known before people began writing about it. If we push back to a time when the Algonquians and the Greeks, now on separate continents, shared a common language and starlore (let us say 20 or 40 thousand years ago), a bear might have been traceable from the Dipper and a few of its surrounding stars. On the other hand, at least one graduate of the Monty Python School of Archaeoastronomy has argued that bears once looked more like dippers than they do today; hence the name.

Dubhe (also known as Alpha Ursae Majoris, or the Dipper's lip) is approaching the Sun at 8.9 kilometers (5.5 miles) per second from a distance of almost 105 light years. Like approximately half of all stars within range of our telescopes, Dubhe is a binary system (a family of two stars).

The companions are separated by a distance of several astronomical units (an astronomical unit equals about 8 minutes of light travel time, or 149,637,000 kilometers—the average distance between the Sun and the Earth), and they revolve about each other with a period of 44.66 years. The total mass of the system, including associated planets (if such exist), is about three times that of our Sun.

Because the two stars orbit equidistant of their common gravitational center, their masses must be nearly equal. Yet one star far outshines the other; the system is an anomaly. Stars of equal mass are supposed to burn with equal brightness. Dubhe, not knowing this, burns in apparent violation of mass-luminosity rules.

A star's brightness—the rate at which luminous energy is shed into space—is dependent upon its surface temperature and its surface area. White dwarfs tend to be hot and bright (attaining surface temperatures of 10,000°C), but the surface areas—through which they radiate light into space—are small.

Most white dwarfs are no larger than the Earth. If a star of this kind were observed from a distance of one light year, it could be discerned only as a faint point against the sky. Red giants, although four times cooler at the surface, are broad enough to engulf the orbit of Mars, and they are the most luminous objects for 100 light years in every direction.

According to surface area/luminosity relationships, one member of the Dubhe system must be smaller and denser (and presumably hotter) than the other. It is not quite a white dwarf but something close to it.

Opposite Dubhe, at the end of the Dipper's handle, is Alkaid (also called Eta Ursae Majoris). As near as anybody can tell, Alkaid is a single star; a single star that shines with the luminosity of 630 Suns. We view this giant from a distance of 210 light years. It is approaching us at a velocity of 10.5 kilometers (6.5 miles) per second.

Mizar (also called Zeta Ursae Majoris) is the next star in from Alkaid; it is located at the bend in the Dipper's handle. Receding from the Earth at a distance of 88 light years, it carries with it a whole family of companion stars.

Through a small telescope or a pair of binoculars, the most easily seen companion is Mizar B Ursae Majoris. Mizar B is almost as luminous as the Sun—70 times dimmer than Mizar A—and orbits Mizar A at a minimum distance of 380 astronomical units (approximately 10 times the distance separating Pluto from the Sun). A single orbit evidently takes some 20,000 years.

Mizar A is itself a double star. Its binary nature can be observed only by means of a spectroscope. That is why it is called a spectroscopic binary rather than a visual binary. As one star approaches us, the wavelengths of light in front of it are compressed. As the other star recedes, wavelengths are stretched out behind it. Both stars have nearly identical mass and luminosity. They whirl about a common center of gravity with a period of 20.54 days, and are much closer to one another than Mercury is to the Sun. They bask in each other's fires, sucking and dragging through space, exchanging matter, and evolving in strange ways.

Mizar B is also a spectroscopic binary, but the two stars are hardly as close as the Mizar A pair. The second star, fainter than our Sun, has an orbital radius comparable to Venus. It completes a single circuit in 182.33 days. To make matters more interesting, tantalizing wobbling motions indicate a third, darker body with an orbital period of 1350 days. In terms of our own Solar System, that would put it somewhere between Mars and the asteroid belt.

One or all of these bodies might possess orbiting planets or moonlets (just as globes of turbulent gas orbiting our Sun—Jupiter, Saturn, Uranus, and Neptune—have evolved into small-scale solar systems within a solar system). We could speculate endlessly about where around these stars habitable zones might exist and what orbits suitably sized planets would have to follow in order to develop life. Such an exercise would be pointless. For a specific and interesting reason, to which I shall return, the Mizar system is undeniably lifeless.

Also without life, and at least three light months away from the double, double Mizar system, is Alcor (often called 80 Ursae Majoris). It too is a spectroscopic binary. The two stars have a total luminosity of 15 Suns, and the pair orbits Mizar A and Mizar B once every 10 million years.

If a family consisting of two double stars in orbit around a double star does not seem confusing enough, consider that Mizar and Alcor, coursing away from Earth at 8.9 kilometers (5.5 miles) per second, are moving parallel with as many as 100 other stars. This moving group—the Ursa Major Stream—includes the central stars of the Big Dipper (those located between Dubhe and Alkaid) and apparently Sirius, "the Dog Star."

If the middle of the Big Dipper is pictured as moving ahead of our Solar System, then Sirius is creeping up behind us. These traveling companions occupy a volume of space that surrounds the Sun. They are moving southeast across our sky, toward the eastern portion of Sagittarius at an average velocity of 14.5 kilometers (9 miles) per second.

Many of these stars (excepting Sirius, which has a small white companion that might be several billion years older than our Sun) seem to be about the same age as the Pleiades star cluster. Born during the reign of Earth's last dinosaurs, long after Split Rock came to rest on the floor of Taurus-Littrow, they would thus be in their infancy. Any worlds circling them must be too young even to support a life-building chemical evolution. Near Mergrez, in the Big Dipper, the first seas might now be forming on a rough world—a likeness of the Earth some 4.5 billion years ago.

Where do moving groups come from? Evidently, traveling families of stars share a common origin. We have learned from the oldest nuggets of matter in our Solar System (pieces of the Allende meteorite) that the collapse of gas and dust into the Sun and planets was probably triggered by the out-racing shock wave of an exploded star—a supernova.

Looking outward from our Solar System, we can observe expanding spheres of supernova ejecta. At their periphery, collapsing nebulae studded with associations or clusters of very young stars are sometimes seen. Rafted along on a spherical shell of slowly expanding hydrogen and helium, newly formed stars— mixed with a few older ones caught up in the wave front—travel parallel on a trajectory pointing away from the explosion center.

Some members of the moving group will swell to red giantism, become supernovas in their own right, and scatter traveling companions in odd directions. Others will be swung off course by close encounters with passing stars. In time moving groups should dissipate.

Today there is little doubt that the Sun was born in the wake of a supernova. It should once have had traveling companions of its own, but it is impossible to identify any of these with certainty because their paths diverged long ago.

408 light minutes; that is the distance the Sun has traveled in the Galaxy since a year ago today . . . 3.4 days of light travel time between the years 1972 and 1984. Somewhere out there, riding the night at immense distances, are stars and perhaps planets born in the same place on almost the same day as our Sun. Like our Sun they are very old now. Very old indeed.

Let us return to the Big Dipper, a subject that will be with us for the next 100 thousand years of our backward journey. Alkaid, the tip of the handle, is moving northwest in our sky. Between the years 1972 and 1984, it shifted 1.44 arc seconds. To notice the shift, you would have to superimpose photographic negatives made through a telescope a dozen years apart, and then view them through a microscope.

The distance involved corresponds to the length of a garden-variety ant seen at 500 meters (1,630 feet) or a quarter seen at 12 kilometers (7.5 miles). It might not strike you as a very great distance even if you could see it multiplied across the span of all human history.

Nevertheless, proper motions of Alkaid and other members of

the Big Dipper are more noticeable than the 2-centimeter-per-year incease in the distance between New York and London. In the following chapters, the constellation will stretch out of shape and become unrecognizable far more rapidly than the configuration of continents on Earth.

Cold empty space, we now know, is neither truly cold nor entirely empty. The average density of the universe is presently estimated to be about 2 hydrogen atoms per 10 cubic meters, or 10^{-30} the density of water (meaning 1 gram of water per cubic centimeter—approximately 10^{24} atoms—*divided* by ten 30 times).

At one time, it was believed that atoms in the gaps between the galaxies, receiving virtually no starlight at all, might exist at a temperature at which no more energy could possibly be removed from them.* This temperature, equivalent to $-273.15°C$ ($-459.67°F$), is called *zero degrees Kelvin* or *absolute zero*.

In 1965, Arno Penzias and Robert Wilson of the Bell Telephone Laboratories at Holmdel, New Jersey, discovered a background of microwave radiation emanating from every direction in space with a temperature of 2.8 degrees Kelvin. As is often the route to exotic discovery, they were looking for something else.

Any number of researchers, making this same observation, might simply have described the observation and there let the matter rest. What earned Penzias and Wilson the Nobel Prize was that they followed the obvious question—what the hell is that doing there?—with other questions.

If there is a moral here, it is that the pathway to new insights lies not in describing what you have observed, but in asking the right questions about what you have described.

Now almost all cosmologists agree that we live in a Big-Bang universe whose beginning can be traced to a condition of very high density and temperature. Thinned by expansion, the 2.8°K background radiation survives as a lingering echo of the Big Bang.

The universe expands. Therefore, looking backward in time, the space in which the stars are embedded will become gradually denser and hotter. That we must eventually encounter a kind of

---

*Some very tiny quantity of residual energy must always remain—in keeping with Werner Karl Heisenberg's (1901-1976) principle that the position and velocity of an atom can never be simultaneously and perfectly determined—but that there must always remain a residual uncertainty. In the case of atoms at very low temperatures, this uncertainty arises because halving the absolute temperature always requires the same input of energy regardless of the starting point. Therefore, no atom can be cooled to a point where all energy is lost and motion ceases. This is known as the "third law of thermodynamics," and it provides a real-life example of Zeno's (fifth century B.C.) contention that putting one's nose 1 inch from a wall, halving the distance, then halving the remaining distance to ¼ inch, then ⅛ inch, and so on and on, will require an infinity of steps, and still one's nose would never actually touch the wall.

"cosmic crunch" seems inescapable. The change will occur slowly. The universe has been 10^{-30} the density of water, heated at 2.8K, throughout all of human evolution—more than 7 million years. So we can set this "hot topic" (pardon the pun) to rest for awhile.

From the year 1972, our tangible records of the past include photographs of the last *Apollo* mission to the Moon. These will be replaced in succeeding chapters by earlier photographs, steel engravings, medieval woodcuts, carved stone, dinosaur tracks, worm trails, and the oldest relics of our Solar System.

And here we stand, in the year of *Apollo's* last hurrah.

Down there on Earth, people had other things to think about. Richard Nixon went to China and established new ties after 22 years of mutual hostility. Three months later he became the first American president to visit Moscow. The voting age in America was lowered to 18. By Election Day, the Watergate affair had mushroomed out of control. There was little doubt in the minds of most voters that the White House was to be blamed, but the alternative was George McGovern, and that seemed too much like being asked to choose between Caligula and Nero.

Nixon won by a landslide.

In Georgia, an obscure fellow named Jimmy Carter, mired in a deepening swamp of personal and political problems, raised his sights on Mr. Nixon's job. Anyone who followed politics knew that the governor must have been joking.

Winter descended on Paris and, while diplomats representing North Vietnam and South Vietnam, the United States, and the National Liberation Front walked under a red canopy in the rain and their suits ran scarlet, Francis Cappola's *The Godfather* was becoming one of the biggest box office grossers of all time. An ounce of gold cost fifty U.S. dollars on the world market. Most economists viewed the metal as a bad investment. A hammer-wielding monster slouched into the Vatican and sent splinters flying from Michelangelo's Piete. Richard Leakey and Glynn Isaac announced the discovery of a 2.5-million-year-old human skull in Kenya, and explorers in the Philippines stumbled upon the Stone-Age people called Tassadays.

That was the year Louis Leakey died.

2 Down from Space

In Italy they had 500 years of bloodshed and they produced Michelangelo, Leonardo da Vinci and the Renaissance. In Switzerland they had brotherly love. They had 500 years of democracy and peace and what did they produce? The cuckoo clock.

Orson Welles

War can sometimes be a stimulating thing. But you can overdo a stimulant.

H.G. Wells

What competition there is between the Soviets and Americans these days is focused more upon the future of space as a medium for military uses.

Earl Lane

We believe that permanently manned space stations with interchangeable crews will be mankind's pathway to the universe.

Leonid Brezhnev

Everything is theoretically impossible until it's done. One could write a history of science in reverse by assembling the solemn pronouncements of highest authority about what could not be done and could never happen.

Robert A. Heinlein

But to place a man in a multi-stage rocket and project him into the controlling gravitational field of the moon, where the passenger can make scientific observations, perhaps land alive, and then return to Earth - all that constitutes a wild dream of Jules Verne.

Lee De Forest, "father of electronics"
(quoted in the June 1957 *Reader's Digest*)

When a distinguished but elderly scientist states that something is possible, he is almost certainly right. When he states that something is impossible, he is very probably wrong.

Arthur C. Clarke

In 1956, the general temperature of the universe was 2.8 degrees Kelvin. No one had really noticed that yet. The Taurus-Littrow Valley looked much as it had throughout all human history. At the University of Chicago, a 21-year-old student named Carl Sagan bet a case of chocolate bars that Americans would walk on the Moon by 1970. The wager was comical. No man-made object had even orbited the Earth as yet.

In late October, just before the start of the Christmas shopping season, Israeli troops invaded Egypt. England and France joined them. With the attention of the Western world focused on the Middle East, the Soviets were free as they saw fit to deal with the rebellion in Hungary. With predictable results, more than 2000 tanks rumbled into Budapest.

Eisenhower was reelected with Nixon as his vice president. Almost everybody in America loved Lucy; and any male still taking in air and in his right mind loved Norma-Jean Baker, who demonstrated her acting ability by so convincingly playing the part of Marilyn Monroe. Marilyn attained immortality; Norma died at the age of 36.

The Andrea Doria sank. The Bell-X-2 Rocketplane soared into the stratosphere at three times the speed of sound (3379 km/hr). Elvis Presley burst onto the scene as the King of Rock and Roll.

The Battery as seen from New York Harbor in 1952. Photomosaic by C.R. Pellegrino.

Parents viewed him with distrust: at best a sinner and a corrupter of youth, at worst Mephistopheles himself. A 15-year-old Paul McCartney viewed him with envious eyes.

In 1924, Vladimir Lenin died, triggering a brutal power struggle in which Joseph Stalin eliminated more than 1 million real and imagined rivals and grasped complete control of Russia's Communist party. Benito Mussolini took office as prime minister in Rome. Adolf Hitler served an 8-month prison term for disorderly conduct. He wrote *Mein Kampf,* and was released early on good behavior.

In America, almost 2.5 million radios were in use. Ford Motor's 10 millionth car rolled off the assembly lines, and the first regular air mail service got under way. The *Draper Catalogue of Stars* was published. British Imperial Airways began operation.

London was 100 centimeters (40 inches) closer to New York than it would be in 1984, and Alkaid was 5.76 arc seconds southeast of its present position, a displacement comparable to the diameter of a green pea seen from a distance of 160 meters (533 feet).

As I write this, four robot spacecraft are hurtling out of the Solar System at velocities up to 30 kilometers (19 miles) per second. At this velocity, relative to the motion of stay-at-home

observers on Earth, *Voyager 2* is traveling forward through time at a rate slightly slower than the 1 second per second measured by our own clocks. At the end of one of our terrestrial years, only 363.5 days will have passed aboard *Voyager 2*. In other words, the spacecraft, according to Albert Einstein's special relativity theory, is moving about a day and a half into our future during each year of its journey.

Still . . . stepping backward to the year 1924, the Moon and the planets and the velocities attained by the *Pioneer* and *Voyager* spacecraft seem impossibly far away. As far away, perhaps, as the stars might seem to we who are witness to the most incredible century *Homo sapiens* has ever known. It opened with the ascent of kite like, motorized aircraft, saw at its midpoint the probing of the ionosphere with rockets, and now the bridging of interplanetary space.

Decades ago, skeptics without number smugly regarded the

The Italian linear Andrea Doria shortly before the final plunge to the bottom of the Atlantic off Nantucket. Photo by Brown Brothers.

gaps between the planets as inconquerable barriers. Other men—Robert Hutchings Goddard was one—peered beyond the visible boundaries of their own time and prepared to challenge infinity.

Goddard began with ordinary Fourth-of-July skyrockets. Instead of firing them into the air, as everybody else was doing, he took them indoors, clamped them into test racks, and measured the thrust they produced against scales. The practice of igniting explosive devices in the enclosure of a campus laboratory proved to be a questionable tactic that came threateningly close to ending Goddard's university career.

The result of all this was a series of calculations integrating the weight of an empty rocket with the weight of its fuel and the velocity of its exhaust. From these figures, Goddard could, at least in theory, predict how high a rocket would travel after all of its fuel was consumed. Then along came his 1919 report in *Smithsonian Miscellaneous Collections.*

The treatise detailed his "calculations of minimum mass re-

Split Rock at Taurus-Littrow in 1924. Courtesy of NASA's Johnson Space Center, Houston, Texas. Photomosaic by C.R. Pellegrino.

quired to raise one pound to various altitudes in the atmosphere." It might have gone unnoticed by almost everybody if not for a scale of calculations that ranged up to the *minimum mass required to raise one pound to an infinite altitude*.

In the winter and spring of 1924, Goddard developed a pump and valve system that injected gasoline and liquid oxygen into a crude combustion chamber. Thus began the building and testing of the first direct ancestors of *Luna, Voyager, Soyuz,* and *Columbia*:

30 December 1925, rocket trembled in its support for 8 seconds . . . 16 March 1926, *first flight* of a liquid-propellant rocket. In air 2.5 seconds. Average velocity 60 miles per hour. Attained altitude of 40 feet . . . 17 July 1929, *fourth flight* of a liquid-propellant rocket. Started to lift at 13 seconds, rose at 14.5 seconds, reached top trajectory at 17 seconds, hit ground at 18.5 seconds, landing 171 feet away. Flight was bright and noisy, attracting much public attention . . . 29 September 1931, a flight took place with streamline casing and remote control. Rocket length was 9 feet, 11 inches; diameter 12 inches; loaded weight 87.2 pounds, and empty weight 37 pounds. Altitude: 180 feet; in air: 9.6 seconds, followed trajectory that was like a fish swimming . . . 13 October 1931, flight effected with simplified combustion chamber, parachute releasing. The 7.75-foot-long, 12-inch-diameter rocket reached more than 1,700 feet altitude, gave loud whistling noise on descent . . . 8 March 1935, flight test

The first air-mail flight prepares to depart from a polo field in Washington D.C. Photo by Brown Brothers.

In 1923, the Thames embankment and the Hotel Cecil (top) and Parliament Street in London (bottom). Photos by Brown Brothers.

equalizer (to prevent liquid oxygen tank pressure from exceeding gasoline tank pressure), pendulum stabilizer, and 10-foot-diameter parachute. The motor fired for 12 seconds, producing a small white flame; velocity of more than 700 miles per hour achieved (may have been supersonic). Rocket tilted to horizontal, landed 9,000 feet from tower . . . 28 March 1935, flight with improved gyro stabilization; rocket was 14 feet, 9.75 inches long, empty weight was 78.5 pounds. Reached altitude of 4,800 feet, range of 13,000 feet. Rocket corrected its path perfectly several times during 20 second flight, which was made at an average speed of 550 miles per hour . . . 18 December 1936, flight test with pressure storage tank. Duration and altitude not recorded, but range was 2,000 feet, rocket impacted with axis horizontal. Noise heard up to eight miles away. Parts scattered over 300 foot area, most being recovered undamaged . . . 26 March 1937, movable air vanes in this flight. Rocket soared to 8,000-9,000 feet (duration 22.3 seconds), corrected while propulsion lasted, then tilted . . . 22 April 1937, flight test with larger movable air vanes; reinforced parachute. Rocket length: 17.75 feet; diameter: 9 inches; duration: 21.5 seconds. Rocket could not be followed to top of trajectory as it was nearly overhead. It landed about a mile from the tower.

The Battery in 1924. Courtesy of the New York Historical Society, New York City.

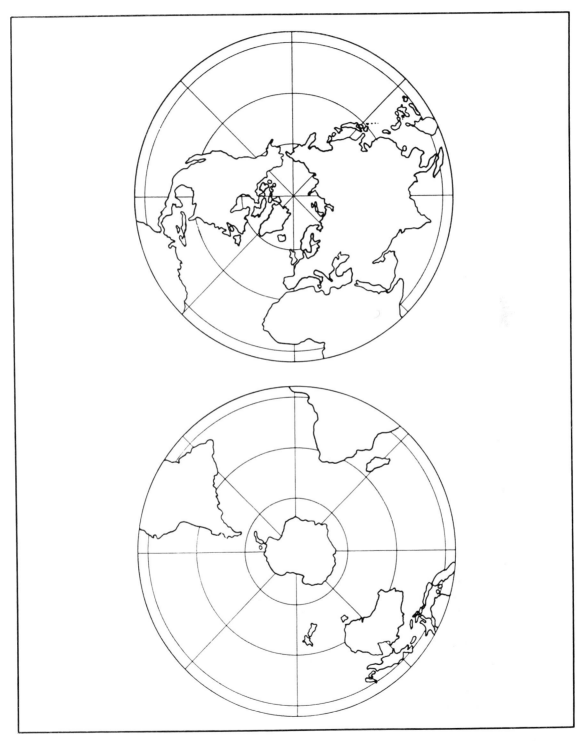

The continents in 1924.

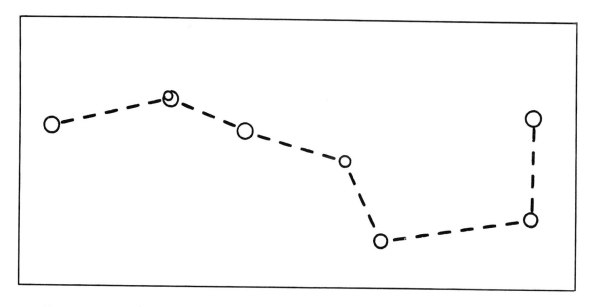

In the midst of all these developments—and despite support from Charles A. Lindbergh and Harry F. Guggenheim—the balding Dr. Goddard had earned for himself a reputation as a crackpot subject to flights of Vernian fantasy. It was a reputation that gave rise to such headlines as: "MOON ROCKET MISSES TARGET BY 238,799-½ MILES."

Meanwhile, under normal international exchanges, his patents had been dispersed to all points of the compass. To the east, the spreading German empire had seen rockets as a niche (or loophole) not covered in the ban on German rearmament imposed by the treaty of Versailles. Suspecting that an approaching European conflict might provide the impetus for rapid development of rocket technology, Goddard warned the military that America should prepare for the eventual emergence of ocean-crossing missiles. His advice was accepted politely, and then dismissed.

At that moment, the Germans were diverting vast sums of money to a 12,000-man team of rocket researchers stationed at Peenemünde.

And that's when things really began to heat up. By 1945, amazingly detailed plans for the world's first reusable, winged spacecraft had been completed. Design specifications called for a manually operated, steerable nose wheel, retractable landing gear, and parachutes to slow the craft during landing. This highly evolved rocket was to have been carried aloft on a first stage consisting of two modified V-2 rockets (or possibly even a cluster of four rockets) strapped together and equipped with air brakes and special parachutes to enable recovery and repeated use.

Once outside the retarding forces of the atmosphere, the on-

Stars of the Big Dipper as they appeared in 1924.

Professor Robert H. Goddard and his rocket. Photo by Brown Brothers.

Charles A. Lindbergh. Photo by Brown Brothers.

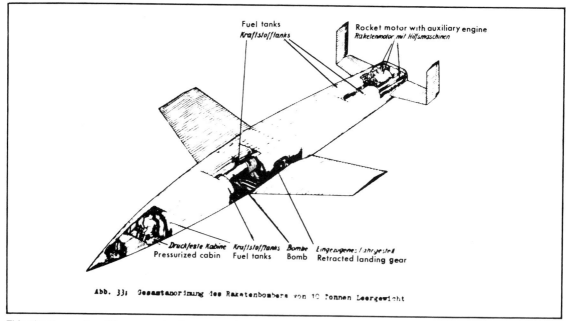

Fuel tanks
Kraftstofftanks

Rocket motor with auxiliary engine
Raketenmotor mit Hilfsmaschinen

Druckfeste Kabine   *Kraftstofftanks*   *Bombe*   *Eingezogenes Fahrgestell*
Pressurized cabin   Fuel tanks   Bomb   Retracted landing gear

Abb. 33: Gesamtanordnung des Raketenbombers von 10 Tonnen Leergewicht

This direct ancestor of the space shuttle was considered by Germany for bombing missions against North America during World War II. Boosted to an altitude of 160 kilometers (100 miles), the rocket bomber was designed to perform a series of undulating skips along the upper atmosphere like a rock skipping on water, loosing energy as it did so until the return to Earth became a long glide. By the war's end, wind-tunnel tests and propulsion-system tests had been completed. George Pallater "borrowed" the design for his science fiction film, When Words Collide. *The U.S. and the U.S.S.R. "borrowed" Germany's rocket scientists for a "space race." This illustration was "borrowed" from captured Luftwaffe documents.*

During World War II, a V-2 rocket being fired from its test stand at Peenemünde, Germany. Photo by Brown Brothers.

board engine could be ignited, and the range of the craft could be sustained for a complete revolution around the Earth by a series of undulating skips off the atmosphere. Like a stone thrown horizontally over the surface of a pond, the first skip would be the longest one (and the most dangerous, in terms of frictional heating), with succeeding skips growing shorter and shorter, lower and lower, until at last the rocket-plane could glide home to a conventional runway landing.

The purpose of this first serious proposal for manned space flight was to bomb Pittsburgh, New York City, and Washington,

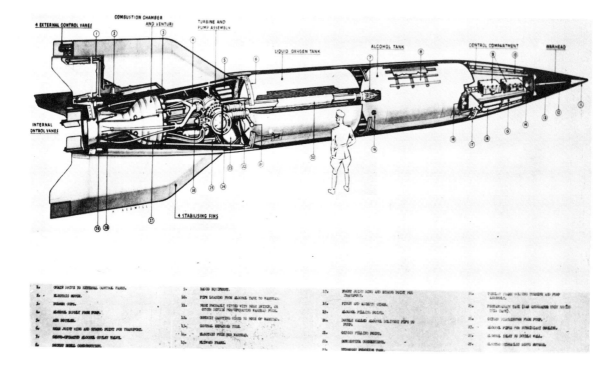

An officially prepared sectional drawing of the German V-2 rocket projectile. The weapon is approximately 46 feet long and 5 feet, 6 inches in diameter. Photo by Brown Brothers.

D.C. from space. What the rocket program lacked was powerful fission bombs. A major reason for this was that the Germans had divided their atomic bomb project into about 10 different government research groups. All of these groups were required to share limited supplies of heavy water and uranium.

This instilled in atmosphere of competition in the program, and some teams became reluctant to share information and materials with the others. Another problem was that the heavy water and uranium had to be shipped from group to group by train, and the first groups to receive these shipments usually didn't leave very much for the groups farther down the line. And of course the trains were getting bombed. All sorts of other ridiculous things were happening. The heavy-water factory was in Norway. The ferry got sunk with all the heavy water, the factory got bombed, and—about a week before the war in Europe ended—one of the teams discovered that they never needed the heavy water in the first place. Meanwhile, the German Post Office was making more headway than just about anybody (the mail service was awful, but they built a good nuclear reactor).

In the post war haze, the Americans and the Soviets divided up the world's first mass-produced, liquid-fueled rockets—and the men who had built them—and brought them home to establish their

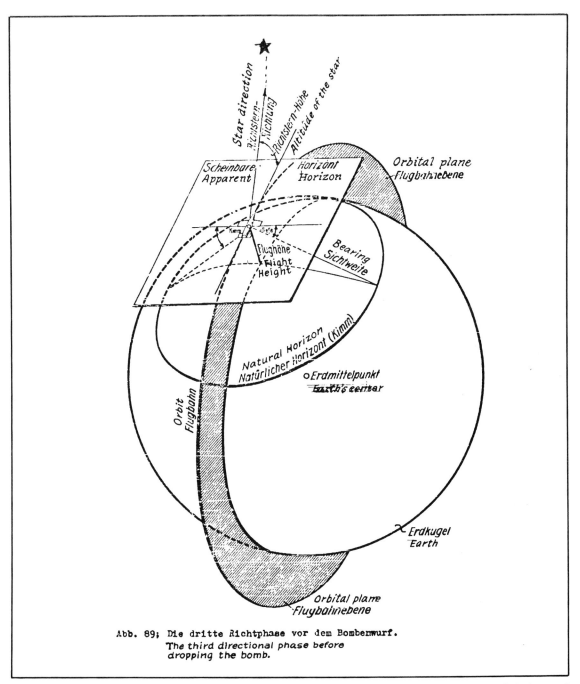

Abb. 89; Die dritte Richtphase vor dem Bombenwurf.
The third directional phase before
dropping the bomb.

Workers on the German rocket bomber, anticipating the difficulties of navigation in orbital and near-orbital flight, invented solutions that are still in use today (including principals of stellar navigation in space). This diagram, reproduced from captured Luftwaffe documents, shows how the pilot would have determined his position and his attitude in order to release his reentry vehicle (a bomb encased in a heat shield) at the proper moment.

Dr. Wernher von Braun with a table model of a space ship designed to fly to the Moon from a space station. Photo by Brown Brothers.

own rocket programs. During one of his initial interrogations, Germany's Wernher von Braun outlined future scientific, economic, and military applications of piloted, winged rockets capable of orbiting the Earth and returning to runways like ordinary airplanes. He proposed their eventual use as "work horses" for the construction of orbital platforms, from which the whole Earth's surface—the movements of storm fronts, icebergs, ships, troops—could be observed in detail through very powerful telescopes. Once in space, the telescopes could also be pointed away from Earth, toward planets and nebulae and galaxies hitherto unseen from a vantage point above the Earth's obscuring envelope of air.

If this sounds like science fiction for the year 1945, consider that von Braun and his colleagues at Peenemünde became the very nucleus of the American-Soviet space race. Add to this, for our astonishment, that even earlier yet the Russian-born Konstantin E. Tsiolkovsky had designed revolving, barrel-shaped orbital habitats with oxygen-producing forests growing on their curved walls and held in place by centrifugal force. "The Earth is the cradle of the mind," he wrote in 1896.

and man will not stay in that cradle forever . . . to set foot on the soil of the asteroids, to lift by hand a rock from the moon, to observe Mars from a distance of several tens of kilometers, to land on its satellite or even on its surface, what can be more fantastic? From the moment of using rocket devices a new great era will begin in astronomy: the epoch of the more intensive study of the firmament.

Tsiolkovsky's designs for liquid-fueled rockets provided the foundations of rocket science many years in advance of its actual use. That the world failed to take quick advantage of his pioneering calculations has made him a classic "man-out-of-his-time" or, as some would say, a member of the world's most exotic minority.

But truly there are no men born ahead of their times. There are only visionaries, and there are circumstances; everything else is hindsight.

It is no "joke of history" that the first practical application of Tsiolkovsky's and Goddard's work came whistling down on London and Dover. Looking back and knowing what has been done since Tsiolkovsky's day, we are tempted to ask how much sooner men could have peered down from space.

The question is pointless. How strange to think that—despite the ingenuity of men like Tsiolkovsky, Goddard, and von Braun—V-2 rockets, *Sputnik 1*, *X-15*, and *Freedom 7* might never

Astronaut Alan B. Shepard, Jr. was the first American to be launched into space. On May 5, 1961, Shepard made a 15-minute suborbital flight in Freedom 7. Photo by Brown Brothers.

have existed (and they might never exist, even given 200 years of the future to work with), if not for World War II and the Cold War that followed.

The one positive thing that can be said for the protracted U.S.-U.S.S.R. conflict is that, overall, it has sustained an ever-accelerating outburst of knowledge. Very rapid progress, it seems, requires crisis. In the absence of deeds that have been performed and must be responded to, men like Goddard find themselves working alone in their spare time and with limited funds. In the presence of a *Sputnik*, they find whole space flight centers named after them (if only posthumously).

The progressive periods of history have been few, and these have generally borne a disturbing resemblance to the evolutionary fits and starts seen in the life histories of some "fossil species." For more than 200,000 years, tool-making humans followed a nomadic, tribal existence. Then, seemingly out of nowhere, there appeared agricultural centers in Egypt, Mesopotamia, and India's Indus Valley—complete with written records, elaborate temples, schools, libraries, sailing ships, wheels, and a knowledge of astronomy.

No one knows why the explosive growth seen between 3400 and 3100 B.C. occurred. Too little information has been preserved. It might have resulted from an accumulation of inventions that awaited merely the fortunate conjunction of circumstances. A new way of life based upon agriculture was evidently one of these circumstances. Surplus grain could be stored or bartered, and shipping or storage required storage containers, which facilitated the development of potter's wheels and kilns. Add to this a need for knowing whose storage containers belonged to whom, how many containers one owned or had traded, or would trade, and the invention of written symbols, for numbers, one's own name—and the names of different "cash crops" is the next obvious step.

There, see what I've done? I've used the word *step*, and I should have known better. If the lessons of history and archaeology are clear on any single point, it is that civilization did not ascend step by sequential step, powered by a gradual increase in understanding. The story of the Sumerians, Egyptians, and the Indus-Valley civilization is one of impressive advancement over a few centuries, followed by almost two thousand years of stagnation and even regression.

By the time Augustus Caesar defeated Queen Cleopatra and Mark Anthony at Alexandria, Egypt had been in cultural eclipse for centuries. Art styles had gone essentially unchanged since the pyramid-building first dynasties, and the country had become impoverished.

Roman civilization—which owed much in its beginnings to the

Cleopatra and Julius Caesar. Photo by Brown Brothers.

Built in 19 B.C., under the reign of Augustus Caesar, the Point du Gard aqueduct is one of the finest examples of Roman engineering in existence. Photo by Brown Brothers.

Greeks—came to its height between A.D. 50 and A.D. 150 (*after* the so-called "rise of moral decay," characterized most prominently by the reigns of Tiberius and Caligula, and cited by Jerry Falwell and his kind as the cause of the empire's collapse).

Roman engineers possessed an advanced knowledge of metallurgy, pistons, primitive steam engines, and differential gears with shifting devices that allowed two shafts to rotate at different speeds (a principle later applied to the hour and minute hands of clocks and to the transmissions of cars). Although some of these devices were connected in order to open doors and to create sophisticated toys for display at public games, no one seems to have thought of mounting a steam engine on wheels or under the deck of a galley. No urgent need called for work to be done more efficiently than was already being done by manual labor. Had a competing country started transporting trade goods by railroads and steamships, a response would have been required from Rome, and the industrial revolution might have preceded Columbus by 10 centuries.

But there were no competing countries.

Napoleon at Waterloo. Photo by Brown Brothers.

Kaiser Wilhelm and army officers at Graf Zepplin. Photo by Brown Brothers.

Rome at the time of Augustus (emperor: 31 B.C. to A.D. 14) had successfully engulfed every nation within range of its influence. In the absence of great external disturbances, Rome descended into nearly 350 years of technological stasis. That the last surge of Roman creativity ran in parallel with the Germanic invasions can hardly be ascribed to coincidence.

Roman control of the Mediterranean was brought down late in the fifth century by the Vandals and other invaders. Rome seemingly invited the invasions by its increasingly feeble existence (just for a start, the Roman army of A.D. 450 was made up almost entirely of foreign mercenaries who couldn't have cared less).

In the Middle Ages, the focus of empire building had shifted away from the Mediterreanean and to the north. England, Spain, Portugal, France, the Netherlands, and others were rising nation-states that competed in trade and frequently warred with each other but never succeeded in establishing a universal empire. There were several close calls: Charles V (holy Roman emperor: A.D. 1519 to 1558), Napoleon, Kaiser Wilhelm, and Hitler—to name a few.

All seem to have been frustrated to varying degrees by inde-

43

pendent nations that knew how to exploit natural barriers such as penninsulas, mountains, bogs, endless tracts of snow, and of course, the moat surrounding England.* By the time the European contest began to quiet down, America and Russia had emerged as new and ominous powers.

*Robert G. Wesson, professor of political science at the University of California in Santa Barbara, points out that in Eastern Europe—where natural geographical divisions are generally less clear-cut than in the west—nation-states have been less stable, there has been less political freedom, scientific and technological progress has been relatively slow, and multinational empires have prevailed.

Squirrels have nested in the ascent stage of America's First Lunar Module. Seen in these odd surroundings (odd for a Rome after the death of Augustus. At this writing, Assistant Air and Space Curator Joshua Stoff is overseeing the spacecraft's

Since World War II, a chancy "balance of terror" has maintained the longest unbroken strategic peace humankind has seen for several centuries. Although there is danger in presuming that our electronic civilization can survive indefinitely under a policy that reads like the golden rule applied to atoms, $1 will get you $5 that we'd have seen World War III two decades ago were it not for the terrifying marriage of rockets and deuterium. Instead, we have enjoyed the benefits of sustained competition force fed by crises.

One such crisis arose when the Soviets managed to hang a few

spaceship, at least), Apollo LTA-1 *is a shrine to a program of planetary exploration that succeeded too well and became like transferral to the Cradle of Aviation Museum at Mitchel Field, Garden City, New York.* Photos by C.R. Pellegrino.

kilograms of magnesium on the other side of the ionosphere and, in so doing, challenged the salability of American technology overseas. Not to be outdone, Americans demonstrated that we could walk on the Moon, without considering that in so doing we had performed a deed for which there could be no response.

The world watched and nothing happened. Truly nothing. No other nation answered the challenge and our drive soured. Near stagnation followed. Plans for the exploitation of lunar resources and a permanent platform in space were scrapped, half-built Lunar Modules (LMs) were packed up and shipped off to any museum that would take them, construction of a space shuttle was set back more than a decade (and almost cancelled entirely), and planetary probes were put on "indefinite hold." Some projects were halted in mid construction, much to the dismay and frustration of our European allies who are presently stuck with *their* half of a solar-polar spacecraft.

Today, in an old garage at Sands Point, New York, LM Test Article 1 rests half-buried in broken dining-room cupboards, aircraft parts, horse-drawn carriages, and a demolished lunar rover. Squirrels have nested in the ascent stage. The world's first completely fitted and rigged Lunar Module is a shrine to a program of planetary exploration that outdid itself and became like Rome after the death of Augustus.

Meanwhile, the Soviets are constructing a space station and a space shuttle *, and Japan and Western Europe have entered the arena. The Chinese have already launched small animals into space, and they are planning to put a man in orbit by 1990.

During his recent visit to New Zealand, a high-ranking Toyota executive renewed the challenge: "If our company had built the space shuttle," he said, "the tiles would never have fallen off."

Whether or not we care to recognize it, a second space race will soon be upon us. And this time they'll be playing for keeps.

---

*Today the Soviet space effort brings yawns in Washington, D.C. Barring any radically new spacecraft design, a manned mission to Mars would require about eight months of travel time in a weightless environment, followed by at least several weeks in the gravity of the Martian surface, and then eight additional months of weightlessness during the return trip. Such a venture would probably also require the launching of supply modules that could be inserted in Mars orbit and docked with as needed. Such modules are routinely launched into Earth orbit to supply the *Salyut* space station, where Cosmonauts endure a weightless environment for as long as eight months without pause, return to Earth for a few weeks, and then go right back into space for another extended stay. The Soviets also appear to be developing a giant rocket with up to twice the lifting power of the *Saturn V* that nudged *Skylab* into orbit. These activities cannot be without purpose. The Soviets do nothing without purpose.

3 Shrinking Horizons

All moons, all years, all days, all winds, take their course and pass away.

A Mayan Prophet

Our disquieting thought is that this is not the Earth of our past, but only a fragile blue globe amid a void so black as to be brilliant . . . Now, so far from childhood's home, we see the full planet revolve beneath us. All the works of man's earlier greatness and folly are displayed in our window in the course of a single day. The world of ancient Rome, explorer's paths around continents, trails across old frontiers, and migrations of peoples take on added significance in our act of seeing.

Harrison "Jack" Schmitt

Most people are puzzled by curved space, even those who live in curved spaces.

Edward R. Harrison

In 1860, Abraham Lincoln became the sixteenth president of the United States; Mark Twain was 25 years old; Charles Darwin, aged

President Abraham Lincoln with General George B. McClellan (right) and Allan Pinkerton (left). Photo by Brown Brothers.

48

Samuel Langhorne Clemens is best known as Mark Twain. Photo by Brown Brothers.

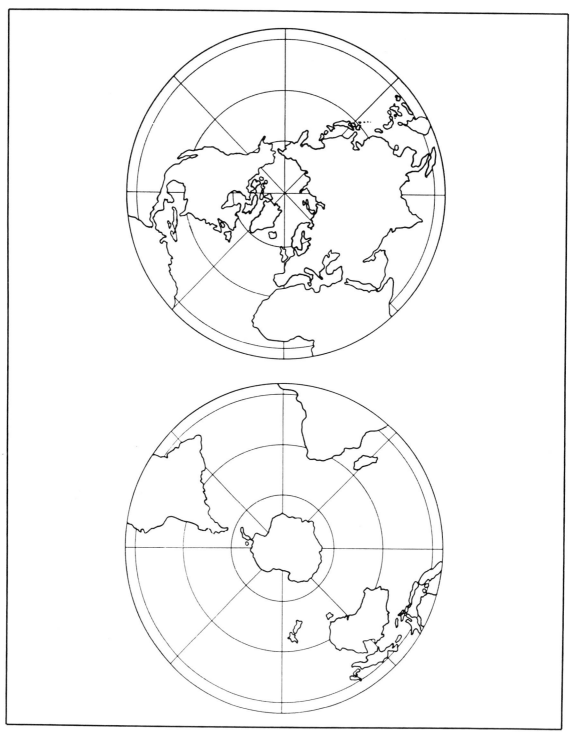

The continents in 1860.

51, had just published his *Origin of Species*; and London was 2 meters (80 inches) closer to New York than it would be in 1984.

New York would have been unrecognizable to you and me. Times Square was then an island of rectilinear farms. Country homes stood north of Canal Street. Mulberry Street was where you found the tastiest mulberries in town. There were tall pines on Pine Street, cedars on Cedar, apple trees on Orchard, and cherries on Cherry Street.

George Washington had spent a presidency in number 3 Cherry Street, the site of America's first White House in America's first capital city. Number 3 Cherry Street is long gone, they built the Brooklyn Bridge there. During the Revolution, on Wall Street, Washington's followers had built a wall to keep the British out. At least they tried to build a wall. New Yorkers kept stealing the lumber.

Water Street ran knee deep with every high tide. A cool stream flowed down Maiden Lane, where Dutch girls came to do their

Departure of the 69th regiment from New York City on April 23, 1861. The Irish headquarters around St. Patricks Cathedral, corner of Prince and Mott Streets. Photo by Brown Brothers.

The Battery and the lower Manhatten skyline (top photo) are seen from New York Harbor in the 1860s. The tallest skyline structure was then the steeple of Trinity. The church is still there today (on Church Street, of course). If you scraped away some of the black marble, you'd see that the building was originally white, in the days before the news media began to list air quality among its weather predictions. Wooden sailing ships are seen in a view looking toward Manhattan (bottom photo). At this time, Times Square was covered with small farms. Photos courtesy of the New York Historical Society, New York City.

laundry. On warm days, Maiden Lane was indeed lined with maidens (Broadway was not). South Street was never south (it is east).

To the north and to the south, where latitude and longitude converge on specific points at the Earth's poles, two frontiers remained to be explored. Southward the record had been held since 1841 by the Scottish explorer James Clark Ross. He had located a seaway into the Antarctic continent, which he naturally named the Ross Sea. He sailed south until, at 77.50 degrees S, at 1418 kilometers (882 miles) from the South Pole, his progress was halted by a wall of pale blue, wind-polished ice. It stood close on 100 meters (333 feet) high. This was the snout of a vast ice front that radiated from the pole, spilled off the continent, and ran seaward. Not surprisingly, Captain Ross named it the Ross Ice Shelf. He also named Ross Island, Ross Point, the White Cliffs of Ross . . ..

In the north, an abundance of major ports and easy access to such technological developments as steamships with centrally heated cabins facilitated penetration into the Artic. The northern record, set in 1855 (while Alex Haley's ancestor, "Chicken George," was becoming one of South Carolina's most celebrated gamecocks), brought Elisha Kane and his crew within 810 kilometers (503 miles) of the North Pole, exceeding Ross' southward penetration by 4.7 degrees of latitude.

It was 128 years earlier—when George Washington was born and Catherine the Great of Russia was four years old; when Benjamin Franklin, who would one day be declared "the most dangerous man in America" (by King George III), opened the Philadelphia Public Library and Hadley invented the sea quadrant (a major navigational tool used in measuring angles and heights of stars to fix latitude)—and Vitus Bering held the official record for pushing north the human frontier, at 66° N, on the margin of the Artic Circle.

Commissioned by Czar Peter the Great to find the limits of Russia's possessions, Bering set forth, in 1724, traveling east from St. Petersburg across 8000 kilometers (4972 miles) of Siberian wasteland to the superpeninsula of Kamchatka. There he supervised the construction of ships and followed the far-eastern coast north to the Bering Strait (65° N). Eighty nine kilometers (55 miles) across the strait lay Alaska, which Bering explored and Russia claimed.* There can be little doubt that Bering's northernmost

---

* Russia held Alaska and the Aleutian Islands until Czar Alexander II sold them to the United States in 1867 to recoup his losses over a section of land contested by Turkey, France, England, and Russia. This was the Crimean War, best known for a foolish bunch of British cavalry that charged headlong against Russian cannons . . . and won. The charge was led by Lord Cardigan—who knitted for himself sweaters that he loved—yes, Cardigan sweaters. The charge that put America's largest state up for grabs is well known as the Charge of the Light Brigade.

New York in 1732, with Trinity Church dominating the skyline. Replica steel engraving by Joshua Stoff.

55

Benjamin Franklin and his printing press. Photo by Brown Brothers.

Vitus Jonassen Bering explored the far northeast for Peter I. The expedition wrecked on Bering Island. Photos by Brown Brothers.

incursion had been surpassed by Eskimos who, traveling overland, breached 70° N.

Sailing south into the Bering Sea, Russian explorers became the first to map the coasts of Alaska, British Columbia, Washington, Oregon, and northern California. Near San Francisco, Russian settlers ran into Spanish explorers heading north. This standoff did not end until after Napoleon, scrounging for money to finance his wars, persuaded France to sell the United States all the land between the Mississippi River and the Rocky Mountains—1803's Louisiana Purchase—and in doing so triggered America's expansion west of the Rockies.

Toward the South Pole, England had held the record since 1578, when Francis Drake emerged through the Strait of Magellan into a storm and was pushed south into a body of open water. He named it the Drake Passage. This was in the vicinity of Cape Horn, about 3850 kilometers (2393 miles) from the South Pole at 56° S. As

Natives of Siberia. Photo by Brown Brothers.

in the case of Vitus Bering, Francis Drake's was not a very significant record. Cape Horn had been settled by nomadic tribes thousands of years before he got there.

Stepping back two centuries and 56 years, there is no point in mentioning the highest latitudes penetrated by ships because longitude now provided humanity with a limitless horizon.

In 1476, 16 years remained before Columbus would discover Haiti and the Bahamas. Michelangelo was one year old. Copernicus

Celebrating the Louisiana Purchase. Photo by Brown Brothers.

was three. Leonardo da Vinci would soon be inventing the parachute. Handguns were becoming all the rage in Europe, and Caxton was preparing Chaucer's *Canterbury Tales* for its first printing. In that year, Western Europe was the technological master of the world.

But there were the Aztecs, the Inca, Polynesians, and Japanese—a planet full of disparate civilizations that had not yet found each other. Nobody knew, at the time, that a master had emerged.

A.D. 964: the focus of human civilization has shifted. Chinese civilization entered the Bronze Age between 3500 and 3000 B.C.. It came to its creative zenith in the era of the "Warring States," centered at 500 - 250 B.C. and coincident with the Renaissance of Indian civilization. The China of A.D. 964 was the most technologically advanced power in the world, having developed paper, gun-

Francis Drake was the first Englishman to circumnavigate the globe. In 1577, he navigated the Strait of Magellan in his ship the Golden Hind. **Photo by Brown Brothers.**

The charge of the Light Brigade. Photo by Brown Brothers.

Leonardo da Vinci and his sketch of a flying machine. Photo by Brown Brothers.

powder, the widespread use of steel, and the first magnetic compass.

The nation grew even stronger during its subsequent campaign to drive out the Mongols. It spread to dominate Indonesia, Malaya, and Ceylon, becoming a united empire while Europe remained a collection of divided and largely uncooperative nation-states. That very division of powerful countries probably gave Europe the eventual lead. Under a series of unifying dynasties, China drew mysteriously within itself and became increasingly bound by tradition. The empire waned static and enfeebled from within.

China was the technological master, yet it was Arab ships that—in the tenth century—ruled the Indian Ocean. In Baghdad and Samarkand, Islamic scholars studied botany, medicine, and mathematics. They calculated the circumference of the Earth and determined the Moon's influence over tides. Tales of far-flung lands became a folklore that still exists today in the stories of *Sinbad the Sailor* and *Antar of Arabia*, the Bedouin Lancelot who braved wild beasts for a fair maiden's hand. Such epics, carried north by Christian Crusaders, paved the way for medieval Europe's age of chivalry.

While the Arab Empire spread Islam east to the people of Indonesia and the Philippines, Viking ships challenged the cold northern reaches of the Atlantic. In 982, banished for one offense or another, Erik the Red sailed west from Iceland to explore Greenland. He found its southwestern coast capable of supporting a colony and, in 986, returned to Iceland to bring settlers back to Brattahlid.

It was 16 years or so later that Leif, Erik's son, led a party of explorers farther west, to North America, where he founded the Vinland colony (much to the surprise and frustration of the Skelling people, whom Columbus, thinking he had circled the world and found a short cut to India, would later call Indians).

There is no mention in the sagas of Erik and Leif that their voyages back and forth between Greenland and Iceland and Vinland were impeded by drifting ice. But the early sagas do speak of excellent growing conditions and great numbers of cattle that could be pastured in Greenland.

Manhattan Island in 1476. Courtesy of the New York Historical Society, New York City.

The port at Genoa, Italy in 1476. Replica wood cut by Joshua Stoff.

65

At the time of Leif's death, some 200 farms dotted the Brattahlid and Godthåb settlements, now located at the snouts of glaciers. Archaeological studies tell of a climate that was clearly more benign than the present one. Eskimo legends tell of old houses and churches buried under the ice.

The Vikings, Europeans, and Chinese fell upon hard times in the 1300s. This was the time of an enigmatic event known as the "Little Ice Age," which produced the greatest extensions of ice on land and sea since the Laurentide ice sheet. Icelandic descriptions of the Baltic Sea as an unbroken ice field during winters of the fourteenth century—of wolves crossing from Norway to Denmark on a bridge of solid ice—bear testimony to an apparent cooling of the Earth's climate that spread drift ice on the North Atlantic and forced sailing routines deeper and deeper south. Contacts between Iceland and her western colonies became increasingly difficult to maintain.

Then the black plague struck. Left to fend for themselves, the colonies eventually succumbed to Eskimos and Indians.

Far to the southwest, the Maya of A.D. 964 were in the grip of a horrible spasm. Palenque—where 300 years earlier had ruled the god-king Pascal, and where the preceding generation had known markets and public pools and orchards—now crumbled in silence.

The landing of Lief Erickson in the New World by Edward Moran. Photo by Brown Brothers.

Someone built cooking fires in Pascal's abandoned temple. We know from pathological studies of his contemporaries (preserved skeletons) that this nameless intruder probably suffered from malnutrition.

Palenque was the first to fall. In its palace courtyard, dark green foliage began a crazy garden. The jungle crept up the avenues and climbed the steps. The city belonged to the lizards.

During Europe's dark ages, the Maya plotted the wanderings of Venus to an accuracy of 13 seconds a year. Their astronomers learned to predict solar and lunar eclipses and invented a calendar system more precise than that developed by Augustus Caesar of Rome. Time, above all, obsessed the Maya. It drove them to pioneer the mathematical concepts of zero and infinity. They viewed time in strange ways past and future shooting away in opposite directions from the present and then knotting together—becoming indistinguishable. They might have been onto something.

At that time, the horizons available for human exploration were limited to how far a ship's crew could take her and return to tell the tale. The horizon seemed endless—restricted only to the number of undiscovered lands on the other side of the sea and to whatever lie beyond those undiscovered lands—just as our present horizon extends to and beyond the Hubble limit (about 15 billion light years away, where the recession velocity of galaxies in expanding space equals the velocity of light). The horizons of both sea and space are endless, but neither is infinite.

Endless but not infinite? Can that be true?

Sure it can. Ships do not, as Columbus was forewarned, sail in straight lines and run clear off the Earth. You can advance in any direction, over land and sea, without ever coming to an insurmountable barrier and, if you stay true to your course and travel far enough, you will come right back to where you started. The earth is finite and unbounded; it is curvilinear. The same might hold true for the universe, where the curvature of space-time is Einstein's general theory of relativity.

We now encounter a variety of endlessness that is different and less intensely endless than the endlessness represented by an infinity of points on the surface of the Earth.

(?)

Quick! Which is bigger? An infinite number of points on the surface of the Earth or the number of points on the surface of a bigger sphere on which the Earth is itself only a speck? Questions like that are unwelcome in an orderly universe. They are the stuff of nightmares, albeit fascinating ones.

If we wake up in a universe that is intensely infinite and unbounded, then common sense drops dead and we become slaves

Columbus ridiculed at Salamanca (top) and Columbus before Ferdinand V and Isabella I (bottom). Photos by Brown Brothers.

De Jnſulis inuentis

Epiſtola Criſtoferi Colom (cui etás noſtra multū debet : de Jnſulis in mari Jndíco nup inuetis. Ad quas perquirendas octauo antea menſe: auſpiciſs et ere Jnuictiſſimi Fernandi Hiſpaniarum Regis miſſus fuerat) ad Magnificum dñm Raphaelez Sanxis: eiuſdē ſereniſſimi Regis Theſaurariũ miſſa. quam nobilis ac litterat⁹ vir Aliander d Coſco: ab Hiſpano ydeomate in latinũ conuertit: tercio kl⁹ Maÿ. M.cccc.xciÿ. Pontificatus Alexandri Sexti Anno Primo.

Q   Quoniam ſuſcepte prouintie rem perfectam me pſecutum fuiſſe: gratũ tibi fore ſcio: has pſtitui exarare: que te vniuſcuiuſcp rei in hoc noſtro itinere geſte inuenteꝗ admoneāt. Tricefimotertio die poſtꝗ Gadibus diſceſſi: in mare Jndicũ perueni: vbi plurimas Jnſulas innumeris habitatas hominib⁹ reꝑeri: quaꝝ oim p feliciſſimo Rege noſtro: preconio celebrato τ vexillis extenſis: cōtradicente nemine poſſeſſione accepi. primeꝗ earum: diui Saluatozis nomen impoſui (cuius fret⁹ auxilio) tam ad hāc ꝗ ad ceteras alias quenim⁹. Eam vero Jndi

Columbus landing in America (top) and the first letter of Columbus giving an account of the discovery of America. Photos by Brown Brothers.

Eskimos in Labrador. Photo by Brown Brothers.

The Black Death swept Europe and parts of Asia during the fourteenth century, killing perhaps 25 million people. Photo by Brown Brothers.

70

Paris in A.D. 964. Replica tapestry by Joshua Stoff.

to a peculiar arithmetic: $00+1=00-1=00\times00=00/2=\sqrt{00}=00^2=00$.

This same arithmetic dictates that the number of points on the Earth's surface—indeed, the number of points on a millimeter-long line on the Earth's surface—must equal the number of points in all of space. We have become victims of a cosmic joke.

University of Massachusetts astronomer Edward R. Harrison is not laughing. He points out that, in an infinite and unbounded universe, where one could go in a straight line forever and ever into the unobservable space that lies beyond the Hubble limit—well, billions and billions of Hubble lengths (forgive me this trespass, Dr. Sagan) are nothing compared to infinity.

If between all those Hubble lengths lie an infinity of planets, then there must also exist every kind of planet, including planets exactly like Earth (except with Chicago mobsters or Romans or feral children ruling). As if to provide relief from infinite horizons, Rudy Rucker of Randolph-Macon College, Virginia, argues that this is not necessarily so because an infinity of planets does not *have* to

The ruins of Palenque qualify as one of the world's most mournfully beautiful sights. By A.D. 964, this center of Mayan culture had been left suddenly and mysteriously to the rule of lizards and malnourished vagrants. In the "palace courtyard," dark green foilage had begun a crazy garden. The jungle crept up the avenues and climbed the steps. In writings that have survived are Mayan interpretations of zero, infinity, and of time itself and hints of a universe that was not rediscovered until Albert Einstein came along. Photos by C.R. Pellegrino.

*Edwin P. Hubble. Hubble's law
states that the greater the distance
between any two galaxies the
greater is their relative speed of
separation. Photo by Brown Brothers.*

contain, say, an identical version of yourself living an identical life.
"We can see this by considering a numerical analogy," he writes:

> Let E be the "universe" of all even numbers. E contains
> infinitely many numbers, yet it does not contain every possi-
> ble type of number, to wit, it contains no odd numbers.
> Although an exhaustive collection of planets would (probably)
> have to be infinite, an infinite collection of planets need not be
> exhaustive.

It probably doesn't matter. Roman Earth's or not, a straight
line, unending universe—Isaac Newton's universe—runs us smack
into the same dilemma raised by medieval Europe's concept of an
Earth that runs flat in all directions. Does nothing exist except
endless expanse? Nothing more?

Columbus comes to the rescue, reminds us that the Earth is
finite and unbounded. In this sense, the world can be truly endless,

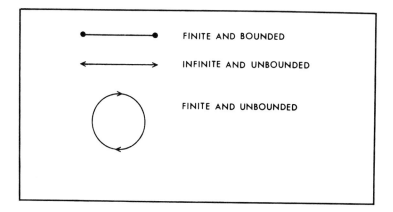

FINITE AND BOUNDED

INFINITE AND UNBOUNDED

FINITE AND UNBOUNDED

but at the same time finite because you can travel all the way around it without ever falling off an edge or running against a wall. Nonetheless you must eventually re-cross your paths.

Varieties of the infinite.

Einstein provided a similar means of escape from the fate of a straight-line universe: "Gentlemen, if you will observe the next eclipse of the sun carefully, you will be able to explain what is wrong with the perihelion of Mercury."

This meant that the planet Mercury, being 92 million kilometers (57,000,000 miles) closer to the Sun's gravitational influence than the Earth, was aging at a slightly slower rate—at a measureable rate—and was thus "out of sync" with the rest of the Solar System. The deviation of Mercury's orbit resulting from this turned out to be quite small, a mere 4.3 seconds of arc per year, but it was large enough to shatter Newton's universe beyond recovery.

In Newton's rectilinear universe, three-dimensional space runs flat in every direction and a body will move at constant velocity in a straight line unless acted upon by a force. The *force* of gravity then accounts for the circular motions of Mercury and Earth around the Sun.

In Einstein's universe, gravity is a product of geometry, and space-time becomes a physical reality in its own right: the geometry of space and time is controlled by matter (matter tells space-time how to bend) and motion is controlled by geometry (bent space-time tells matter how to behave). An important feature of general relativity is that space-time can exist independent of the existence of matter; that is, even something as close to nothing as empty space must still be something.

If there are holes in the universe—regions devoid of matter—space-time will be perfectly flat. A billiard ball thrown into such a region (where gravity equals zero) will travel at constant velocity in a straight line. If, after a period of time, the ball approaches our Sun—a body wrapped in curved space and slowed time—it will accelerate as it swings around the Sun in a curved path. The

Albert Einstein. Photo by Brown Brothers.

centrifugal force resulting from acceleration cancels the effect of gravity; their sum is zero.

If you could travel with the ball, you would not notice the acceleration and would think that you were still moving in a straight line, which, if Albert Einstein's theory has anything to say about it, you are. The Sun alters the geometry of space-time just as a man standing in the middle of a trampoline alters the geometry of the canvas about him. The billiard ball is still following a straight path, but it has become a straight path transposed onto curved space-time. Thus the ball and Mercury and Earth are responding to a warp in space and time, not to a force.

We have seen that the shortest distance between two points on the Earth's surface is part of a great circle—a curved line—because the two-dimensional surface of the planet is bent in three-dimensional space onto a sphere. On a larger scale, the four-dimensional space-time of our universe (as indicated by clusters of gravitationally bound galaxies) might bend into a finite but unbounded range of spherical space-time. All the geometry associated with spheres must then apply.

To see what this can add up to, consider that space is expanding, that the distance between every galaxy is slowly increasing (with a corresponding decrease in the density and temperature of the universe), and that—whichever galaxy you happen to be located in—you perceive yourself as being at the center of the expansion. Now imagine that you can look out into space from a point in our galaxy (the Earth will do nicely) for a billion light years in every direction. You then have a sphere of vision with a radius of 1 billion light years.

Now allow that sphere to expand to 5 billion light years, to 10 billion light years, to 15 billion . . .. If four-dimensional space-time is, by analogy, the surface of a sphere, there comes a time when the surface outside our expanding sphere of vision is itself a large sphere; the circumference of the large external sphere then contracts into a point and disappears on the other side of the universe.

To understand how this happens, imagine yourself at the North Pole on the spherical surface of the Earth. From there, extend your range to Latitude 40° N, which runs through Peking and Philadelphia. Push your range to the equator and from the equator to 40° S, which runs close to Wellington, New Zealand and San Antonio Oeste, Argentina. 70° S carries you into Antarctica, where it becomes apparent that the area outside your expanding range is a large circle with a circumference that has been shrinking ever since you crossed the equator. The shrinkage continues as you advance toward a point at Latitude 90° S on the far side of the world.

In the three dimensions of space, with the fourth dimension of time added, contracting circles are ominous reminders that as we look out into space—as we look back into time—we might eventually find ourselves and the whole cosmos squeezed into a single spot. This disquieting concept was foreshadowed by Pascal: "God is an intelligible sphere, whose center is everywhere and whose circumference is nowhere."

All well and fine, and harmless enough, so long as we do not take the spherical universe too literally and imagine it as being contained in a higher dimensional space (i.e., the ball and the room that contains it and, heaven forbid, whatever lies outside the room). To do this would be to impart extrinsic significance to space-time, and in most scientific circles that is called blasphemy.

The fact that ships sailing the Atlantic are tracing the curve of the Earth is an intrinsic property of our planet's geometry. The fact that we can step away from the Earth and take a grandstand view is an extrinsic geometric feature. But space-time has no extrinsic geometry. Travel in any direction as far as you want and you are still within it. If the universe is indeed a finite and unbounded sphere, then its radius is time itself and we cannot step outside and take an extrinsic view—which is just as well for us.

4 Islands

Out of the chamber of the south cometh the storm, And cold out of the north.

The Book of Job

Prehistoric peoples (in Britannia first, of course) watched sunrises and moonsets from behind aligned stakes, until the stakes rotted; and then they discovered that stones worked just as well and didn't rot. Amazing! Moving on to rock art appreciation, boy, did that Crab nebula supernova get around—no, not the carvings and paintings, but the star itself! In New Mexico the star appeared both north and south of the crescent Moon, in Utah east of it; in Arizona on it, and in California the star positively went into (lunar) orbit. So much, in my mind, for archaeoastronomy as a serious science.

Philip C. Steffey

We expect rough treatment from our colleagues whenever we produce something shoddy . . . The essential factor which keeps the scientific enterprise healthy is a respect for quality.

Freeman Dyson

Dyson makes a good point, but he should have extended
it to say that criticism shouldn't be shoddy either. If it is,
it should be treated just as roughly.

Timothy White

Alkaid moved.

In 60 B.C., the star at the tip of the Big Dipper's handle was 184.32 seconds of arc southeast of its A.D. 1984 position. You could almost see the difference with your naked eye. It was equivalent to a pinhead held out at arm's length.

The distance between London and New York was shorted by 32 meters (107 feet). Niagara Falls, their brinks eroding steadily, were 2 kilometers (1.2 miles) down river of their present location.

This was the year of Rome's ill-fated triple pact, formed by Pompey, Crassus, and an ambitious little fellow who in his youth had been forced to seek a new hiding place almost every night, and to bribe householders to protect him from dictator Sulla's secret police. Pressured by public opinion, Sulla relented with these words: "Very well then, you win! Take him! But never forget that the man whom you want me to spare will one day prove to ruin of the party which you and I have so long defended. There are many Mariuses in this Julius Caesar."

Ten years later, this Julius Caesar would establish a Roman encampment in France. He would call it Paris. Five years after that, in the first year of Caesar's reign as Emperor (49 B.C.), his legions in Britannia would come upon Stonehenge (already in ruin), shrug at it, and move on to found Londinium.

Augustus Caesar was three years old in 60 B.C.. The Servile Revolt, led by Spartacus, had occurred 10 years before. Near

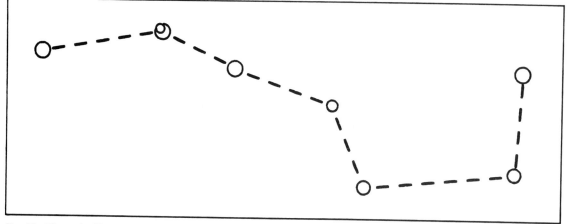

The Big Dipper in 60 B.C.

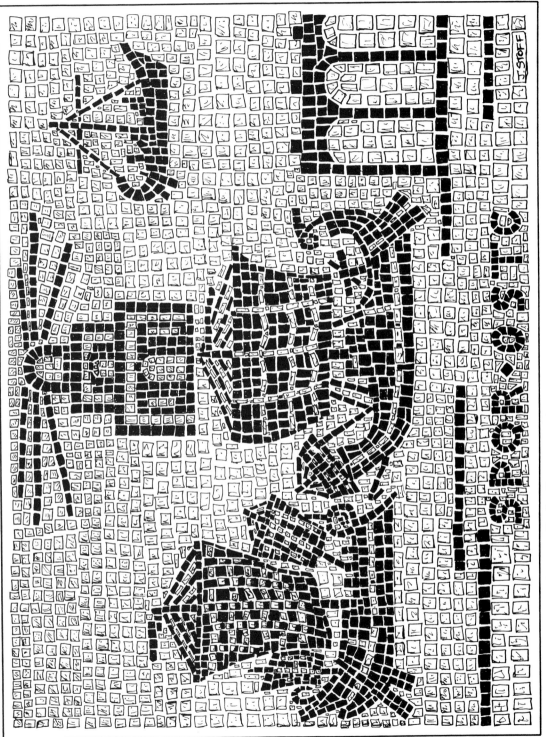

The port and lighthouse at Ostia in 60 B.C. Replica Roman mosaic by Joshua Stoff.

81

Naples, Rome's wealthiest citizens were building villas, along the beautiful shores of Mt. Vesuvius, in the resort towns of Herculaneum and Pompeii.

Caesar crossing the Rubicon. Photo by Brown Brothers.

On the other side of the Atlantic Ocean, Peruvian artists had begun decorating the bleak plains of Rio Nazca with giant intersecting lines, trapezoids, spirals, monkeys, spiders, and birds. Today, some of the lines stretch more than five kilometers (3 miles), ending at the bases of mountains and continuing in perfect alignment on the other side. Animal figures are drawn from continu-

Landing of Julius Caesar. Photo by Brown Brothers.

83

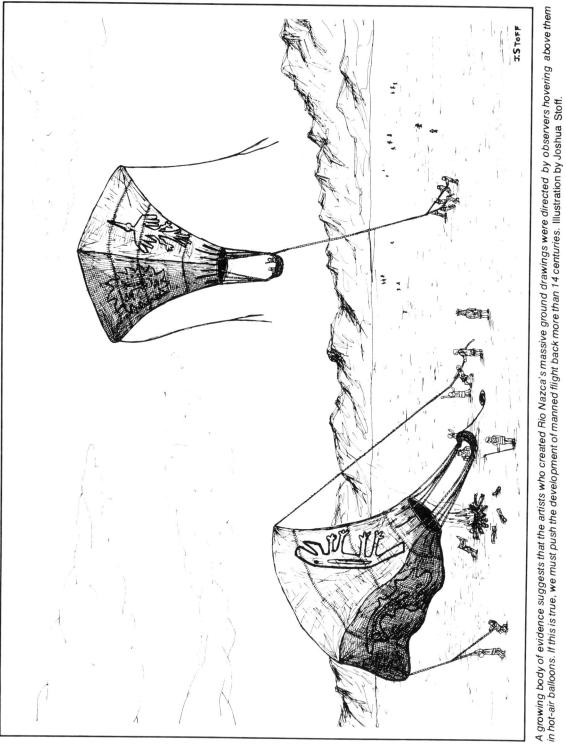

A growing body of evidence suggests that the artists who created Rio Nazca's massive ground drawings were directed by observers hovering above them in hot-air balloons. If this is true, we must push the development of manned flight back more than 14 centuries. Illustration by Joshua Stoff.

One June 5, 1783, Joseph and Jacques Montgolfier inflated a hot-air balloon near Lyons, France. Later that year, a Montgolfier balloon sailed over Paris. Photo by Brown Brothers.

ous lines more than a kilometer long and are recognizable only from the air.

Although this does not by itself permit us to jump to the conclusion that the Nazcas actually did view their ground drawings from on high, clues have begun to pile up. In 1975, members of the International Explorer's Society discovered a compelling document at Portugal's University of Coimbra. An eyewitness account spoke of a Brazilian-born Jesuit missionary named Bartholomew de Gusmão who, in 1709, traveled to Lisbon and was granted an audience at the palace. There he sailed a textile bag on a column of hot air rising from glowing coals in a clay pot. The method, he said, had been used by prehistoric Indians. It was 74 years after Gusmão's demonstration that France's Montgolfier brothers floated a full-scale model over Paris.

In the graves of Nazca Indians have been found woven textiles suitable for making hot air bags. Other excavations have turned up fire pits among the desert drawings, and a figure on a ceramic pot looks astonishingly like the envelope of a balloon.

We know that the last ground drawings were made about A.D. 600. Facing us is the possibility that Nazca's artists were directed by observers hanging above them in hot air balloons, and that we can push the development of manned flight back more than 15 centuries.*

The Great Pyramid at Giza was practically new (a mere 500 years old) in 2108 B.C. All gleaming and clear cut, its sides overlain with white marble, it stood hard and silent over the commotion of a thriving port. This was the time of Egypt's Isis and Osiris cults, and its first libraries.

There were other islands of civilization. The Chinese had determined the Sun's equinoxes (which occur about March 21 and September 22, when the Sun crosses the plane of the Earth's equator) and solstices (when the Sun is farthest from the equator) and developed a calendar that varied in accordance to solar and lunar cycles.

---

*It should not surprise us that these very same people—whose other accomplishments included successful brain surgery (usually to remove splinters of skull), aquaducts, and suspension bridges—had no wheel. Elsewhere in the world, you could capture a wild animal, tie its legs together, fill it with good food, and hope it would learn to like you and pull your cart. Unfortunately, horses and oxen were unknown to the New World until the Spaniards arrived. And jaguars were out of the question. Nor should it surprise us to learn that ancient people got around quite a lot, as indicated by Nazca drawings of animals from Brazil and by the 1982 discovery, in Brazil, of a ship wreck dating to the first century B.C.. The wreckage contains several hundred long-necked urns with distinctive handles. The urns were used to carry water, wine, oil, and grain on long voyages. They are called amphora and—there can be no doubt about this—they were manufactured in Rome. If the ship had managed to get back, an American Declaration of Independence might have been signed 2000 years ago and children might now be playing Romans and Indians.

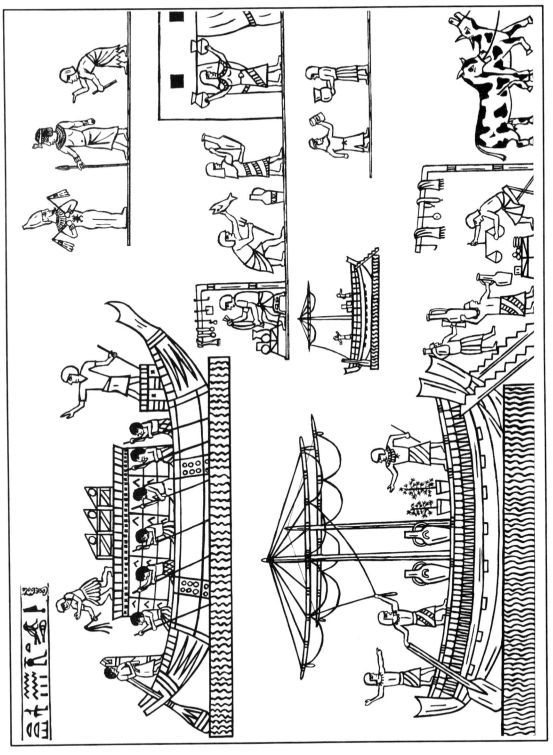

The port of Tyre in 2108 B.C. Replica limestone relief by Joshua Stoff.

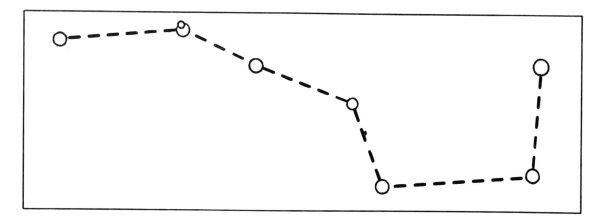

The Big Dipper in 6204 B.C.

Under a climate that was milder than today's, warmer by about 1 to 3°C (2 to 6°F), the Indus civilization flowered. The Peruvians were cultivating cotton. The earliest temple-building Maya were not only cultivating cotton and corn, but they were actually breeding it for desired traits (with each step backward into successive layers of dirt, archaeologists have uncovered harder, more abrasive corn specimens). They were, according to paleopathologists (about a dozen people in the world who study ancient disease), taller than today's Maya, generally better nourished, and prone to arthritus and sinus infections.

Across the Atlantic—narrower by more than 60 meters—the early Minoan period had begun in Crete and Thera. It was six centuries later that this maritime empire would die abruptly and at its zenith. Thera's 120-megaton convulsion sent a 92-meter (300-

Manhattan Island in 6204 B.C. The coming of sky scrapers and paved roads and sewage systems in the twentieth century A.D. did not stifle completely the streams that once ran through Manhattan. One still runs beneath the Empire State Building, where, three floors below 7th Avenue, water pumps are constantly at work. Painting by C.R. Pellegrino.

The three pyramids of Gizeh. Photo by Brown Brothers.

foot) wall of water impacting against Crete. The Minoan fleet vanished under this towering monster.

At almost the same moment, a wave of heavy air laced with ash and steam rolled across the devastated coast, defoliating highland trees and burying farms. There are things in the writings of Plato and in the Bible, glimpses of whole cities going up like the smoke of a furnace and being swallowed by waves—Atlantis, Sodom, Babylon—you wouldn't have wanted to be in the Mediterranean when Thera exploded.

6204 B.C. We have crossed into prehistory. No battles, no kings, no explorers, no centers of population have names.

Cereal grain was being cultivated in Iran. People in Thailand were growing beans and manufacturing wood-fired pottery. A pottery industry had also developed in Japan.

About 2000 years earlier, the Polynesians began their spread from island to island, radiating from Indonesia and Australia and covering thousands of kilometers in canoe like ships. By 6204 B.C., they had probably extended their range to Micronesia, Fuji, Samoa, New Caledonia, and New Zealand. Out of sight of land, with nothing but the Pacific stretching out to the horizon in every direction, navigation by those stable coordinates in the sky—stars—became requisite.

Photos by Brown Brothers. *Using stellar navigation, the Polynesian cultures Cook encountered has begun their island-by-island colonization of the the Pacific some 10,000 years before he set sail. Cook's death in Hawaii is believed to have been triggered when his navigator panicked and ordered his men to fire on the natives (his navigator's name was William Bligh, and he survived Cook to became captain of the H.M.S. Bounty).*

Among the most remarkable tales of celestial navigation (if not *the* most remarkable) is that of a group of men and women who left Tahiti seeking religious freedom. They brought with them the eldest people who had memories of an ancient legend. According to this legend, if they aligned their ships to the Southern Cross, and then followed the stars in a certain way, they would reach a promised land.

As the canoes slid forward on the curving Pacific skin, new stars began to rise on the edge of the ocean. No one had seen these stars from Tahiti. Certain stars were followed, in accordance with the dictates of legend, until the Tahitians came upon the Hawaiian Islands.

If such pinpoint navigation across some 4023 kilometers (2500 miles) of ocean does not sound dramatic, consider that Hawaii's first settlers are said to have made a second voyage to Tahiti and back long before Columbus—bouyed on an Equatorial Current that pointed him in the right direction—came upon land masses spanning the entire west atlantic.

It was 8000 years ago that *Homo sapiens*, essentially a tropical mammal with a preference for temperatures around 22°C (72°F), had radiated from the equator to latitudes as high as 60°. It was the control of fire and the capacity to build that allowed human beings to spread almost from pole to pole. There were no more than 10 million of us then. Although we occupied every major land mass except those higher than 60° north and 60° south, scarcely any individual pockets of humanity knew any more of the earth's surface than their immediate settlements—no more than their own fields, their own valleys, their own shores.

The Taurus-Littrow Valley looked exactly as it would in 1972, before Eugene Cernan arrived and sketched his wife's initials there. The temperature of the universe was still 2.8 degrees Kelvin. Its density was still 10^{-30} the density of water . . ..

14,396 B.C.. The ice had come; and not on little cat's feet. The Laurentide blanket rivaled todays Antarctic ice fields. It piled up more than 3.2 kilometers (2 miles) high over northern Canada. The pressure of overlaying ice pushed it out across the face of a continent. It edged into Idaho, Nebraska, Kentucky, and New Jersey. In spring, its edges softened and surged. On its eastern margin, meltwater drained into the Hudson River in such profusion that rocks the size of cricket balls were carried seaward.

If you stood on Staten Island, in the middle of the Hudson, and looked several kilometers north, you would have beheld horizon-spannng cliffs of ice. To the south, the Hudson River cut through 161 kilometers (100 miles) of uninterrupted coastal plain where today there is water. The water that formed the giant ice caps came from the sea, and their formation had lowered global sea levels by

Ice Age Manhattan as it might have appeared in the year 14,396 B.C.. (Photos of Antarctica's Dry Valley Region by Andy Frost.)

Changless, in contrast to Manhattan, the Taurus-Littrow Valley is seen in the year 14,396 B.C.. Courtesy of NASA's Johnson Space Center, Houston, Texas. Photomosaic by C.R. Pellegrino.

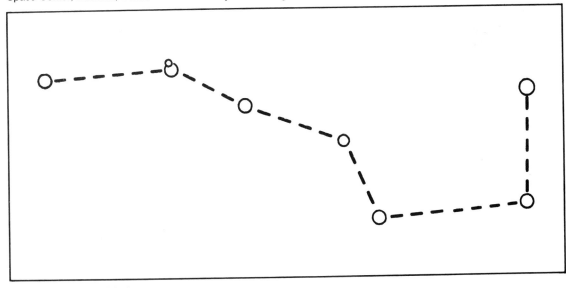

The Big Dipper in 14,396 B.C..

almost 92 meters (300 feet) so that new lands rose out of the oceans.

The climate in upper Egypt was less arid than today's. There were tributaries and there was rain to feed them. Hippopotamus bones found 4 kilometers (2.5 miles) away from the Nile are evidence of swampy areas where none presently exist. Up and down the Nile Valley, a stone-tool industry flourished. Farmers grew wheat, barley, lentils, chick-peas, capers, and dates. Interestingly, they did not adopt a village lifestyle. Instead they remained nomads who planted seeds, moved on, and returned the following season. They apparently saw agriculture as just one more source of food.

In Thailand, domestication of beans and the invention of pottery might have occurred about this time. People were manufacturing partially polished stone tools in Australia. The first settlers had reached South America at least 2000 years earlier. Their descendents would be waiting on Cape Horn when Francis Drake arrived.

Near 12,000 B.C. began the great flood. The ice retreated. The Mississippi River discharged as much as 12,600 cubic kilometers (2000 cubic miles) of water in a single year. From this alone the worldwide rise of sea level would have been about 2.5 centimeters (1 inch) annually. With the Cordilleran, Scandinavian, and Antarctic ice sheets, melting back at comparable rates, sea level could easily have risen twice as much. On the broad, flat continental shelves, oceans lapped menacingly at coastlines, advancing inland 60 meters (197 feet) per year.

In western Montana, the shelf of ice that dammed Lake Missoula gave out. It fell like an express elevator, unleashing a foaming hell that stuck along the southeastern part of Washington State. The water sought lowlands, glutting itself with debris, scouring the land clean, and leaving behind a maze of channeled scablands that looks eerily like the flood-outwash plains of Mars. To the humans of that time, the glacial retreat might well have seemed like the end of the world. To the animals it just about was.

At the height of the last glaciation, the continents supported a rich and varied fauna of mammals. North America alone once housed an assortment of bears, bear-sized beavers, horses, elks, camels, and mammoths. There were peccary, tapir, rhinos, giant sloths, cats—the list goes on and on. What followed, as the ice melted, was an extinction almost on a scale with that of the dinosaurs 63 million years earlier.

The tempo of extinction increased in parallel with the rate of glacial recession, reaching its peak about 6000 B.C. A comparable biological tragedy struck Europe, Asia, and Australia, but not Africa. While the decimaton of large herbivores and carnivores was assisted by humans roaming the planet with spears in hand, their persistence in Africa—a main population center of *Homo sapiens*—seems to

absolve humans of total blame. What was the *other* major cause for extinction?

A proposal for climatic stress does not stand up because the extinction did not coincide with the glaciation itself (presumably the time of greatest climatic stress). Instead, the tempo of extinction was at an all-time high when the glaciers were shrinking at their maximum rate, when the climate was supposed to be getting warmer and milder.

If this is the case, then perhaps the postglacial whodunit has no suspects other than man. After all, New Zealand's Maori burned down most of the South Island forests in their prehistoric hunts for Moas, the largest birds that ever lived (they live no more). Our forebears are also suspect in the extinction of giant ground sloths and wooly mammoths. There can be no doubt about who threatens today's whales. But what about all those other Ice-Age animals? Does the evidence support it?

No, it does not. Just for a start, there's that anomaly in Africa to be contended with, and does all that melting ice really mean a warmer climate?

Let's return to the Mississippi River. Up to 12,600 cubic kilometers of water drained into the Gulf of Mexico during a single summer; 12,600 cubic kilometers of *cold* water. Now consider that it takes 3000 times as much energy to warm a given volume of water 1° C as to warm an equal volume of air by the same amount. This means that the heat gained by a cubic kilometer of water on warming 1° C, in air, must lower the temperature of 3000 cubic kilometers of air by 1° C. This is equal to a volume of air a kilometer on a side stretching from San Francisco to Kansas City.

Put another way, 12,600 cubic kilometers of water, warmed 1° C, would cool a layer of air 100 meters (333 feet) thick and covering the whole United States (with a little left over for Europe) by 22° C (30° F).

True, the earth was getting warmer in the year 12,000 B.C. The *ice* was getting warmer, but warm ice becomes cold water and cold water (cold fresh water) rides the currents at the sea surface and cools the overlaying ocean of air.

To use the Mississippi as an example, the Gulf Stream would have run cold during the glacial retreat—flowing east and across the North Atlantic, as it does today—and have a profound effect on western Europe (perhaps retarding the melting of its glaciers).

Running south along the coasts of Portugal and Morocco, water from the collapsing North American ice fields exerted a penetrating effect even into the tropics. Shrinkage of stable climatic belts probably induced wholesale migrations on continents where land areas were being steadily reduced by encroaching seas.

For many species, this would have been the final *coup de grâce*: They would have had to compete for limited space and resources in areas where changing rain shadows now turned savanna and woodland habitats into hyperarid plains and vice versa (as in the case of Florida, which was transformed by rising waters from desert plateau into lowland marsh). In short, some migrants found themselves in new habitats unsuited to their previous life styles.

The Little Ice Age, which seems to have routed the Vikings and spurred Europe's textile industry, is perhaps a reminder that our present era of global warmth is merely an anomaly amid a cycle of glaciations. Since about 1975, the academic opinion of scientists who propose links between astronomical effects and weather and long-term climate has swung from intense loathing to curiosity to widespread acceptance.

The ice ages result, at least in part, from the periodic wobbling motions (over thousands of years) of the Earth's rotation axis, which varies the amount of solar radiation falling on the ocean masses during perihelion (the point at which our slightly elliptical orbit carries us nearest the Sun). The significance of this lies in the fact that most of our planet's ocean surface, which absorbs heat and radiates it slowly into the wind, is concentrated around the equator and in the Southern Hemisphere.

Other factors, including the Sun itself, seem to affect planetary climate. Cores drilled in compacted snow and ice at the South Pole reveal annual bands of deposition whose thickness over the last 1000 years has varied in parallel with the 11- and 22-year sunspot cycles. One of the more interesting features in the ice is its decreasing nitrate (NO_3) content during the years of the Maunder minimum (a period from 1645 through 1715), during which sunspot activity was almost totally absent), coincident with the height of the Little Ice Age.

In 1981, radiocarbon in the rings of North America's oldest pine trees yielded evidence that the ratio of carbon-14 to carbon-12 has varied in the past, particularly during the Little Ice Age.

Carbon-14 is produced by the transformation of cosmic radiation entering the upper atmosphere. One of these transformations produces showers of fast-moving neutrons (electrically neutral particles, located in the nuclei of atoms). These collide with abundant nitrogen nuclei in the atmosphere, chipping off a positively charged proton and replacing it with an uncharged neutron of approximately the same mass.

A nitrogen-14 atom has 7 protons (+ charge), 7 neutrons (no charge), and 7 electrons (− charge). A carbon-12 atom has 6 each of protons, neutrons, and electrons. A carbon-14 atom has 6 protons, 8 neutrons, and 6 electrons, and is thus unstable (radioactive). It achieves stability through a process called beta decay (whereby a

high-speed electron is ejected from the nucleus via the transition of a neutron to a proton, which raises the atom's atomic number, or + charge, from 6 to 7 and changes it into nitrogen again).

Plants and animals take up both carbon-14 and carbon-12. Death halts the uptake; the organisms's carbon-12 remains, but the carbon-14 changes back into nitrogen with a half-life of 5730 years.

Woods Hole assistant scientist Ellen M. Druffel has verified a carbon-14 anomaly in the skeletons of banded corals growing in the Florida Straits. The ratio of carbon-14 seems to have increased against carbon-12 in the shallow waters from A.D. 1642 to 1710. She also found that the ratio of oxygen-18 to oxygen-16 in these same corals indicates a slight cooling of the Gulf Stream in 1720 and 1760, near the close of the Little Ice Age. *

At present, this seeming paradox of cooling Gulf Stream water during a period of climatic warming is being attributed to changing patterns of ocean circulation, including such unlikely events as southward currents from the Sargasso Sea.

If we turn our attention to the hundreds of tributaries feeding the Mississippi River, a more likely scenario might include spring and summer meltwater. But that is beside the point. Druffel's data support the theory that a decrease in solar activity can modulate the Earth's magnetosphere (a region where particles and radiation are governed by the Earth's magnetic field). This can trigger an influx of cosmic rays that in turn increases atmospheric carbon-14 production and, at the same time, reduces atmospheric nitrogen content, which may be expressed as decreased nitrate content in Antarctic ice.

It seems that we can, therefore, read the Sun's signature on a glacial advance. The obvious next question is how constant is the solar constant? Sooner or later, we are going to have to come to terms with *that* question.

. . . Alkaid!

In 30,780 B.C., the star at the tip of the Big Dipper's handle was 2949.12 seconds of arc southeast of its A.D. 1984 position. You could easily see the difference. Its displacement was equivalent to the diameter of the Moon.

With much of the Earth's water tied up in continent-sized ice sheets, forests grew in what is now the Java Sea. Humans took advantage of the lowered sea level to cross into New Guinea and Australia. The 100 kilometer-wide (62 miles) Exmouth Trench prevented them from making the crossing entirely on foot. They

---

*Ancient water temperatures can be estimated because of the tempeature dependence of the isotopic ratios of oxygen-18 to oxygen-16 during the accretion of calcium carbonate (Ca CO$_3$) to build coral skeletons. Ellen Druffel cautions that the observed decrease in oxygen-18 might also indicate periods of higher salinity of sea water. It is difficult, at this time, to distinguish between the two effects. Nevertheless it is important to note that melting ice produces a *decrease* in salinity.

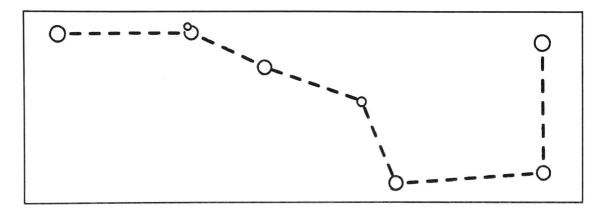

The Big Dipper in 30,780 B.C.

needed boats. And on boats they entered Australia at least 40,000 years ago.

Excavations in Russia show that people near the Aldan River were hunting mammoths, bison, and giant wooly rhinos about 33,000 B.C. The sea that Vitus Bering would one day name was then a stretch of rolling tundra. The first known Americans came out of Siberia, bearing Asian characteristics: wide cheekbones and distinctly shoveled incisors (referring to a curved, "scooped-out" appearance of the front teeth) and, probably, coppery skin, dark eyes, and straight black hair.

By 27,000 years ago, they had occupied the Yukon's Old Crow Basin. Among their relics have been found the jaws of dogs, some of which have been carbon-dated to about 30,000 B.C. Certain minute aspects of bone structure change when animals are domesticated, and these are easily identified and unmistakably present in the Old Crow dogs. They push the era of animal domestication back 20,000 years farther than was previously believed.

Christy G. Turner II of Arizona State University is presently engaged in comparative studies of human dentition throughout time and across geographic barriers. He has learned that, by about 9000 B.C., shoveled incisors became twice as pronounced in American Indians as in their Asian forebears. From this he concludes that America's Paleo-Indians could not have branched off from the Asian stock more than 40,000 years ago because a high frequency of shoveling apparently did not evolve in Asians before that date.

Equally important as fixing a backward limit for the onset of large-scale immigration to America is the suggestion that *Homo sapiens* changed during the course of about 1550 generations spanning the years between 40,000 B.C. and 9000 B.C.

If we pursue the "vulgar version of Darwinism" (not Darwin's version), then small changes in the shape of a tooth were the *perfect* result of a long process of testing and refinement. This view forces us to explain the increase in shoveling among the parent Asian

Prehistoric man carving with sharpened stone. Photo by Brown Brothers.

stock, and then its further elaboration in American Indians (i.e., the spread of a genetic change among individuals), in terms of evolutionary usefulness.

A prehistoric mammoth hunt. Photo by Brown Brothers.

Sounds easy doesn't it? Simply apply the first adaptationist argument that comes along: scooping out the back of an incisor tooth created a more chiseled surface and hence a better edge for cutting and tearing meat. All well and fine, but the Indians had been using fire while the change was taking place, and fire—in a figurative sense—added tens of meters to man's digestive tract. If the meat was tough, it could be softened by boiling (as could cellulose). Fire ushered into the diet a broad range of previously undigestable foods.

See the problem?

How could natural selection modify the form and function of a tooth over many generations—expressing the advantage of a new tooth design by increasing the owner's chances of survival—when a new recipe could provide an equal advantage in the space of a few hours?

In answer, some of the traditional burden of natural selection can probably be lifted from individuals, freeing us from having to break living things down into separate parts (a separate tooth, a separate eyelash), each with its own governing genes, its own history, and its own evolutionary justification.

We need not elevate natural selection to the role of an all-seeing, all-knowing force that works on minutae, scrutinizing every variation and directing organisms as if they were collections of perfect parts . . . an eyelash shaped in detail and located in a specific place for its specific role (?).

American Museum of Natural History paleobiologist Niles Eldredge, and Harvard paleobiologist Stephen Jay Gould have argued that the growth and development of a given part is often linked to the development of other body parts. Shoveled teeth, for example, might be an accidental side effect of some subtle modification of skull shape, which may itself be nothing more significant than a random change occurring in a small, founding population of North Americans (estimated to have averaged 50,000 persons prior to 12,000 B.C.) existing at the edge of humanity's geographic range. Gould writes:

> The principle is as obvious as your big toe, which appears to have developed for no better reason than to keep pace with your thumb. Repeated parts of the body are not fashioned by the action of individual genes. There is no gene "for" your thumb, another for your big toe . . . Repeated parts are coordinated in (embryonic) development . . . It may be genetically more complex to enlarge a thumb and *not* to modify a big toe, than to increase both together.

If he is right, shoveled teeth and other "racial characteristics" that distinguish a Mongol from a Navaho and a Navaho from a Mayan or a European are the ordinary products of geographic variability within our species. Some of these features, it might be discovered, provide no advantage for survival. They might simply be morphologic excursions: changes that neither enhance nor inhibit.

New variants appear to branch off from existing ones in odd, almost random directions. This attests to the hit-and-miss process of variation. Classifying these variants, even when we are dealing with the creature we should know best (especially when we are dealing with the creature we should know best) more often than not invites confusion. Which proves that dwelling too narrowly on the differences between teeth and toes and cephalic indexes can be a mischievous adventure, if not a downright dangerous one.

5 You're Looking Very Neanderthal Today

On Stating the Obvious:

Oxygen consumption (in running cockroaches) was directly related to running velocity.

Science
volume 212, page 331 (1981)

Beetles which seemed to be moving normally were counted as alive, beetles moving but unable to walk were counted as moribund, and those not showing movement within three days as dead.

Nature,
volume 245, page 388 (1973)

Most people who are shot realize what has occurred.
Archives of Dermatology,
volume 96, page 701 (1967)

Development of hydro power in the desert of North Africa awaits only the introduction of water.

Nuclear News,
volume II, page 29 (1968)

Smoking kills. And when you're dead, that's an important part of your life that's gone.

Brooke Shields

Nuclear war is something that may not be desirable.

U.S. Presidential Councellor Edwin Meese

63,548 B.C. seems as good a time as any to define a clear point of divergence in the hierarchy of animal classification. The word species, as used in this book, applies to a population of actually or potentially interbreeding organisms sharing a common gene pool. The phrase *potentially interbreeding* is a key point.

The more than 100 breeds of domestic cats known today are the product of approximately 25 mutant morphological genes, 10 of which contribute in various combinations to the differences between a Persian and an orange tabby. Though different in skeletal structure and outward appearance, Persians and tabbys are both *Felis catus* and, left to their own devices, will produce offspring that are capable of eating, sleeping, spitting, and doing all the things that cats normally do—which includes (of course!) making more cats.

Similarly, all domestic dogs are members of the same species (*Canis familiaris*), but here you can begin to see the emergence of physical isolating mechanisms. The sheer range of sizes places a barrier between Great Danes, at one end of the scale, and Chihuahuas at the other. Although the two could not form an *actually* interbreeding population in the wild, they are nevertheless a *potentially* interbreeding population because a female Great Dane can be artificially inseminated with Chihuahua sperm and will produce healthy offspring (not so the other way around).

The Big Dipper in 63,548 B.C.

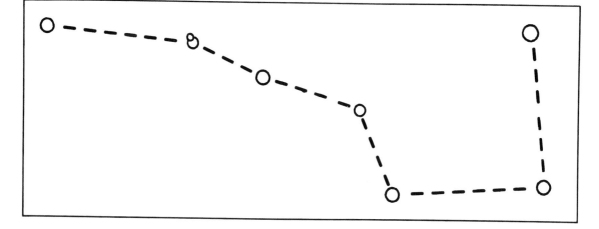

Fine. No one is going to argue about the species concept applied to domestic cats and dogs, especially living ones. Start talking about variation in human beings, especially fossil ones, and you are bound to expose a whole bunch of raw nerves. Ask two paleoanthropologists when *Homo sapiens* broke from an apen ancestor and you will get four different answers. That leads us to the question of Neanderthal man.

He was the original club-bearing "ape-man" brute who, according to folklore, dragged his women around by the hair, lived in caves, and had awful table manners. For various reasons, including religious ones, Neanderthal man is still regarded in some quarters as a creature not yet graced with true sapience. Steven M. Stanley, professor of paleobiology at Johns Hopkins University, is less than flattering of the Neanderthals:

I suggest that we cast off the biases that have led us to embrace Neanderthal as one of our own and instead give him the recognition he was commonly accorded in past decades: status as his own species, *Homo neanderthalensis* . . . The limb bones of Neanderthals were heavier than ours, and it is inferred that their grip was more powerful. Apparently, they were in general considerably stronger for their height . . . Neanderthals were built for strength rather than for swiftness. We must be much better long distance runners . . . average brain volume for some Neanderthal populations seems to have been greater than in our species. This does not mean that Neanderthals were smarter. The difference in volume is slight and may relate to the need for extra neurons to control the Neanderthal's more massive musculature . . . Finally—and I am inclined here to ask whether sexual fantasies have been at work—there is the notion that *Homo sapiens* of our type must have interbred with Neanderthals. Given the great breadth of human sexual behavior, interbreeding probably did take place, but we cannot be sure that resultant offspring were healthy, fertile, or socially acceptable even to their parents.

The observations upon which these statements are based can be affirmed as having substance (after all, even in our twentieth-century "enlightenment" the children of interfaith or interracial marriages too often bear a social stigma). It is the conclusions drawn from these observations that we should question.

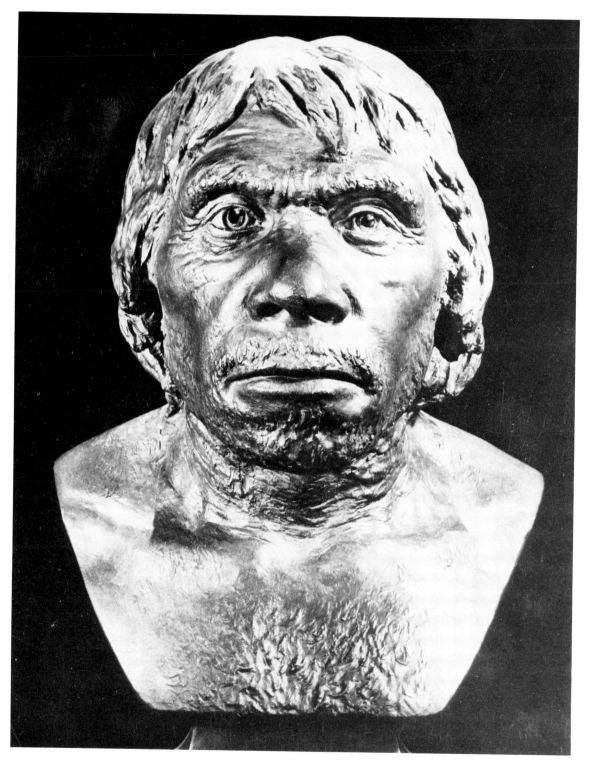

Most Neanderthal fossils are essentially "modern" in skeletal anatomy. Dissimilarities arise from the relative heaviness of Neanderthal bones, and muscles that must have been correspondingly heavier. Their bones are nonetheless fully human in structure, just as Mongol and Navaho incisors—though different in certain details of shape—are derived from the same basic tooth design.

The chief difference between modern man and the Neanderthals is that they weighed more than most of us do today. The "extra" weight was not fat; it was muscle. You wouldn't have wanted to get into a scrap with one. Their distinctive build (which makes them nowhere near as different from us as a Chihuahua is from a Great Dane) might signify nothing more than variation within our species—even specialization—and not "primitive features" belonging to subhuman brutes.

Iran's Shanidar burials, dating to about 58,000 B.C., provide a more civilized picture of the Neanderthals. One individual had lost an arm and the use of one leg. He was unable to take care of himself, yet somebody sheltered him and fed him for several years before he died. And when he died, somebody grieved for him and placed him gently into a grave and provided him, even in death, with food and tools.

At a number of burial sites in Europe and the Near East, bodies were placed on their sides, with the legs drawn up, and with the head resting comfortably on the right arm as if death were regarded as a kind of sleep. The graves contain finely crafted flint tools, charred animal bones (indicating roasted meat) and pockets of pollen (the remains of flowers). It is not likely that the dead were provided with fine tools and cooked food unless these things were somehow meant to be used.

We are witness to hope, and to a deeply felt loss experienced by people who were probably no less human than you or I—brutes that never were.

Human fossils with a pattern of Neanderthal skeletal features extend from Portugal across Europe into the Near East and Soviet Central Asia. Their greatest concentration appears to be in Western Europe, with a focus on France.

The most distinctly Neanderthal features include a low cranium (compared with your own) prominent brow ridges, enlarged nasal cavities, and a forward projection of the face that frequently brings the wisdom teeth ahead of the lower jaw's ascending branch. Notably, these features are variable across intervals of time and geography. Minor deviations from the "classic" Neanderthal pattern, a less dinstinct brow, for example, are known to grade into patterns seen at neighboring sites. The variants are suggestive of evolving lineages (or tribes) that branched off in different directions.

Neanderthal man. Photo by Brown Brothers.

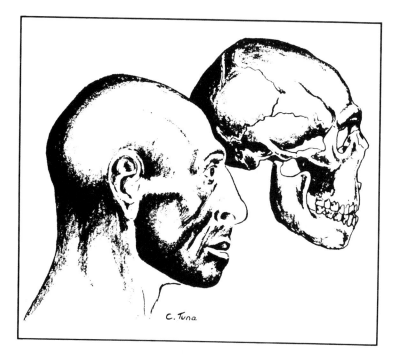

A Neanderthal skull, turned into a fleshed-out individual, would look much like this. Look familiar? Illustrated by C.R. Pellegrino.

Geography and time and (possibly) in *some* cases time *alone**
provide the isolation that leads one lineage to look morphologically
distinct from another. This implied process of branching off in odd
directions, with some of the youngest branches occasionally finding
and fusing with each other (interbreeding) and others terminating
abruptly (extinction), opposes a widely held view of evolution as a
connect-the-dots sequence of ancestors and descendents.

Instead, men migrate across Beringia into the Americas, the
glaciers melt, Beringia is drowned, and one population diverges
into two, each with a distinctive tooth structure. We look today at a
polymorphic species called *Homo sapiens*, the product of untold
branching events whose most striking outward sign is our present
range of skin color.

Today the branching process is hampered by advanced trans-
portation and by the one truly "international language." Except in a
few "religious" circles where self-imposed isolation endures, in-

---

*This message was driven home during my still-in-progress studies of morphologic
excursions in New Zealand crabs belonging to the extinct genus *Tumidocarcinus*.
Fossil evidence hints that an entire interbreeding population underwent a surge of
variation during an episode of climatic cooling(there are clues that the surge corre-
sponded with a population decrease). Time, assisted by environmental stress, can
trigger speciation as surely as placing a mountain range down the center of a
population and then changing the climate on one side. It is time that forbids us from
interbreeding with our remote ancestors, providing a barrier more powerful than any
ocean or range of mountains.

terbreeding is taking place and will continue to take place on a global scale. Given the rate at which this is occuring, we might, in two centuries or so, see today's color lines grading away to an almost universal hybrid (assuming we don't blow ourselves up first).

Of course, 65,000 years ago branching would have been greatly accelerated by limited transport (feet and possibly dug out boats) and by mankind's much smaller numbers (in the hundreds of thousands, compared with today's billions). These conditions were more conducive to rapidly diverging morphologic excursions (genetic change). The population sizes were small and evolutionary rates were apt to be rapid in separate islands (branches) of human occupation.

New Zealand's Wellington weta (*Hemideina crassidens*) provides a convenient analogy. This flightless, cricket like insect is found on the southern coast of the North Island and around Nelson's flooded river valleys on the South Island. It grows to about 6.5 centimeters (2.5 inches) in length. Hiding in dark corners during the day, it crawls out at night to feed on vegetation.

As the latest ice age ended, hills near Wellington became islands and, in the space of 6000 years, a population of wetas isolated on at least one of those islands appears to have diverged. The population currently numbers only a few hundred individuals, ranking them among the world's rarest insects (for this reason, their island habitat is not named here). They are also the world's largest insects. They weigh nearly twice as much as an averaged-sized mouse.

Ballooning proportions must have involved a considerable reorganization of structure and habits over the "short" span of a few thousand generations. Prevailing explanations for the giant weta's existence call for their previous distribution all over New Zealand. It is then proposed that the first Polynesian settlers, and the rats they brought with them, ate all the giant wetas that lived, except for those on one particular island.

There is no fossil or historical evidence to suggest that giant wetas ever lived on the mainland. The claim that they did seems to rest entirely on the belief that even very *small* populations isolated from their ancestral group cannot evolve so quickly as post-glacial divergence would imply.

Examples of rapid evolution abound. Some of the most striking are discussed in Steven M. Stanley's *Macroevolution, The New Evolutionary Timetable* and in the December 1982 issue of *Natural History* (special Hawaii issue). Among these are two species of moths (*Hedylepta maia* and *H. meyricki*), which have evolved in Hawaii to feed exclusively on banana plants. Bananas were first brought to the islands by Polynesian settlers about 1600 years ago. The new moth species can be no older.

It is important to note that, whereas some species appear to emerge in evolutionary fits and starts, the evidence is not yet strong enough to support claims that all (or even most) speciation occurs in this way. It would be a mistake to think that species arise through one mode alone. Nature is not so simple.

Simplistic thinking, what we call tunnel vision, leads inescapably to the *either-or fallacy*. This fallacy pervades the current controversy over rates and modes of evolutionary change. This is particularly true for *punctuated equilibrium* versus *gradualism*. Both views can be true. We should not be surprised to find examples of *"punctuated gradualism,"* whereby one feature—such as shape—changes suddenly while size increases gradually, as appears evident in the shells of some ammonite lineages. It looks as if, in these days of overspecialization, too many scientists are focusing on too narrow a world picture. The result is too much nitpicking aimed at too few new insights.

For the Neanderthals, from which we have little more than fossils to read from, the evolutionary picture is even less clear—if not downright chaotic. These "archaic" *Homo sapiens* might or might not have been direct ancestors of "modern" *Homo sapiens*. In some circles, modern man is believed to have diverged from an even more ancient stock, with Neanderthals occurring as a "side-branch." We simply don't know yet. The evidence is too sparse.

What we do know is that the Neanderthals became established in Europe and the Near East before or during the last interglacial period (a warm period extending from about 130,000 to 80,000 years ago). We know that they spread to the Pacific and possibly across Beringia into America (although no conclusive North American remains have been found), and that they departed abruptly between 45,000 and 40,000 years ago.

In Western Europe, they seem to have vanished utterly and without heir. There are no European intermediates between archaic ancestors and modern descendents, nor are there any skulls suggesting an archaic/modern hybrid. The record suggests local displacement by an invading population, presumably without subsequent interbreeding.

Outside Europe the record looks different. Two sites in Israel have yielded skeletons seemingly intermediate between the Neanderthals and us. The Skhūl specimen, named after the cave in which it was found, has the distinct projecting face and brow ridges of Neanderthal man combined with a modern cranial vault. The specimen dates from about 35,000 B.C.

Skeletons at a neighboring site in Tabūn predate the Skhūl specimen by about 5000 years. They are essentially Neanderthal. A skull from Djebel Qafzeh, presently believed (but with no great confidence) to predate the Tabūn people by about 10,000 years,

110

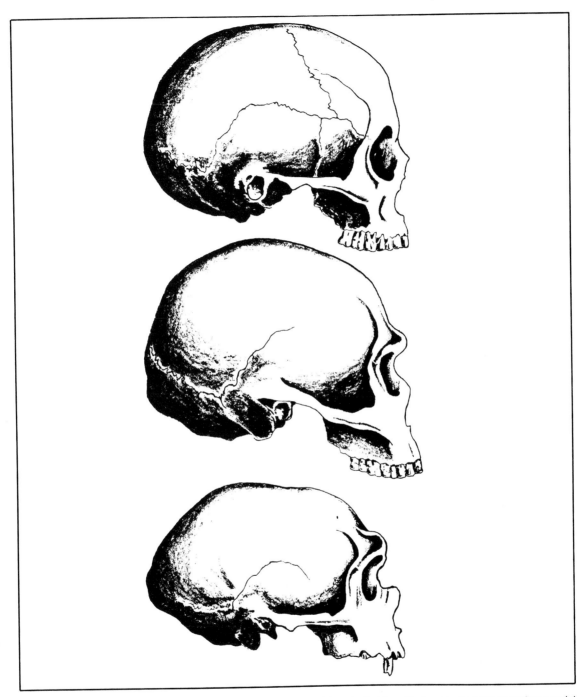

A skull from Skhūl cave in Israel (center) is suggestive of having a Neanderthal face (bottom) tucked into a modern cranial vault (top). Whether the "hybrid" represents an intermediate stage in the evolutionary chain of events leading from archaic men to modern men, or the offspring of interbreeding populations of both, or an evolutionary "side branch," is a question that remains to be settled. Illustrations by C.R. Pellegrino.

more closely resembles the Skhūl skull: a Neanderthal face tucked into a modern cranial vault. Whether the Skhūl and Tabūn specimens represent an intermediate stage between archaic and modern man, the result of interbreeding populations of both, or a side branch is anybody's guess.

A modern-appearing skull from Borneo might date back as far as 38,000 B.C. At about that time, the first humans crossed the Exmouth Trench into Australia. The oldest Australian skulls possess heavy brow ridges and projecting jaws displaying the characteristic Neanderthal gap between the wisdom teeth and the ascending branch. The full Neanderthal pattern is not present, however, and the younger skulls that succeed these earliest known Australians are modern.

It seems unlikely that the "Australian Neanderthals" evolved directly into more modern-appearing men because migrants probably continued to filter in from mainland Java and Borneo throughout the last Glacial Age. There is no reason to believe that, once the first people came to Australia, they simply stopped coming.

It follows that the Australian record could be one of constant influx of people who were undergoing a loss of Neanderthal robusticity in one or more places beyond Java. This record perhaps reflects an episode of outward migration (with Australia on the

Manhatten Island as it might have appeared in the year 129,084 B.C., during the warm interglacial period. Photo by C.R. Pellegrino.

Taurus-Littrow in 129,084 B.C.
Courtesy of NASA's Johnson Space
Center, Houston, Texas. Photo-
mosaic by C.R. Pellegrino.

receiving end) wherein one breed—a newer and less robust one—
somehow out performed the others and eventually won for itself an
entire planet.

129,084 B.C. passed. The interglacial period began, and thick
ice covering West Antarctica's mountains was draining seaward. By
125,000 B.C., Staten Island would be swamped by tides rising 5.5
meters (18 feet) above their present level. London was 2 kilometers
(1.24 miles) closer to New York than it is today. This scarcely made
a difference to migrating eels and bluefin tuna.

If you stood in the Taurus-Littrow Valley that year and compared its rocks and massifs against photographs taken in 1972, you
would have seen immediately how changeless a place can be.
Somewhere in the valley, one or two or perhaps as many as 100,
fist-sized splash marks were missing. You'd have to look awfully
hard to figure out which ones. Only the sky would tell you that
anything had really changed. To a visitor from futurity, the desert
regions and ice caps on Earth wouldn't look right. You could see this
from Taurus-Littrow even without a telescope. And the stars? The
Big Dipper was unrecognizable.

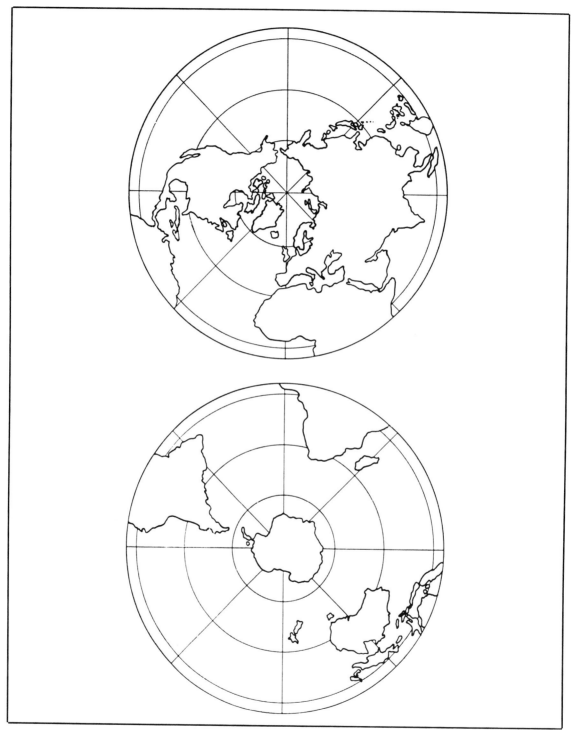

The continents in 129,084 B.C.

The general temperature of the universe was still 2.8 degrees Kelvin. Its density was still 10^{-30} the density of water. The Sun and its neighboring stars, sweeping in a great arc around the galactic center, would cover a distance equal to 1220.64 years of light travel time between 129,084 B.C. and A.D. 1984.

There are no signs that humans had penetrated into Australia or the Americas by this time. The Neanderthals were then concentrated chiefly in Europe and the Near East. Other "archaic" races occupied Africa and the Far East.

Some of the earliest Neanderthal remains are tentatively dated to about 130,000 B.C., although they could be somewhat younger. These are scraps of skull representing two individuals from the Kibish Formation, in the Omo, on Ethiopia's side of Lake Turkana. Both were recovered from the same general horizon in the sediments, yet there are important differences between them.

One individual has an elongated cranial vault that is heavy of bone and does not rise as high above the brow as modern man's. Its cranial capacity (brain volume) is about 1400 cubic centimeters (slightly greater than the average 1330cc for modern man). The other skull displays more modern characteristics: a higher, more lightly boned cranial vault with a less elongated profile at the rear.

The skulls might represent exceptional morphological variation within a population of archaic humans or, more likely, differences between two separate but contemporary populations. Perhaps it represents a split between Neanderthals and moderns.

How such branching progressed is unclear. This is especially true if we pursue an adaptationist line of reasoning. By this time, people had already mastered the use of fire. They were building

The Big Dipper in 129,084 B.C.

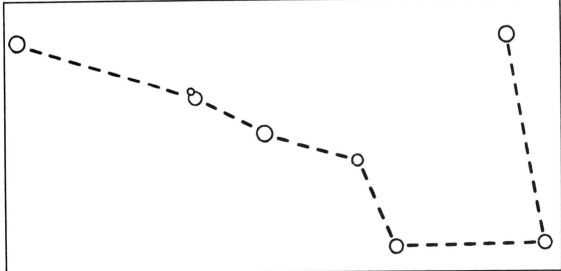

huts and could produce clothing appropriate to the demands of climate. Natural selection's power over human evolution was diminished, and most morphologic change should have been "nonadaptive" in nature (neutral).

This complicates explanations for the reorganization of cranial patterns that seems to define the arrival of anatomically modern man. We don't know what (adaptive) importance the overall loss of robusticity has or if it indeed has any importance at all, but this does not stop some theorists from focusing on the human skull as if it were a collection of individually crafted parts. Such focusing leads to, among other things, proposals that Neanderthal man's large nasal cavities were "useful" because they provided additional volume for warming inhaled air in a chill climate. This might be true but the same enlarged cavities, which gave the Neanderthal nose a broad, flattened appearance, are found in Europe before the cold of the last glacial advance and in zones that were warm during the Ice Age.

Although a strict adaptationist might argue that nasal morphology could have become fixed during a previous glaciation, the counter argument is that an animal-skin scarf would have done the job just as well and been genetically less complex. Enlarged nasal cavities ("useful" or not) might simply be a "side-effect" of overall Neanderthal robusticity.

Peering back into the cellars of time—to European Neanderthals and the Omo fossils—we are reminded, perhaps, that ours is not a straight and narrow ancestry. Instead, we appear to be located at the tip of a branching pattern that knows no end. Look back far enough and we might encounter any number of side branches converging on a single point at the base of the *Homo* limb. A devotion to "either-or" hypotheses and to the naming of things, rather than to an understanding of the variation on which names are based, can easily blind us to a broader view of life.

6 The Naming of Names

What's in a name? That which we shall call a rose
By any other name would smell as sweet.

William Shakespeare

I don't want to classify you like an animal in the zoo But
it seems good to me to know that you're a Homo Sapien
too.

Pete Shelley

The period we are now probing, 522,300 to 260,156 B.C., witnessed the final branching and decline of a lineage called *Homo erectus*. These people had a skeletal anatomy similar to ours, except in the weight of their skulls, shoulder blades, and limb bones. They were, in fact, more robust than the Neanderthals. There can be little doubt that *Homo erectus* was our ancestor. Whether we emerged from their Neanderthal descendents or branched more directly from *Homo erectus,* with the Neanderthals side-branching in a different direction, is still an unanswered question. In either case, both roads lead back to *Homo erectus*.

We know from diggings near the villages of Toralba and Ambrona, in north-central Spain, that about 400,000 years ago bands of 20 to 50 individuals came together and participated in well-organized hunts. Judging from analyses of fossil pollen, the Toralba Valley was then warmer and wetter than it is today.

The Mindel glacial period was in its birth stages. The region was more heavily wooded than present, with tall grass flanking its massifs and lowland swamps. Hunting parties set brush fires in strategic locations and drove migrating herds of deer, horses, wild cattle, and elephants (especially the elephants) into the swamps.

One fossil swamp bed contains hundreds of bones belonging to an extinct variety of straight-tusked elephant that stood higher at the shoulder than today's African species. It's all there in the sediments: tools of stone and bone, even wood, and widely scat-

The Big Dipper as seen in the years 260,156 B.C. (top) and 522,300 B.C. (bottom).

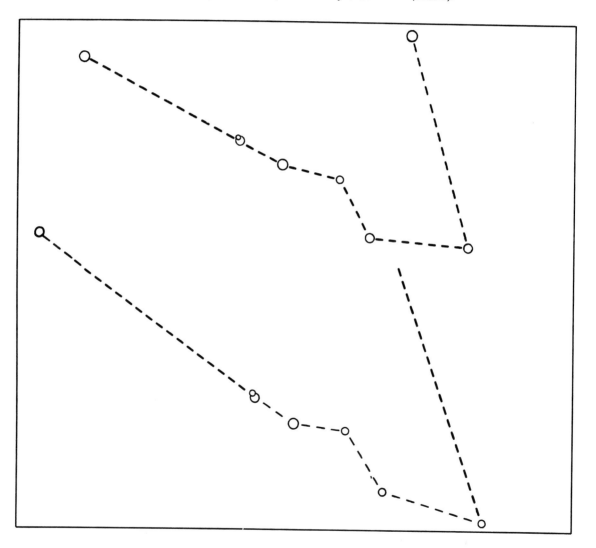

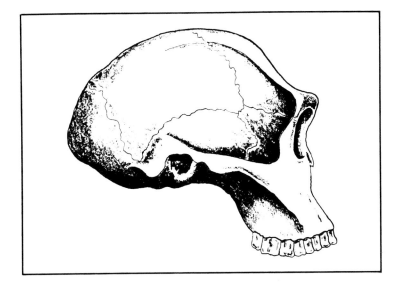

A Homo erectus skull *(partly recon-structed) from the eastern shore of Lake Turkana, Kenya.* Illustration by C.R. Pellegrino.

tered traces of burned trees and grass. Elephants' legs were severed and arranged in rows. No one knows why. One elephant had the entire top carved away from its skull. The brains were eaten. Bones were cracked to expose the marrow. It was eaten. Muscle, soft internal organs, hides—they were all taken.

At about this time in Terra Amata, France, people were leaving their footprints near a beach that no longer exists. They trimmed saplings and leaves and fashioned from them temporary dome-shaped shelters. They built cooking hearths, they slept on animal skins, wrapped their bodies in them, and began to move away from the subtropics into regions of more rigorous climate such as northern China.

You don't do such things—build huts, plan intertribal hunts, set dry grass ablaze and drive herds of wild animals into just the right place—unless you have a means of communicating very specific ideas. It begins to look as if our ancestors knew language a half million years ago. We can probably push its origin back farther yet.

And now the question of species. It's not an easy question to answer. This is especially true because we are dealing with fossil material and only a small portion of an animal's genetic information is expressed as lasting, fossilizable hard parts (as, for example, bone or shell).*

---

*Niles Eldredge describes the problem: "One instance that springs readily to mind is that of lions and tigers. None of us has any problem telling these beasts apart when confronted with the living, breathing animals—or even stuffed ones in a museum. But even those most familiar with the skeletons of big cats find it difficult or impossible to discriminate between them with only the bones to go on. And bones are all the paleontologist ever has."

Clues have been provided by Allan C. Wilson and Vincent M. Sarich, both of the University of California at Berkeley. They have compared a variety of blood proteins, each coded by a sequence of DNA, and demonstrated that, at the molecular level, men and chimpanzees (*Pan troglodytes*) differ from each other by only 1 percent. The genetic rift between humans and chimps is thus smaller than the average for tested pairs of *sibling species* (two species that differ little in morphology but function as separate reproductive communities in the wild).

In other words, if you took the entire genetic blueprint for a chimpanzee and changed one out of every hundred coding sequences, you could build a man. Apparently, it is the quality of the genes changed and not the quantity that counts. Wilson proposes that changes in a few key regulatory genes might alter the tempo and duration of developmental events (cranial growth, for example), and trigger branching between two populations without any great amount of genetic differentiation.

Support for Wilson's hypothesis comes from Frankfurt Museum anatomist D. Stark's morphometric studies of primate skulls. He concludes that humans and chimps differ only in relative sizes and rates of growth: man is unique only in the quantitative sense.

"So small are the genetic distances that separate us," writes Stephen Jay Gould, ". . . interbreeding may well be possible . . . But, lest we fear the rise of a race comparable to the heroes in *Planet of the Apes,* I hasten to add that the hybrids would almost certainly be sterile—like a mule, and for the same reason."

Now *Homo erectus* is obviously a closer relative to modern man than is the chimpanzee. Superficially there are differences—the low sloping forehead, the thick brow ridges, the protruding jaw—but the differences between us seem to be merely that: superficial. Such genetic reorganizations as have taken place over the last half million years probably do not involve the chromosomal inversions and translocations that would preclude fertile *Homo erectus/Homo sapiens* offspring. If this be true, then according to the species definition given at the start of Chapter 5, *Homo erectus* is *Homo sapiens.*

Except for one technicality.

Homo erectus and *Home sapiens* might be "potentially interbreeding organisms," but they will never "share a common gene pool." The two populations are reproductively isolated by time.

Caution: do not take this technicality too literally because, in its broadest application, your great-great-grandmother 100 years ago must be counted as a species separate from our own. Yet there is no question that she could mate successfully with humans living today.

In order to avoid the predicament of having to provide each generation of humans with a different species name, we must seek a clearer definition of time as an isolating mechanism. We will therefore fix a time boundary (in this case, for the life history of *Homo sapiens*) at the species level. No small task when you consider that scientists are still fighting about what constitutes a species.

Looking from our vantage point in the present, tracking backward the arrow of time, we do not observe a clear-cut line for species distinction. Instead we encounter a series of ever-strengthening barriers that begins with such things as different languages and mating rituals, and leads finally to your own built-in warning system: the instinct not to breed with creatures whose behavior and/or appearance are different from your own. This instinct seems as deeply rooted as sexual desire. It protects our species by preventing its members from spreading their germ plasm where it can be of no use (for example, in a genetically incompatible species).

In its most extreme manifestation, a strong predilection for seeking out other members of our species and then differentiating "self" from "nonself" can build up to all sorts of conflict between coexisting geographic variants; that translates to racial arrogance. Consider South Africa's apartheid laws, Europe's neo-Nazis, and America's Ku Klux Klan.

Seeking the backward limit of our species' life history, we can safely bet that most modern men would find *Homo erectus* women a bit too stocky and somewhat "ugly" for their tastes (even Neanderthals might be pushing the issue).

Stepping farther back, *Homo habilis,* who probably qualifies in the true genetic sense as a different species, would be perceived as downright revolting. That is just as well for both species because a *Homo sapiens/Homo habilis* hybrid would likely be sterile. If our species coexisted and interbred with each other and produced sterile offspring, the result could have been a reduction of numbers on both sides, if not extinction.*

The concept of dividing organisms into species is therefore not

---

*It is fascinating to know that thinking in terms of "this is me and that is my mate and that, over there, does not look like me or my mate and must therefore be my enemy" probably had a useful purpose way back when, as we will soon see, the Earth was inhabited by more than one manlike species. But all of today's human races can be interbreed with each other to produce healthy offspring. The instinct has therefore outlived its usefulness. To continue following it and other deep-rooted behaviors, including some of our territorial ones and the urge to breed like rabbits on a world that was already overly crowded at the outbreak of World War I, well—we may make a cosmic joke of ourselves yet. Some instincts—love is one—are good for a civilized species. Others are not. If we go on behaving like tigers with plutonium-tipped claws, then our days are surely numbered. We might endure as a thinking species but not as a technological one.

an artificial one. It has genuine consequences. If we mated all living horses (*Equis caballo*) with all living donkeys (*Equis asinus*), their progeny would be sterile mules and both species would pass from existence in a single generation. The same might hold true for *Homo sapiens* and *Homo habilis*, and it certainly holds for such extremes as *Homo sapiens* and the still undiscovered ancestor of humans and chimpanzees.*

Between these two extremes lies a whole spectrum of less clear-out divisions that includes the nebulous line between *Homo sapiens* and *Homo erectus*, and runs its course through genetically compatible birds that live in different parts of the same tree, mate at different times, and *never* interbreed in the wild (sibling species). Chemists were forced to overcome a similar obstacle involving the naming of acids and bases. A whole range of strengths lies between nitric acid, at one extreme, sodium hydroxide at the other extreme.

The pH scale enables chemists to describe all the observed phenomena occurring between the most powerful acids and bases. If we are to describe life at all levels of variation, we might have to adopt a similar gradational approach; one with a capacity for taking up such borderline cases as *Homo sapiens neanderthalensis* and *Homo erectus* into a more comprehensive species view.

---

*One myth of human evolution states that chimps are the ancestors of *Homo sapiens*. Not so! Humans and chimpanzees simply branched off from a common ancestral type. Humans have diverged farther from that ancestral type; chimpanzees have retained more of its archaic features.

7 On the Origin of the Fittest

Most of this is very confusing to mere mortals living in the 20th Century, A.D.! You are challenging Darwin, Malthus, Glaessner, Mayr, and God knows who . . . You think in funny ways, and I don't know how we are going to bang it out of you.

Anonymous comments
on an early manuscript for this book

. . . even suggesting to a young scientist that it is somehow inappropriate to "question Darwin" is the antithesis of what a young scientist is supposed to learn—to question virtually everything.

Niles Eldredge
(in response to the above)

Are we not men?

DEVO

1,046,588 B.C.

The first thing one notices about *Home erectus* skulls is that,

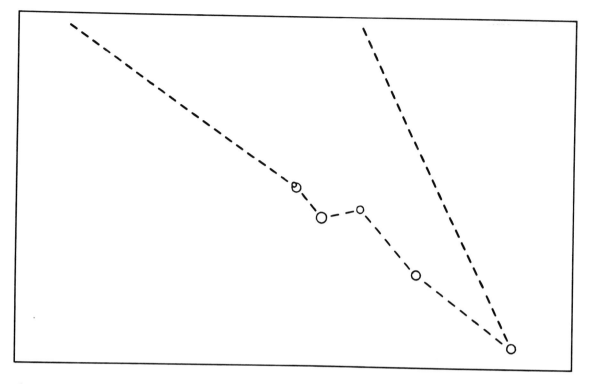

The Big Dipper in 1,046,588 B.C.

placed side-by-side, they exhibit surprisingly little variation over hundreds of thousands of years. The differences between *Homo erectus* skulls dating a million years apart are actually less noticeable than the differences between *Homo erectus* and the Neanderthals, or between the Neanderthals and us. This apparently stable branch of our family tree stretches from about 1.6 million B.C. to as late as 200,000 B.C. That's quite an interval of time. yet attempts to quantify variation in *Homo erectus* have failed to reveal trends that might compel us to believe that any cumulative change of gene content, frequency, or expression took place. There are no major morphologic excursions; merely a thicker brow ridge here, a subtle variation of tooth structure there, and not much else. It looks as if a substantial stretch of human evolution was characterized not by change, but by stasis.

Near the top of *Homo erectus'* stratigraphic range (the youngest and hence the highest rocks in which this fossil species occurs), a nearly complete skull from Dali, in China, was unearthed in 1981. The Dali skull was officially named "an archaic type of early *Homo sapiens.* It has a cranial volume of 1120 cubic centimeters (210cc below the average for modern adults), a long cranial vault with moderately thick bone, brown ridges almost intermediate between *Homo erectus* and *Homo sapiens* and, most interestingly, facial fea-

124

tures reminiscent of modern eastern Asians. American Museum of Natural History anthropologist Eric Delson regards this skull as "the best evidence I know for the now usually discounted concept of locally continuous evolution from *H. erectus* to modern peoples."

On the other side of 1 million B.C., tools and associated animal fossils have tentatively placed the base of *Homo erectus'* range near the Sea of Galilee almost 500,000 years before Homo erectus' earliest *known* occurrence in Africa. Charles Repenning of the U.S. Geological Survey, working with Oldrich Fejar of Czechoslovakia's Geological Survey, believes that the tools could have come from ancestors migrating away from Asia, perhaps driven south by the onset of Pleistocene climate between 2 and 1.6 million years ago.* If *Homo erectus* did radiate into the Middle East and Africa just ahead of the Ice Ages, bringing with him his distinctive tools, he did not find himself the only living branch of man's family tree. There were *Australopithecus robustus, Australopithecus boisei,* and *Homo habilis* to be dealt with.

Australopithecus robustus and *Australopithecus boisei* display an odd blend of human and apelike characteristics. We know from a combination of fingers, knee joints, pelvis bones, and fossil footprints that they and their ancestors walked erect.

Homo habilis had a lower forehead than *Homo erectus,* a longer face (downward projection of the nasal cavities and upper jaw), flangelike cheek bones, and other characteristics that place him somewhere between the slender australopithecines and the more robust *Homo erectus.* He was also a toolmaker, and today he has one particularly special distinction: some workers—focusing more on his name than on the nature of his variability—prefer to deny his existence and do so by kicking his bones aside to either *Australopithecus* or *Homo erectus.*

All four branches clearly coexisted between 1.8 and 1.3 million years ago. Considering the rate at which new skulls are turning up, we should be surprised if four additional branches are not identified before the year 2001. The four branches we already have are enough to show that diverging patterns of variation (apparently rooted in isolation and subsequent radiation from centers of origin) are a fundamental feature of human evolution.

---

*In accordance with Ernst Mayr's *allopatric theory,* wherein genetic change is most likely to arise in small founding populations at the periphery of a species' geographic range, the first appearance of *Homo erectus* was likely the result of geographic isolation that severed genetic communication between more northernly people and their ancestral stocks near Java, Israel, and Africa. The northern populations were thus affected by so-called genetic drift (the Sewall Wright effect): random changes in genes in time. When populations are small and isolated, the effect is apt to be amplified, as in the earlier example (in Chapter 5) of Wellington's wetas.

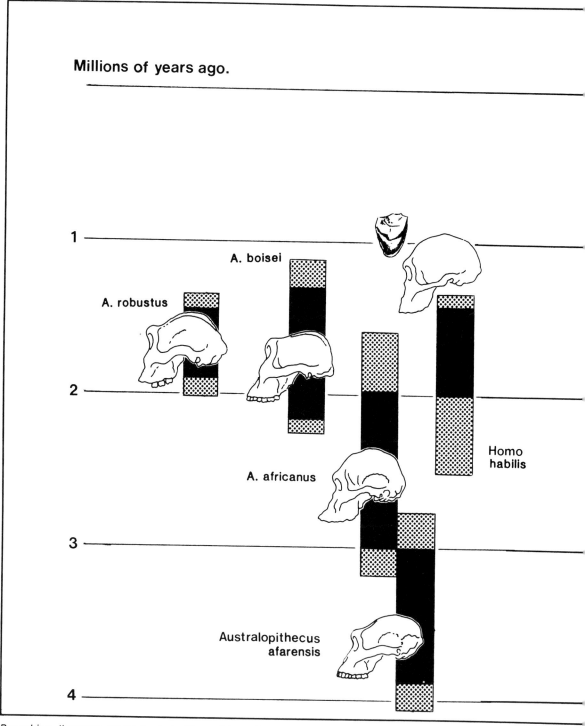

Millions of years ago.

1

A. boisei

A. robustus

2

A. africanus

Homo
habilis

3

Australopithecus
afarensis

4

Branching lineages on the Australopithecus/Homo *"tree."* Illustration by C.R. Pellegrino.

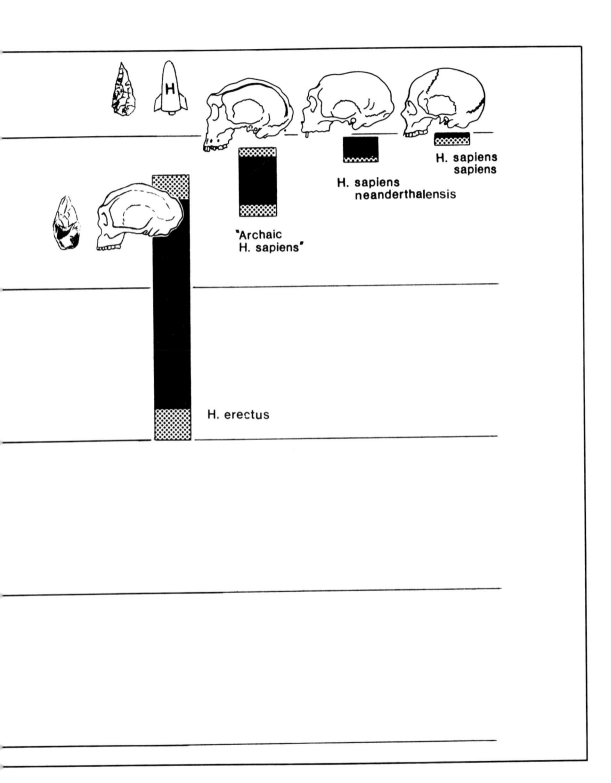

"Archaic
H. sapiens"

H. sapiens
neanderthalensis

H. sapiens
sapiens

H. erectus

Question: if several branches of premen lived side by side, which one was our ancestor?

Given only four choices (so far) and enough well-preserved specimens to permit comparisons, we can come close to an answer. The two australopithecines seem more closely related to each other than to either *Homo habilis* or *Homo erectus*. They are very likely parallel side lines sharing a common ancestry with the (possibly) then-extinct *Australopithecus africanus*. Similarly, *Homo habilis* and *Homo erectus* seem related only to each other, with *H. erectus* having diverged farther from shared ancestral stock. If so, they provide a good example of an ancestral type persisting alongside its immediate descendent.

The abrupt appearance (punctuation) and subsequent stability (equilibrium) of *Homo erectus* as a distinct "fossil species" that endured for more than 1 million years are suggestive of a relatively fast transition from *Homo habilis* to *Homo erectus*. The *punctuated equilibrium* theory, which describes the origin of species as sudden spurts of genetic change followed by long periods of stasis, should perhaps be viewed in a manner similar to Einstein's special relativity theory. Namely two observers moving at different velocities relative to each other view the same phenomena differently.

Some 1000 years to evolve a new kind of Hawaiian moth or New Zealand weta is anything but abrupt in terms of human life spans. But paleobiologists have a peculiar way of looking at time.

Viewed in terms of the geologic time spans we are now approaching in this book, a millenium seems but a millisecond—a mere pulsebeat. On a scale of year-by-year experience, however, gradual change in a population will have real meaning even if the rate of change is punctuational. The theory of punctuated equilibrium places branching events in discrete pockets of time and space, and raises many new and intersting questions about regulatory genes, chromosomal saltations, and geographic isolation.

In other words, the theory focuses attention on *how* species split into new forms. This new focus on modes of evolutionary change (rather than the current furor over rates) might emerge as punctuated equilibrium's most lasting contribution to evolutionary theory.

Splitting species seem to have presented *Homo erectus* with a rather special problem. At the beginning of the Pleistocene Epoch, a main feature in his environment was the presence of no less than three other manlike bipeds. The arrival of each new branch must have been experienced by one or more of the other branches as a deterioration of their environment (i.e., "Damn! There goes the neighborhood."). Food became more difficult to locate, especially if more than one branch expressed the same dietary preferences. An instinctive revulsion toward people who looked familiar and yet somehow were not quite the same increased friction between the branches: the birth cries of racial conflict. Shrinking northern habitats might have added fuel to the fire.

All this makes early Pleistocene Africa sound very hectic. It was. Tanzania's Olduvai Gorge, made famous by the Leakey family, is replete with punctured shards of skulls. Louis Leakey and South African anthropologist Raymond Dart confirmed some of the holes as having been made by leopard's teeth. Other skulls, many others, look like they were opened up with stone tools.*

We do not know precisely what role killing played in our ascent to ownership of the earth, but the picture is clear enough. Chillingly clear. *Homo habilis,* the closest branch, went first. *Australopithecus robustus* followed. Then, just short of 1 million B.C., *Australopithecus boisei* vanished from the fossil record. Man's first world war must have been a real dilly.

It is a sobering fact, but a fact nonetheless, that out of the great radiation and diversification of apes (which occurred about 15 million years ago), only man and four withering branches have survived. Commenting on this development, Donald Johanson and Maitland Edey wrote:

> Send a few more hunting parties into the moutain forests of Ruada, Burundi, and the Congo, and the gorilla will vanish. Continue to cut down the Budongo forest in Uganda, farm the Gombe Stream, waste a couple of other fragile habitats, and the chimpanzee will vanish. Keep up the harassment in Borneo, kill a few hundred more mothers in order to get babies for zoos, and the orangutan will vanish. Turn the remaining hardwood forests of Indochina and Malaya to lumber, and the gibbon will vanish. And that will be the end of the apes. It could happen in another fifty years.

The apes endured in relatively large numbers through the decline of *Australopithecus.* Then they too began to die out.

Go to a zoo and watch the humans and you might understand why. Those gathered around the gorilla and chimpanzee pens tend to express fascination with the similarities (especially the behavioral ones) between us, mingled with disgust at the differences

---

* More recently, anthropologist Tim White, of the University of California at Berkeley, announced the discovery of a partial *Homo erectus* skull bearing marks of butchery with stone tools—"the first known scalping," he says. "It appears to be intentional de-fleshing but it's impossible to say why it was done."

(especially the behavioral ones). Seeing this natural, inbred response, is it any wonder that monkeys—which were relatively rare in australopithecine times, not as closely related to us, and presumably not as competitive with us—have outlived and outbranched *Homo habilis*, the australopithecines, and the apes?

8 Habits from the Good Old, Old, Old Days

Earthmen are not proud of their ancestors, and never invite them 'round to dinner.

Douglas Adams

In the year 2,095,164 B.C., the density of the universe still averaged about 2 hydrogen atoms per 10 cubic meters, and those atoms were still heated at a general temperature of 2.8°K.

If you searched the Taurus-Littrow Valley very carefully and compared it against photographs taken in 1972, you might notice that at least one crater measuring more than a meter across was missing. Here and there, relatively young splash marks and ejected splinters of rock would appear more clear cut than in 1972 photographs. Over a span of 2 million years, the arrival of micrometeorites on the Moon's surface has an erosive power like that of a steady, gentle rain.

In Africa, and near Java too, lived *Homo habilis*. According to Repenning and Fejar, *Homo erectus* seems to have branched off from *Homo habilis* at about this time. *Homo habilis, Australopithecus robustus, Australopithecus boisei,* and an older lineage named *Astralopithecus africanus* were almost exact contemporaries. Tracking back another 0.5 or 1.0 million years, we are likely to find these and one or more still undiscovered branches converging on a common ancestry with A. *africanus.*

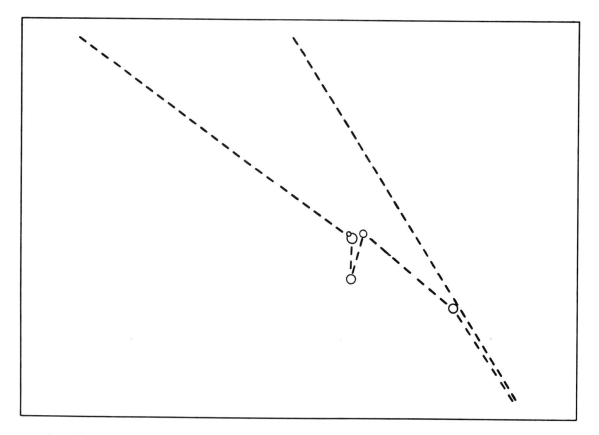

The Big Dipper in 2,095,164 B.C.

A. *africanus* is sometimes regarded as the ancestor of the genus *Homo.* In view of the fact that from the period about 2.5 million years ago there are no other positively identified candidates, this claim is not without some credibility. Most of the relevant fossils are still lying undiscovered within the earth, however, and it might yet turn out that *Australopithecus africanus* is merely another side branch.

This fossil species has left traces of itself spanning from 3 million years to 2 million years ago, although it might well have originated earlier and survived until as late as 1.6 million years ago in East Africa. It was thus one of the longest-lived australopithecine species. It was a two-legged animal; essentially human in form but generally under 1.2 meters (4 feet) tall and weighing less than 23 kilograms (50 pounds). The jaws and teeth were relatively larger than those of modern men, and its brain—although larger than the brains of modern apes of comparable size—was less than half as large as ours.

The most decisive feature of human evolution was a pattern of gradually increasing brain volume (punctuated gradualism?). The australopithecine brain averaged less than 500cc, compared to the

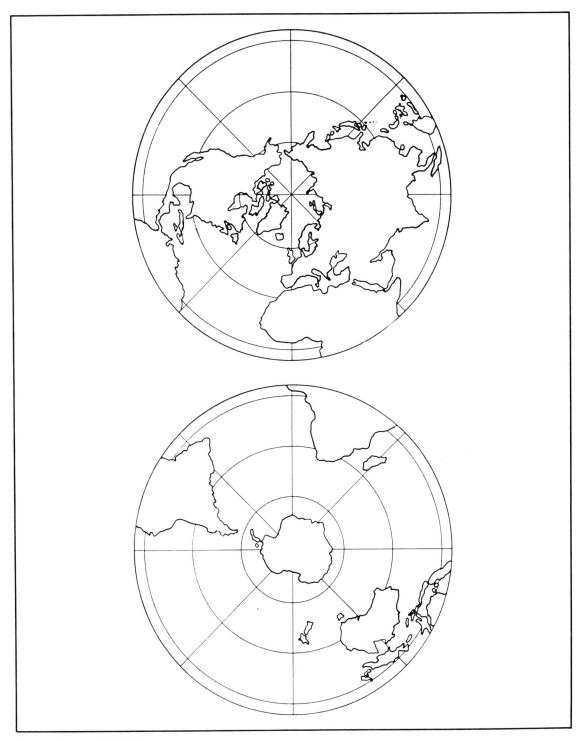

The continents in 2,095,164 B.C.

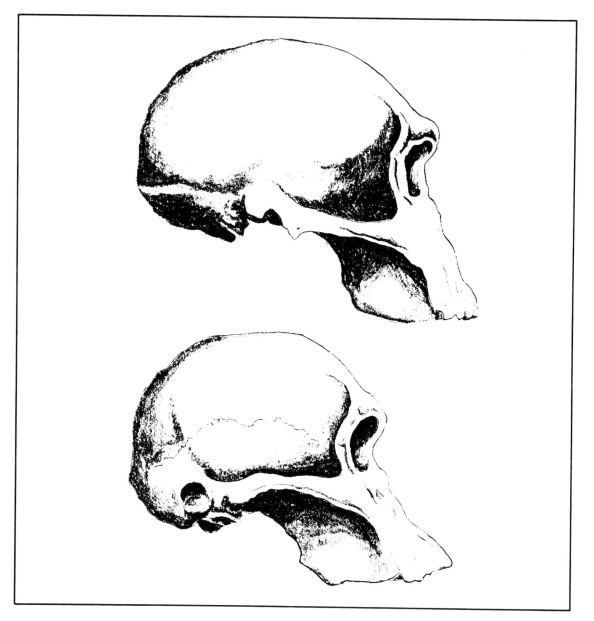

range of 500-800cc for *Homo habilis*, 700-1250cc for *Homo erectus*, and 1000-1800cc for *Homo sapiens*.

Hitler's "master race" became more than a little obsessed with cephalic indexes (a crude measurement of brain size). They allegedly turned up a lot of people whose small brains could be linked to such things as race and creed. One of these small-brained "inferiors," a former patent clerk named Albert Einstein, was hounded clear out of Germany. He seems to have managed quite well with his

A Homo habilis *skull (top: partly reconstructed) from the eastern shore of Lake Turkana, Kenya, and (bottom) the best preserved Aus-* tralopithecus africanus *skull known to date. It belonged to an apparent female from Sterkfontein (about 25 kilometers north of Johannesburg, South Africa). Illustration by C.R. Pellegrino.*

little more than 1200cc brain. Evidently, quality of wits carries more clout than quantity of wits.

Even so, comparison between apes, australopithecines, *Homo habilis*, and *Homo sapiens* seems reasonable because the differences are large. The increase in average brain volume from *Australopithecus africanus* to *Homo sapiens* is so large as to suggest a marked increase in the amount of information that can be retained (memory) and the number of connections that can be made from retained information (thought).

Our brain differs from a chimpanzee's or an australopithecine's brain not only in its size, but in its shape. The front of our brain case, the forehead (which houses the frontal lobes, in which many anthropologists believe the "mind" lives), is greatly inflated. Brain growth by itself would seem to be a rather minor anatomical excursion, but its effect is spectacular.

An assemblage of tools and fossil bones, arranged according to their age and to whom (we think) they belonged, implies that we are set apart from our remote ancestors more by differences in behavior than by differences in anatomy. And even here the differences seem to be only a matter of degree. Chimpanzees modify twigs into tools for catching edible termites, *Homo habilis* apparently discovered how to make blades and choppers from stones, and we pull metal ores from the ground and make from them mechanical and electronic devices.

We know from a trail of footprints uncovered at Laetoli, in Tanzania, that by 3.7 million years ago our forebears had taken their first steps on two feet. Whatever might happen to brains, hands were no longer required for locomotion and could thereafter be exploited for carrying things and making tools and getting us into all sorts of new trouble. Call it happy circumstances if you will. Kangaroos have "free hands," but they are articulated by rather small brains. Whales and porpoises have relatively well-developed brains, but they lack "useful" limbs.

Randall L. Susman and Jack T. Stern of the State University of New York at Stony Brook believe that hands did not entirely give up their locomotor function with the transition to habitual bipedalism. They base their belief on the finger bones of a 1.76-million-year-old fossil hand belonging to *Homo habilis*. The fingers were more curved and more robust than yours or mine, and although advanced in thumb and fingertip morphology (compared with modern apes), were powered by much larger grasping muscles.

In other words, the hand still retained a tree-climbing potential. The two anatomists attribute the hand shaped to phenotypic plasticity, meaning that its appearance results from interaction of the genotype (an organism's genetic constitution) with the environment; its shape is influenced by its use.* If *Homo habilis* did not climb regularly, they conclude, its hand should be similar in overall configuration to ours. Instead it looks more like a chimpanzee's.

As it is today, as it was a million years before *Homo habilis* arrived on the scene, sleeping and perhaps occasionally feeding in trees is a very effective survival strategy. This is especially true if you happen to possess stone tools or sharpened sticks with which to torment anything trying to climb up after you.

The oldest known stone tools come from (tentatively dated) 2.5 million-year-old strata at Hadar on Ethiopia's Awash River. For the moment, they appear to have belonged to *Homo habilis* (we have no conclusive evidence that australopithecines manufactured stone tools, but this too might change). Post dating these first tools by about 1 million years, at Ologesaile in Kenya, is a small "mass grave" containing the bodies of no less than 50 adults and a dozen young baboons belonging to a giant, now extinct, species. Lying with them are several hundred chipped and sharpened stones. The baboons were not makers or users of stone tools. Instead, their skeletons—battered and dismembered and stripped of edible tissue—identify them as victims of formidable hunters.

When Mary and Louis Leakey first started excavating Olduvai Goge in Tanzania, they found not only pieces of australopithecines and *Homo habilis*, but also a scatter of stone tools and broken-up animal bones located in the same strata. These strata date to about 1.7 million years ago, and one tool site contains elements of having been a "factory." They even found curious rings of stones, indicating that someone was living in outdoor shelters similar to those built by *Homo erectus* and some present-day nomads.

On the eastern shore of Lake Turkana, in the Koobi Fora deposits of Kenya, an area 16 meters in diameter was strewn with several hundred stone tools. The tools rested on an ancient ground surface that had once been the sandy bed of a stream. By the time the toolmakers arrived, at least 1.6 million years ago, the streambed was mostly dry. Clustered among the tools are 578 fragments of animal bone, including hippopotamus, giraffe, porcupine, waterbuck, gazelle, wildebeest, an extinct species of pig, and a crocodile.

Such accumulations of animal remains are sometimes produced by stream action, but Berkeley anthropologist Glynn Isaac discounts this suggestion because of the discovery, alongside the bones, of very light flakes from stone tools that would have easily washed away under the same stream action. He proposes instead

---

*For example, your genotype may be that of a 6-foot-tall adult but, if you are poorly fed as a child, the phenotypic expression of the genotype might produce a somewhat shorter individual.

that the people who manufactured and used and discarded their tools at the site were also responsible for the bone accumulation. This being the case, they are presumed to have carried their food to this meeting place from diverse places and (probably) shared it.

The tools consist of small, bladelike flakes struck from a suitable lump of stone (called a stone core) and then shaped according to need. At one Koobi Fora site, where no suitable raw materials occur naturally within several kilometers, toolmakers evidently carried their own core stone with them. They hammered off 50mm (2-inch) long flakes on the spot, shaped them into double-edged points, and cut meat from a hippopotamus carcass.

Crude as this technology might seem, barely a notch above the sticks that chimpanzees have been known to wave at each other, it is nonetheless a skill that requires years of practice—even if it is to be mastered by present-day humans. One must learn how to identify the most suitable core stones; flint, obsidian, and fine-grained quartzite produce flat, sharp-edged flakes. Granite and other crumbly, coarse-grained rocks are useless.

Learning how to trim a flake to shape with a series of precisely angled secondary hammer blows is even more difficult. To pass such skills from generation to generation of *Homo habilis*, I suspect, required communicative abilities—language. And presumably the spoken kind. Grunts will not do.

Somewhere along the line in the evolution of human behavior emerged two patterns: food sharing and a division of labor. Among present-day hunter-gatherers, the females generally contribute the "gathered" foods (plant products, shellfish, small reptiles, amphibians, eggs, and so on), while adult males contribute most of the "hunted" foods. The result is an "energetically profitable" increase in the variety of foods (hence vitamins) consumed by the group.

The existence of this division can be tied to the fact that females are traditionally encumbered with children. Human children require more parental care than those of any other mammalian species, including our cousins in the trees. Our enlarged brains are part of the problem. Human fetal growth is characterized by an acceleration in the development of both brain and body, as the British anatomist Robert Martin of University College has observed: "Human infants have brains and bodies twice as big as you'd expect, given the length of gestation. This must be extremely costly energetically. A high-energy feeding strategy was essential for its development."

The human brain quadruples its volume between birth and adulthood. Other primates double the volume. No primates grow new nerve cells after birth. Postnatal brain growth is limited to supporting brain tissues and to making new nerve connections. In spite of our accelerated fetal development, we are born with an essentially fetal brain, rendering human infants about the most helpless things around. By contrast, a horse stands up within hours of being born and a chimpanzee will out perform a human child in every way during the first year of life.

The burden of support falls upon our parents. A simple comparison of skulls and pelvises permits us to make a good guess at when a marked increase in parental care became necessary. The "explosive" growth of the human brain late in our phylogeny was not without consequences. Incomplete closure of the newborn's skull was very likely one of several inelegant solutions to the problem of ballooning brains.

The female pelvis also changed. The skeletal opening became substantially wider in the region of the birth canal, but enlargement of the pelvic girdle could only go so far before eventually rendering women incapable of walking. The reshaped pelvis is an imperfect, almost jerry-rigged accommodation to large brains, whose only virtue is that it works—sometimes.

Here we encounter a phenomenon that has no name. For lack of a better name, let's call it *selective balance*, whereby requirement "A" (a need for the widest possible birth canal) is balanced against requirement "B" (a need to walk efficiently). In this case, requirement "A," acting in one direction and carried to an extreme, would be harmful (if you make the pelvic opening too wide, women cannot walk). Requirement "B," acting in the opposite direction and carried to an extreme would also be harmful (if you make the pelvic opening too narrow, women cannot give birth to large-brained babies).

Natural selection forces a chancy sort of balance. The result is that bigger brains and mobile mothers are accommodated at the expense of a higher incidence of mortality during childbirth. Nature drives a hard bargain. Prior to the advent of birth control and twentieth-century medical technology, childbirth was the number one killer of women between the ages of 15 and 30.*

According to Robert Martin, the brains of modern infants are about as large as pelvic engineering will allow (meaning an upper limit of approximately 350cc at birth). If we apply the typical

---

*Some investigators have argued that the development of human intelligence will be forever restricted because pelvic engineering will not permit us to grow bigger brains. This view has been extrapolated to suggest that kangaroos have the potential to become brainier animals than us because the greater part of marsupial brain development takes place outside the womb. Hence the idea that spacefaring extraterrestrials are likely to carry their young in pouches. Proponents of this view are overlooking the fact that, once we made the transition from an intelligent species to a technological one, biological constraints on skull size went out the window. We learned to perform Cesareans (which, incidentally, were *not* named for Julius Caesar, nor he for them, and, no, he was not born that way).

primate pattern of postnatal doubling of brain volume, we yield an adult brain size of 700cc.

Basing our predictions upon the pelvic girdle of living humans (because we have no fossil pelvises dating from about 2 million B.C.), it seems as if, near the adult level of 700cc, a limit had been reached beyond which any further brain growth had to be assigned to postnatal life. Hence the brain became less developed at birth, its owner more helpless, and the demands upon parents rose proportionally. The 700cc boundary matches evenly with *Homo habilis*, whose brain was the first outside the australopithecine line to show a substantial increase in volume.

But big brains are energetically expensive and, according to Martin, can be afforded only under certain favorable circumstances such as a stable environment and a high energy feeding strategy. A large body also helps. Living primates range in size from the mouse lemur, weighing in at about 60 grams (about 2 ounces), up to the 275-kilogram (605-pound) mountain gorilla.

If you plot body weight against metabolic rate, you get a slope of ¾. We seem to have in this situation a special relationship, between increased size and increased energetic efficiency, that is consistent with what we know about primate dietary habits. The largest apes feed on leaves, and leaves are relatively low in energy content. Monkeys tend to be fruit eaters. The smallest primates subsist on high-protein seeds and insects (a notable exception is the energy-rich and varied diet of our closest living relative, the chimpanzee).

If this does not excite curiosity, then go ahead and plot the ratio of brain volume to body weight. The result again is a slope of ¾. The fact that both comparisons—body weight with metabolic rate and body weight with brain weight—produce the same slope hints at a relationship between them. "It is the mother's energetic potential that determines the brain size of the developing fetus," says Martin. "After birth, the brain growth then follows a trajectory already set" (by the energy throughput of the mother's metabolism).

Generally, humans are among the largest of all primates, and large size runs in parallel with improved energy conservation. In addition, we subsist on a generalized, energy-rich diet that expands in many directions to include fruits, vegetables, meats, and seafood. Together an efficient metabolism and high-energy feeding strategy might have fostered the development of large brains.

The outcome of all this has been an explosive radiation of the *Homo* lineage away from the tropics and subtropics and into the polar ice fields. We have overrun the planet as no animal has done before. We have burrowed through mountains, sunk shafts into the Earth's skin, penetrated to the deepest reaches of its oceans. As I write this, seven of us are living outside the Earth altogether.

Others, here on the ground, have probed the sands of Mars and the winds of Titan and now, not satisfied with that, we have begun to contemplate antiprotons and sustained 1-G acceleration and time dilation. We dare the stars.

We DARE them.

9 Lucy in the Sand with Foot Notes

What rough beast, its hour come 'round at last,
slouches toward Bethlehem to be born?

William Butler Yeats

He who has seen a savage in his native land will not feel
much shame, if forced to acknowledge that the blood of
some more humble creature flows in his veins. For my
own part, I would as soon be descended from that heroic
little monkey, who braved his dreaded enemy in order to
save the life of his keeper; or from that old baboon who,
descending from the mountains, carried away in
triumph his young comrade from a crowd of astonished
dogs—as from a savage who delights to torture his
enemies, offers up bloody sacrifices, practices infan-
ticide without remorse, treats his wives like slaves,
knows no decency, and is haunted by the grossest super-
stitions.

Charles Darwin

...4,192,316 B.C.... we have pushed back past the beginning of the
archaeological record.

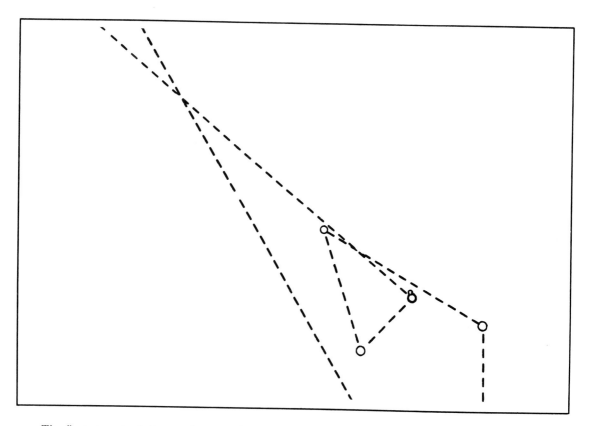

The first stone tools turn up in strata dated to about 2.5 million years ago. This by no means fixes the backward limit of tool use. Not all of the stone tools in the world have been discovered, and—before they began shaping stones—our forebears almost certainly used softer, wooden tools such as sticks sharpened against coarse rocks. Stone tools are virtually indestructible; wood rots and is seldom fossilized, and because of this we may never know how far beyond the Stone Age extends the "Wood Age."

There is no telling whether "Lucy" or any of her contemporaries used wooden tools. Lucy was a young australopithecine woman who died in Hadar (Ethiopia) about 3.5 million years ago. And that was that. At least until 1974, when Maurice Taieb of France's National Center for Scientific Research, and Donald Johanson of the Cleveland Museum of Natural History brought her bones to light. Somehow she became a household name. Perhaps in America even a fossil can aspire to stardom.

The emerging picture of exactly who (or what) Lucy was did not come easy. It required a long, careful comparison with thousands of australopithecine bones. And that was just the start of it. Surprising results led almost inevitably to a violent shaking of man's family tree, and to a clash of personalities that verged on all-out war and did not

The Big Dipper in 4,192,316 B.C

stop short of character assasination. The name-calling proved little except that sacred cows (in this case all previous family trees or cladograms) fall hard.

The evidence now at hand suggests that Lucy was a "stem" species ancestral to both *Australopithecus africanus* and the *Homo* branch. Although she might have been able to interbreed with *Australopithecus africanus* or even *Homo habilis* (in any case, this is a question we can not yet answer), she is, for the time being, given the convenient label *Australopithecus afarensis* (named for the Afar triangle, where hers and similar bones were found).

Her "species" flourished from about 4 million years ago to about 3 million years ago. During that time, the *A. afarensis* line seems to have undergone little or no evolutionary change. Once again we encounter a long span of stasis—in this instance about a million years of it—followed by a surge of relatively sudden change that includes the parting of branches from an *Australopithecus/Homo* junction.

The features of *Australopithecus africanus* are not like those of either *Homo habilis* or *Australopithecus afarensis*, but hint at creatures markedly more apelike than either. Lucy was fully bipedal—this we know from her pelvis and leg bones and from footprints at Laetoli—but she stood somewhere between humans and chimpanzees, and possibly closer to chimps.

She was just over a meter (3.5 feet) tall and probably weighed about 25 kilograms (almost 55 pounds). She represents the smallest adult *Australopithecus afarensis* known. The largest members of her

Based upon anthropologist Tim White's reconstruction of an Australopithecus afarensis skull, and anatomist Jay Matterne's reconstructions of muscle placement, "Lucy" probably looked something like this. Because A. afarensis was a tropical creature living in an exposed savanna habitat, and assuming that reduction of body hair was an early development in hominid evolution (which exposed the skin to more ultraviolet radiation, against which increased melanin production became a convenient means of protection), it is likely that Lucy was dark skinned. The fossil record has revealed neither the quantity of hair that covered australopithecine bodies nor the color of their skin. Reconstruction (sans hair) by C.R. Pellegrino.

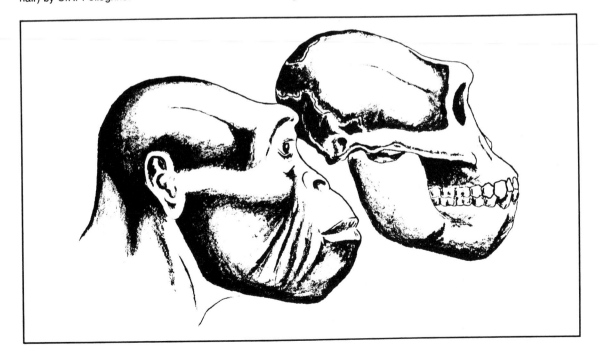

species were males standing about 1.5 meters (5 feet) tall and weighing up to 55 kilograms (121 pounds). Her hands were like human hands, except for being attached to arms relatively longer than yours or mine. Her fingers were more curled and more robust than ours, being powered by heavier muscles.

Like *Homo habilis*, she retained the tree-climbing potential of her predecessors. Certain of her wrist bones were strikingly apelike, yet her feet were so like those of modern humans that they leave unanswered the question of how knuckle-walking apes became erect-walking australopithecines.

The chimpanzee foot also resembles very closely the human foot, suggesting that the foot itself was not the focus of change. Above the thigh, the difference between chimps and australopithecines is overwhelming. Chimps have a long, saddle-shaped pelvis characteristic of quadrupedal apes. *Australopithecus afarensis* had a pelvis almost identical to modern man's.

A chimp can walk on its hind legs only for short distances because the innominate bone (which forms the sides of the pelvis), in particular the broad upper portion called the ilium, is very poorly shaped for erect walking. It causes the muscles leading down to the leg from the pelvis to fatigue after only 20 meters (65 feet) on two legs. Consequently, chimps prefer to walk knuckle down on their long arms, keeping the shoulders high.

The mechanics of Lucy's pelvis were appropriate for bipedal walking, but—not surprisingly—were inappropriate for the delivery of high-browed babies. The *A. afarensis* brain ranged in volume from 380cc to 450cc. This range slightly overlaps the 300cc to 400cc brains of chimpanzees, whose body weights are comparable with *A. afarensis*. Notably, the range falls short of the low end of the *Homo* scale (460cc for the smallest known adult *Homo habilis*).

Because of her small brain, Lucy's face was small and chimp like above the nose. Her brows were heavy of bone and above them the forehead appeared to be missing. Thinking about the process of change, it seems clear that if we change the shape or size of one part (in this case the brain), other body parts are effected (in this case skulls and pelvic girdles and, carried along with the pelvis, the leg bones and spine and even the rib cage).

Lucy was probably hairier than modern women. The exact quantity and color of her hair is anybody's guess. Her skin, like the skin of chimpanzees and tropical humans, was probably dark; no one knows for sure.

Like present-day chimps, sexual bonds between individuals were probably variable. As with chimps, some females and most males are likely to have courted and mated with several members of the opposite sex, especially during the first years after puberty. Looking around, things don't seem to have changed very much since the chimp and australopithecine days.

Hoping to reveal details of behavior, Al Ryan of the University of Michigan has focused on Lucy's teeth. Using the high magnifications attainable with a scanning electron microscope, he first examined the surface features of living Eskimos' teeth and compared them with those of American Indians excavated from burial mounds. In both populations, he found chipped enamel—micro flaking—resulting from jaws being used as tools for holding bone, cutting hides, tying knots and, in modern times, opening soda bottles and turning bolts.

Looking at modern apes, he learned that gorillas—living entirely on coarse vegetation growing on the forest floor—have a distinct pattern of scratches and pits on the incisors. The pattern arises from the abrasive action of silicon in the cells of plants and from sand adhering to stems and roots, which gorillas pull through their teeth—stripping off whatever can be chewed and digested. In the process, they wind up eating a lot of dirt.

Whereas the gorilla might eat two dozen kinds of leaves and some fruit, the chimpanzee diet covers 200 kinds of berries and seeds and ranges to include insects, bird's eggs, and occasionally other primates. The soft fruit in the chimpanzee diet polishes the incisors and the grinding down of small, hard seeds slowly wears the tooth down to its dentine layer.

When Ryan examined *Australopithecus afarensis* teeth he found microflaking, pitting, and scratching, and evidence of gradual wear through the enamel and into the underlying dentine. In other words, Lucy was an omnivore, and omnivore spells a high-energy feeding strategy. As indicated in Chapter 8, increasing size in primates corresponds with increasing metabolic efficiency. A high-energy diet combined with improved energetic efficiency can support energetically expensive big brains. This agrees exactly with what you see when you examine man's family tree through the fossil record.

Homo habilis generally stood about 1.5 meters (5 feet) tall, and our large-brained (compared with apes) australopithecine omnivore was smaller yet. Branching in a different direction from the *Homo* genus, *Australopithecus robustus'* brain did not grow beyond the *Australopithecus afarensis* volume, and actually seems to have gotten smaller. Its reduced canines ("fangs"), massive molars set in heavy jaws, and a sagittal crest—or ridge that ran from front to back along the top of the skull and supported powerful jaw muscles (as does the gorilla's sagittal crest)—betrays an energy-poor diet of leaves.

In terms of physical appearance, a great deal of change separates us from *A. afarensis*, even if—according to detailed comparisons between us and modern chimpanzees—the overall genetic change is less than 1 percent. You can't just stop and look at evidence like this without starting to wonder about what causes the change.

The discovery of *transposons* (stray bits of DNA that wander about the cell "looking for home") has thrown a wild card into discussions about morphologic excursions. According to Cold Spring Harbor geneticist Barbara McClintock, transposons (sometimes called "jumping genes") can raise all sorts of havoc. They might, for example, get inserted next to a gene that controls the rate at which certain bones grow, and then switch that gene on or off, throwing the whole choreography of embryonic development awry.

Working with changing patterns of color on kernels of "Indian corn," McClintock identified *structural genes* (these are the genes responsible for specific traits such as pigment production) that are regulated by two *controlling elements*: an AC (activator gene) and a DS (dissociator or repressor gene). The activator, as its name suggests, switches the dissociator on and off, and the dissociator, when switched on, produces a protein that prevents the production of pigment by the structural gene.

McClintock learned by 1965 that the location of these controlling elements, and hence their influence over the structural gene, is not fixed. Their effectiveness—and their recent recognition—arises from their tendency to "jump around." This tendency provided McClintock with a lifetime of interesting questions. Just when she thought it was safe to announce their positions, the next generation of plants turned up with the same controlling elements in new locations—next to new structural genes on the same chromosome—or, almost unbelievably, on a different chromosome altogether.

From such surprises Nobel Prizes are made. Here were regulatory genes that could not only get up and go, but they could go to and exert their control over new structural genes, with the result that a whole new feature might become subject to mutation.

Jumping genes do not live in corn alone. They seem to be everywhere: in bacteria, yeast, the fruit fly *Drosophila*, and now, we think, even in humans. But the genetic game of musical chairs does not end with the transposon. Some bacteria spontaneously release strings of DNA into a growth medium or into the cells they happen to infect. Other organisms seem able to pick up and occasionally use stray bits of DNA.

A variety of mustard plant (*Arabidopsis thalina*) carries a hereditary defect that renders individuals unable to produce thiamine, a type of vitamin B. When it appears, the defect is expressed as a lethal deficiency in the seeds that die shortly after germination. But many bacteria manufacture thiamine. When clumps of DNA from thiamine-producing bacteria are applied to the

146

mustard seeds, they absorb the *necessary* genes and grow into flowering plants that are capable of producing healthy seeds. What is noteworthy here is that the bacterial genes are incorporated permanently into the genotype of the mustard plant to produce what is essentially a new organism.

Viruses can be viewed as wandering collections of genes. They are not merely carriers of flu, or herpes, or random death, but compulsive communicators whose "function" is to keep snatches of genetic information in widest circulation amongst us. Commenting on this view, Lewis Thomas, of the Memorial Sloan-Kettering Cancer Center in New York, wrote in 1974:

> . . . we live in a dancing matrix of viruses; they dart, rather like bees, from organism to organism, from plant to insect to mammal to me and back again, and into the sea, tugging along pieces of this genome, strings of genes from that, transplanting grafts of DNA, passing around heredity as though at a party.

In support of this view, and hinting at the mechanisms of genetic change yet to be discovered, R.E. Benveniste and G.J. Todaro, both of the National Cancer Institute in Maryland, have isolated, from the chromosomes of certain cats, genes that are quite distinct and do not occupy the chromosomes of any other cats. The genes, however, are identical to genes found in monkeys and baboons; they are also known to exist in a particular virus.

Looking at a potential chaos of shuffled genes, one wonders what on Earth may be inferred from it. To Benveniste and Todaro, it points to the viral transfer of genetic information between species that are only remotely related. That tempts one to ask what might happen if controlling elements got transferred from one organism to another and became functional in their new environment. It is something one has to stop and think about for a moment.

To what extent might the branching process implied by homonoid fossils (and let us not forget Darwin's Galapagos iguanas, tortoises, and finches) be a consequence of "something in the air?" The answer can only be guessed at.

According to the best current knowledge, Lucy was a scavenger and gatherer who sampled a broad range of foods and lived a nomadic existence. She probably belonged to a "tribe" of 30 to 50 individuals. She walked upright, and she stood at or near the base of the *Australopithecus /Homo* tree.

And that is the current story of human genesis.

We might have to change our minds. As Stephen Jay Gould once put it, new prehuman fossils are coming to light almost every day, changing our picture of man's family tree with such rapidity that this chapter is likely to become outdated even as it is being written.

A UPI release; June 11, 1982: The oldest ancestor of man yet to be found has been discovered near Ethiopia's Awash River. Claimed by Berkeley anthropologist Tim D. White to provide new evidence that human ancestors were bipedal eons before they developed large brains and began using tools. Tentatively classified as the species *Australopithecus afarensis* . . . 400,000 years older than Lucy . . ..

10 A Geography Lesson

We tend to think of ourselves as the only wholly unique creations in nature, but this is not so. Uniqueness is so commonplace a property of living things that there is really nothing at all unique about it.

Lewis Thomas

Just because everything looks different doesn't mean that anything has changed.

The Christchurch Wizard

You tell me that it's evolution—
Well you know, we all want to change the world.

Lennon and McCartney

The Taurus-Littrow Valley was 486.54 kilometers (302.39 miles) closer to the Earth in 8,386,260 B.C. That's what the Moon's present recession velocity of 5.8 centimeters (2.38 inches) per year adds up to over the stretch of almost 8.4 million years. Today the Moon's maximum surface-to-surface distance from the Earth is 376,007

kilometers (233,690 miles); the minimum distance is 348,200 kilometers (216,408 miles).

If the Moon's present recession velocity has remained constant throughout time, then 1 billion years ago it dipped within 58,000 kilometers (36,047 miles) of the Earth's surface. This is about 18 percent closer than it is today. This put it almost within the Roche limit; the frictional tug-of-war between the two planets would have been spectacular.

Gravitational effects do not increase linearly with distance. They increase logarithmically. Moving the Moon almost one-fifth closer to the ground increases the tug of gravity somewhat more than one-fifth: Frightful tides rush east to west across the Earth, reflecting off continents with amplitudes that could sink 30-story buildings and displace garage-sized boulders; lunar bedrock creaks, softens, and flows liquid—but the Moon did *not* bleed lava 1 billion years ago. This we know from the ages of rocks collected during the *Apollo* and *Luna* missions.

The youngest-known lunar basalts solidified by 3.2 billion years ago. Obviously, the Moon could not have resided inside the Roche limit 1 billion or even 3 billion years ago. It follows that the Moon's present recession velocity must have been some 10 to 15 times slower in the past, and for a good reason. If the gravitational bond between two bodies increases logarithmically as they get closer to each other, then—when you set the Moon aloft near the Roche limit and try to push the two worlds apart—you notice immediately that it takes about 16 times more pushing to force a 5.8-centimeter gap between them. Farther out, their hold on each other weakens and the same amount of push has greater effect.

You might be wondering where the push comes from. It's in the tides. The oceans bulge out toward the Moon, following it westward across our skies, sloshing into bays and mud flats—dragging there, and releasing frictional energy that every second costs the Earth a little bit of angular momentum.

According to unbreakable equations governing the conservation of angular momentum, what you subtract from the Earth you must add on someplace else. The Moon, obedient to unbreakable equations, absorbs the loss as a tiny push away into space. On Earth, this loss adds up to a steady running down of the transition from day

Manhattan Island, as it probably appeared in the year 8,386,260 B.C. Photo by C.R. Pellegrino.

to night to day again. Our days are almost one-half second longer than they were in 8,386,260 B.C.

Some 8.4 million years ago, none of the main Hawaiian Islands had broken the ocean surface. The Gardner Pinnacles were then a shield volcano located approximately where Kauai is today. Since then, it has edged 998 kilometers (620 miles) northwest to its present site. Subsiding under its own weight, assailed every inch of the way by pounding waves and wind and rain, it has dwindled from a mountain with a cone that once poked through the snow line to a few small pinnacles of rock.

In the future, as the pinnacles sink and erode, coral reefs growing around and over them will form an atoll similar to Midway Island. Eventually, even the atoll will sink and carry the coral below the reach of sunlight. Like Koko Seamount, it will become a submarine volcano that is inactive and capped with dead coral.

Many geologists now believe that "hot spots," plumes of molten rock, are long-lived and relatively stationary with respect to each other. They rise thinly against the Earth's crustal plates, that, urged by convection, ride over them. The Hawaiian Islands are a linear chain extending with increasing age through 28-million-year-old Midway Island and 48-million-year-old Koko Seamont (located 3540 kilometers northwest of Kauai). The entire chain of islands and seamounts seems to have formed one at a time as the Pacific plate moved over the plume at about 10 centimeters (4 inches) per year.

Kauai, the northernmost of the Hawaiian Islands, is "only" about 5.5 million years old. Hawaii, the largest and southernmost of the Hawaiian Islands, is no more than 750,000 years old.

All plants and animals on the islands are descended from relatively recent arrivals that became founding populations driven to divergence by a combination of isolation, time, and new environmental settings. The outcome has been an extraordinary series of branching events that includes over 40 known varieties of honeycreepers, all descended from a single avian species (compared to Darwin's 12 varieties of Galapagos finches).*

Small moths have radiated into more than 1000 new species, and the fruit fly *Drosphila,* in entomologist Elwood Zimmerman's words, "is found in a range from unusually small species to absolute giants up to a centimeter across . . . there may be as many as 300 species concentrated in an area smaller than the little state of Massachusetts . . . where else has such a drosophilid fauna developed?"

---

*The Hawaiian fauna also includes one interesting case of stasis. An upland goose has remained a single species uniquely adapted to its environment and found nowhere else in the world.

Although birds, moths, flies, and so forth cannot have arrived prior to the formation of the islands, the islands do not set a backward limit for how long any of their inhabitants have remained isolated from genetic exchanges with the continents. Some 48 kilometers (30 miles) southeast of Hawaii, located directly above the hot spot, an underwater volcano called Loihi is becoming the next Hawaiian island. When it breaks the surface, it will eventually be populated by moths and flies presently residing on the other islands.

What do you suppose happened on Kauai when it first emerged some 5.5 million years ago? Like passengers abandoning sinking ships, Kauai's first settlers must have arrived from neighboring, now submerged, northwesterly islands. How long have flies and moths and birds been leapfrogging from island to island? For all anyone *really* knows, their ancestry could extend as far back as Midway and Koko. Perhaps it does. Go out to the Gardner Pinnacles, Midway, and all the islands in between and look for surviving descendents of early settlers, and you might come up with an answer.

Far from the Hawaiian Islands, on both sides of the Pacific, Australia and South America provided their own brand of isolation: continent-sized islands. In both places could be found animals that lived nowhere else in the world. Examples are the marsupials or pouched mammals.

Some 8.4 million years ago the Panama isthmus was closed, blocking the way for faunal exchanges between Columbia and Mexico. South American marsupials had flourished throughout Cenozoic time (the "age of mammals"), evolving pouched versions of rhinos, horses, and saber-toothed cats.

Between 4 and 2 million years ago, the general temperature of the Earth fell almost 5.6° C (10° F) with apparently deadly effect. South American rain patterns changed. The change was quickened by the rise of the Andes from 2000 to 4000 meters between 4.5 and 2.5 million years ago. Southern South American forests and savannas turned into pampas and the pampas turned into deserts.

Many subtropical and savanna-woodland animals found themselves restricted to the warmer, wetter Amazon region. About 2.5 million years ago, the isthmus rose and North American migrants began to arrive and settle amid an already beleaguered South American fauna: 21 migrant genera spilled into South America and radiated into 49 secondary genera. Moving in the opposite direction, into Mexico, 12 South American genera gave rise to only three secondary genera.

Why the greater "success" of North Americans? If we choose the supposedly obvious explanation of competitive displacement of southern groups by northern invaders, we are forced to invent a series of unlikely scenarios to explain, for example, how a jack

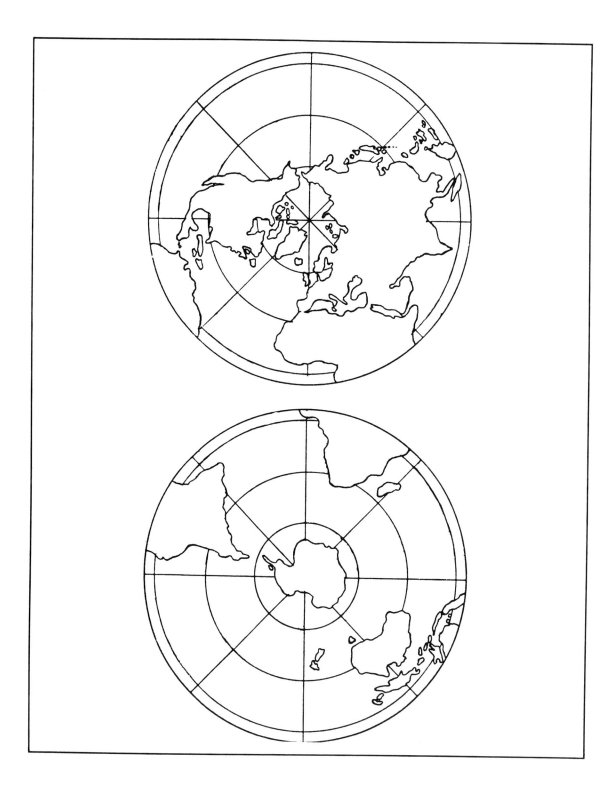

rabbit—in spite of its different food preferences and housing requirements—managed to or even needed to express "competitive superiority" over an opossum.

Perhaps most northern forms simply walked into the very habitats that southern forms were shrinking away from and found these new habitats well-suited to their life-styles. For example, opossums prefer wooded areas whereas rabbits can and often do live on pampas and semideserts. We should think twice before accepting the old story of advancing waves of superior invaders and subsequent displacement. More likely than not the tale is one of *replacement*.

Only recently have humans, along with their cows and horses and cats, replaced Australia's extinct, forest-dwelling marsupials. One such animal was a giant kangaroo with a giraffe like neck.* Like giraffes on the African plains, it browsed on the branches of trees.

The largest known marsupial was a fossil called *Diprotodon*. It grew up to 3.5 meters (12 feet) long and was shaped like a rhinoceros. *Thylacoleo* was a tree climber the size and shape of a lion, with molars that resembled razor blades. Some researchers argue that it climbed trees merely to get at fruits and used its shearing molars to cut the hard ones. That doesn't explain why it needed projecting, spearlike incisors.

What did it really eat?

Probably anything it wanted.

Some 8.4 million years ago, Australia was 629 kilometers (391 miles) south of its present position. As the Ice Age began, the continent continued to drift steadily northward, toward warmer equatorial reaches. But it apparently did not move fast enough to escape the climatic effects of melting glaciers. The same Late Pleistocene extinction that struck North America, Europe, and Asia was also at work in Australia.

By about 6000 B.C., the giant marsupials had died out. Only one large carnivore survived into modern times: *Thylacinus,* the so-called Tasmanian wolf. This pouched "wolf" was an efficient hunter that more than welcomed the sheep provided by immigrant ranchers. Unfortunately, ranchers and bounty hunters were not as appreciative of *Thylacinus*. The last known living example died in 1933 at the London zoo.

About 50 million years from now, Australia will have made its first physical contact with Southeast Asia. Peninsulas and chains of

In the year 8,386,260 B.C., the Panama isthmus was closed, blocking faunal exchanges between Mexico and South America. Australia and India were 650 kilometers (400 miles) south of their present positions. The Atlantic Ocean was 130 kilometers (80 miles) narrower than it is today, and the Mediterranean Sea was drying up.

---

*When Captain James Cook first set foot in Australia, one of the first things he asked the locals was, "What are those odd, hopping animals?" They answered in their native tongue, "I don't know," which is pronounced kangaroo; and we have been calling them that ever since.

islands will touch, enabling the descendents of present-day kangaroos and sheep and whatever new creatures might branch from them to begin a faunal exchange like that across the Panama isthmus. The zone of contact between the two land masses will grow until the sea between them shrinks into a patchwork of lakes and disappears under upthrust peaks.

That's exactly what was happening in India around 8,386,620 B.C. Creeping north at about 5.0 centimeters (2 inches) per year, the continent had already begun an uneasy marriage with Eurasia, one that was plunging seabeds under Tibet and pushing up Mount Everest and the Himalayas.*

The Earth's skin wrinkled. The Tibetan Plateau, seen from on high, resembled a squeezed-up accordion. The world's longest crustal splits opened across Indochina and became rivers whose banks periodically shuddered, slipped, and swayed.

Elsewhere the Mediterranean Sea was drying up. Africa's northward drift had triggered an episode of mountain building that slowly bridged Spain and Morocco and put a natural dam across the

The Rock of Gibralter. Photo by Brown Brothers.

---

*Before the time of its first contact with Eurasia, India housed no mammalian life. The oldest known fossil mammals in India date from about 45 million years ago and are similar to Mongolian fossils of the same age.

Strait of Gibraltar. By 6 million B.C., the entire sea would evaporate, leaving behind a desert basin and endless flats of salt. Here and there on the basin floor, rivers would cut deep gorges—until about 5.2 million B.C., when the Atlantic Ocean breached Gibraltar dam.

And *that* must have been something to see.

The Atlantic was 128 kilometers (79.6 miles) narrower than it would be in 1984. To the ancestors of European anguillid eels, this meant a migration route to the Sargasso Sea that was shorter by almost 3 percent. It is not a very large difference; hence it is safe to guess that European and American eels, though sharing the same breeding ground, still mated at different times and therefore lived as two separate species.

We know practically nothing about the evolution of our prehuman ancestors between about 8 million and 4 million years ago. Digging down through the Pliocene, the spade strikes a wall near 4 million B.C. Beyond that point stretches Miocene time and very few homonid fossils (creatures with humanlike features). On our side of the wall stands Lucy, already walking around and gathering high-energy foods as her forebears had been doing for—how long?

Alkaid moved, shifted more than half way around the circle of the sky. Not one of our present-day constellations looked even remotely familiar, and—look there! The temperature and density of the universe have begun to creep upward.

The Big Dipper in 8,386,260 B.C.

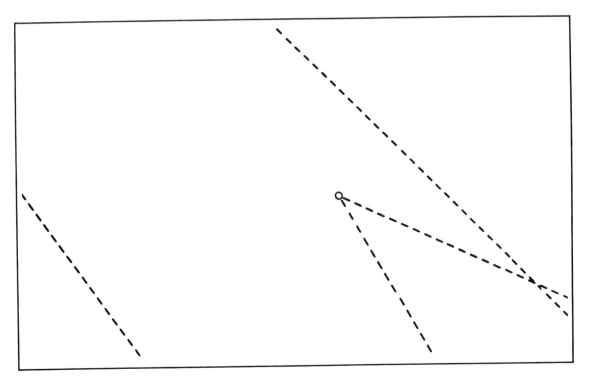

11 The Face of Siva

Norman Ness, from the Goddard Space Flight Center, principal investigator on the magnetic field team, explains how the Voyager passed through Saturn's bow shock wave at 4:50 P.M. when Titan was inside the magnetic field envelope of the planet. He speaks of the solar wind, the flow of ionized gas given off by the sun that hisses through the solar system. There is no poetry in the words . . . only in the way he speaks of it. Norman Ness barely realizes he has looked on the face of the Almighty.

Harlan Ellison

Now and then, though I rarely admit it, the universe projects itself toward me in a hideous grimace.

H. G. Wells

I can equate natural selection with just two members of the Hindu Triad—with Siva the destroyer and Vishnu the preserver, but not with Brahma the creator.

Lyell

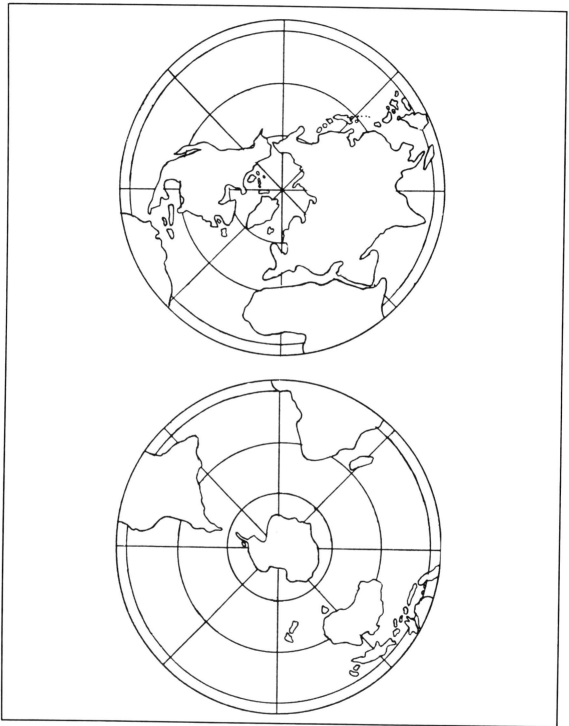

The continents in 16,775,228 B.C.

A long, long time ago, in fact right here in this galaxy . . .. The general temperature of deep space was 2.82 degrees Kelvin. The density of the universe amounted to at least 3 hydrogen atoms per 10 cubic meters of space; in other words, about 50 percent more atoms than you would find today.

In 16,775,228 B.C., the Moon was 973 kilometers (605 miles) closer to Earth than it would be in A.D. 1984. The year was 5 minutes and 36 seconds shorter, and the Atlantic Ocean was 256 kilometers (159 miles) narrower. *Anguilla anguilla* and *Anguilla rostrata's* forebears might then have shared a common gene pool.

During this warmest part of the Miocene epoch, lush forests advanced into northern Alaska. Even the Antarctic coastline was green with plant life. Across the forests and savannas of Europe, East Africa, and Asia had spread the cosmopolitan dryopithecine and ramapithecine apes.

They came out of Africa near 17 million B.C., crossing over the island continent's first physical contacts with Eurasia. And yes they were apes. This was the zenith of apen radiation and diversification: A great branching of new lineages in which ape species came to outnumber monkeys by about 20 to 1. Uncountable branches died off during the next 2 or 3 million years. One line, probably a still-undiscovered one, pointed in the direction of chimpanzees and australopithecines—beasts that became us.

Dryopithecus africanus (also known as Proconsul) spread quickly through Asia and Europe. In the late 1970s, remarkably complete limb bones and skull parts began to turn up. Based on Johns Hopkins University anatomist Alan Walker's and Kenya National Museum anthropologist Martin Pickford's analyses of these bones, *D. africanus* was close to, if not at the stem of, the dryopithecine line. It was a tree-dwelling creature that weighed in at about 11 kilograms (24 pounds). Its feet and lower leg bones were strikingly ape like in appearance, as were the shoulders and elbows. But the hips and hands looked like they belonged to monkeys. Its ratio of brain weight to body weight seems to have been much larger than that of monkeys, almost at a level seen in today's gorillas, orangutans, and chimpanzees.

By 16 million B.C., the ramapithecine and sivapithecine branches were living in northern Pakistan. Both branches are named after members of the Hindu Triad: Rama, the reincarnation of Vishnu, and Siva, the destroyer.

Through the 1970s, the two genera were known only from splintered teeth and slivers of jaw, and there were not enough of these to fill a cookie tin. In 1980, Yale University student Mark Solomon unearthed a *Sivapithecus* face. It was all there: the lower jaw, every tooth, parts of the braincase—a whole treasure trove of new information.

Assisted by Harvard anthropologist David Pilbeam, Solomon has constructed the following picture of Middle Miocene apes. *Sivapithecus* does not belong on a line leading to gorillas, chimpanzees, or australopithecines. Instead, certain features of the jaw, eye sockets, and nasal cavities point to a link between it and the Asain genus *Pongo* (the orangutan). *Ramapithecus*, once thought to possess a mixture of ape and human characteristics, seems to have been related only to *Sivapithecus*, making it part of a group of species that came in various shapes and sizes and whose only surviving branch is the modern orangutan.

Looking to the genetic timetable (to the evolutionary history written on our globin genes), we know that humans differ from chimpanzees by only 1 percent. This difference is slightly less than that between humans and the genus *Gorilla*, and only half that between humans and orangutans. The genetic contrast increases successively from orangutans to gibbons (*Hylobates*) and monkeys.

If rates of evolution at the molecular level are more gradual than

This simplified evolutionary "tree" combines the genetic history written on the blood proteins of living primates with clues from the fossil record. According to this interpretation, dryopithecine apes (probably several species) radiated out of Africa into Asia and Europe about 17 million years ago. One branch, leading to orangutan like creatures, split off from a lineage ancestral to gorillas, chimpanzees, and humans some 16 million years ago. The gorilla split next, between 10 and 7 million years ago, while proto chimps and proto australopithecines parted ways between 7 and 5 million years ago. Compiled by C.R. Pellegrino.

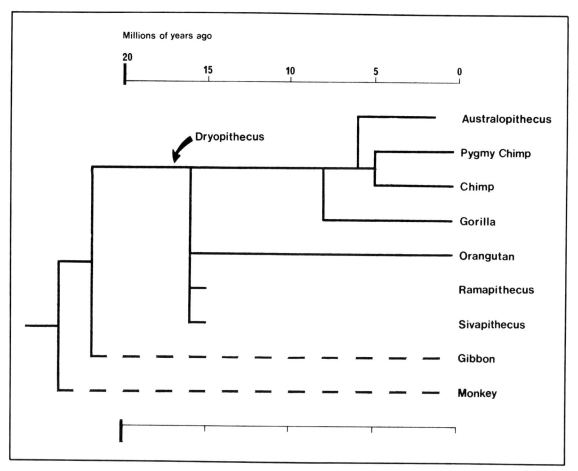

changes in outward appearance, then a synthesis of genetic dates and fossil dates is in agreement (for the moment at least) that the orangutan branch split off from a lineage ancestral to gorillas, chimpanzees, and humans some 16 million years ago.

The gorilla split next, between 10 million and 7 million years ago, while protochimps and protoaustralopithecines parted ways between 7 million and 5 million years ago. All of this means that, in ramapithecine times, there existed nothing that even resembled humans. Protoapes were the newest and brightest things around.

And into their world came a great calmity.

It came from the west, dark and heavy. Frighteningly heavy. Moving at 32 kilometers (20 miles) a second, 5 million tons of rock and rock-ice carried with it the potential explosive force of 500 hydrogen bombs. Somewhere above France it slid into the atmosphere. A billion years of accumulated boulders and dust blew away from its surface like a spray of dazzling diamonds.

The underlying bedrock blazed instantly, and brighter than the Sun. Twenty seconds later, a giant meterorite detonated on the forested countryside near Stuttgart in southern Germany. Forests vanished in a searing white glare, and from the smoke of their burning—preceding the very sound of the explosion—came tight swarms of molten glass that had only an instant earlier been sand and stone.

Still liquid, the glass splashed 32 kilometers (20 miles) up into the vacuum of near space, boiling there. Trapped gases swelled into bubbles. Within seconds, the glass solidified and, as it flew east across the heavens, internal gases cooled and thinned.

Almost 260 kilometers (161 miles) downrange, the swarms began to fall against denser layers of the atmosphere, scattering at hypersonic speed. The leading edge of each glass spherule began to melt. The outermost surface became vapor, while cooler glass immediately below flowed toward the rear and—sculpted by the wind—formed an aerodynamic tail.

Booming through to subsonic speed, thousands of warm, green teardrops thudded down on Czechoslovakia's forests. They formed strewn fields along two parallel streaks near the Moldau River. One streak runs 130 kilometers (80 miles) south of Prague. The other lies 150 kilometers (93 miles) southeast of the city.

Within the strewn fields, the glassy pearls all have the same potassium-argon isotope and fission-track ages: about 15 million years.

Almost 300 kilometers (187 mi.) away, in southern Germany, the floor of Nordlinger-Ries Basin is filled with breccia (rock composed of angular chips of older rocks crushed and fused together). These rocks are studded with coesite—a dense, high-pressure phase of glass—and lechatelierite, a type of glass known only from

places where lightning bolts frequently strike ground. Passing through quartz sand, the bolts produce 1710° C (3110° F) images of themselves. Melting sand solidifies to become "fossil lightning."

The Ries Basin lechatelierite and coesite have been isotopically dated to 15 million years ago. They and the Czechoslovakian glass solidified at the same time, indicating a common origin.

Ries Basin is a saucer-shaped depression measuring 24 kilometers (15 miles) across. Throughout 15 million years, earthquakes, wind, and vegetation have softened its features, but still it is structurally similar to craters that scar the Moon. It should be because it was created by the same celestial trapshoot that has pitted every square meter of Taurus-Littrow.

Unfortunately for scientific investigators, the green glass was thrown to a region of Europe known for ancient glass making. While the rest of civilization was occupied with such things as World War I and II, scientists found time to argue over whether tectite glass (from the Greek *tektos*, meaning melted) belonged to the archeologists or the astronomers. The question was partly resolved after a group of scientists succeeded in turning vast quantities of sand instantly into tectite like glass. This was accomplished on July 16, 1945, when the world's first atomic bomb was exploded in New Mexico.

In the end, the archaeologists were glad to be rid of the tectites. Too many bizarre scenarios were getting into the act:

☐ Sunspots spat them at the Earth.
☐ Antimatter struck the Earth.

Testimony of a violent moment in the history of life, this Moldavite was jetted into near space, where it traced a 300 kilometer (187 miles) path from southern Germany to Czechoslovakia's Moldau River. This event appears to have been partly responsible for such things as the extinction of giant crabs in New Zealand and the eventual origin of Homo sapiens. Photo by C.R. Pellegrino.

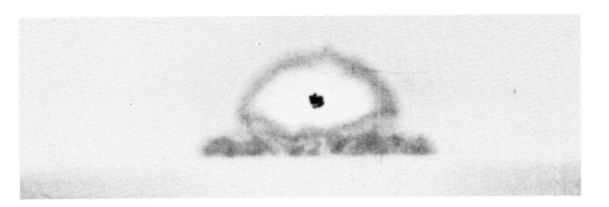

The first atomic bomb was successfully tested near Alamogordo, New Mexico on July 16, 1945. Photo by Brown Brothers.

Destruction caused by an atomic bomb detonated over Hiroshima, Japan on August 6, 1945. The Ries Basic explosion was 3 million times more powerful. Photo by Brown Brothers.

☐ A mini black hole passed through the Earth.

☐ A flying saucer dropped its ballast—or blew up—or both.

☐ The Earth once had rings, like Saturn, and tectites are pieces of the rings.

None of these scenarios stood the test of time, if indeed they ever stood at all. What we find when we probe the Moldau River

tectites (called moldavites) for such isotopes as helium-3, neon-21, and aluminum-26—all of which, like carbon-14, originate from exposure of glass or other materials to cosmic radiation—is nothing. Even at the highest possible resolution: nothing. Moldavites could not have spent even 100 years outside the Earth. Perhaps they were never really there at all.

What we have then is a shower of glass and, a few hundred kilometers away, one heck of a hole. It begins to look as if the shower came from the hole. Nevertheless, there remain a few die-hards who strongly dispute this view, and insist that tectites are lava ejected from lunar volcanoes.

As this chapter is being written, geochemists at Rutgers University and California Institute of Technology's "Lunatic Asylum" are dropping a few bombs that, as far as arguments about glass meteorites are concerned, should lay to rest the Earth-or-lunar-origin issue.

Certain tectites have been found to contain about 100 million atoms of beryllium-10 per gram (1 ounce = 28.4 grams). This isotope of beryllium has a half-life of about 1.5 million years and, if the tectites originated in a lunar volcano, they could have acquired the observed amounts of beryllium-10 only if they had sat on the Moon's surface and then—within 15 million years prior to their arrival on Earth—been pulled down into the Moon and melted.

This requires a geologically active Moon, at least during the last 15 million years or so, and—as we know from nearly a decade of manned and unmanned expeditions—the Moon has been quiescent for more than 3 billion years. On Earth, the levels of beryllium-10 found in tectites are easy to explain if the material from which they were made spent several thousand years at the Earth's surface— soaking up atmospheric beryllium-10 from rain and ground water—before being turned suddenly into glass.

The list of radioactive isotopes pointing to glass that could have come only from earthly sediment is beginning to pile up: samarium (element number 62), neodynium (element number 60), strontium (element number 38), and rubidium (element number 37). These collectively poke a hole, a 24 kilometer one, to be exact—in the traditional anticatastrophic thinking of many geologists, and point to rough times for Middle Miocene apes.

Across Europe and into Asia, the noise of the first shock wave must have been literally deafening. Unknowable thousands of apes lived their remaining years with a permanent, maddening ringing in their heads. They were the lucky ones.

From southern Germany spread a growing black curtain laced with sheets of lightning and made heavy with hot, descending ash. It ran like a liquid over the ground, faster than a plane, slashing down trees as it moved. Far above, cubic kilometers of ultra fine powder entered the stratosphere and began to form a global dust cloud. The sky's transparency changed.

In years to come, sunlight striking the particles would radiate some of its energy far from the ground, triggering climatic effects that could span into centuries and probably amplifying a world wide cooling that seems to have already been under way. Ice sheets were driving across the Antarctic, marking a geologically rapid transition from a world characterized by limited polar glaciation to a climate more like today's.

Carbon and oxygen isotopic changes in the shells of deep-sea organisms suggest that the rate of change was greatest between 14.8 and 14.0 million years ago. Middle Miocene fauna were correspondingly unstable in contrast to a relatively stable early Miocene record. The instability seems to have been global in extent. In the waters near Christchurch, New Zealand, the lush subtropical assemblage of early Miocene plankton was replaced abruptly by a more temperate, less diversified fauna.

The giant crab, *Tumidocarcinus*, vanished, as did several molluscan species. In more northerly reaches, the tropical forests that girdled the planet receded toward the equator. As they retreated, most of the Miocene apes died out, and thus began the great diversification and branching of monkeys.

On May 11, 1983, the comet IRAS-Araki-Alcock became a chilling reminder that we do not live in a sealed vessel, isolated from the environment of space in our bubble of air and water. This comet missed the Earth by a margin of 4.7 million kilometers (2.9 million miles). If this sounds like a large number, consider that if the comet had arrived 27 hours later, it would have found itself in the same place as the Earth. Civilization would have ended that day. Courtesy of NASA/JPL.

It was a bad time to be an ape. They found themselves in eclipse, limited to a few isolated branches in steadily shrinking habitats. From where we stand today, that might not have been an entirely bad thing. Decrease the number of animals you have to work with, increase the stresses upon them, and—if you can bring them close to the brink without actually pushing them over the edge to extinction—you might end up with a surge of variation on your hands. Remember? Speciation works best on small populations isolated from genetic communication with each other. Environmental stress keeps the numbers small. These are the conditions from which new branches emerge.

And here we stand as the youngest twig on a very old tree. But suppose the tree hadn't been pruned. Suppose the competition hadn't been cleared away and the great Miocene blooming of apes had continued unimpeded. The line leading to chimps and australopithecines might never have pulled through. A descendent of *Sivapithecus* or some entirely unknown apen line might now be the most sapient of creation's achievements. Think upon that. We might owe our dominion over the Earth to nothing more glamorous than luck in the form of bad weather made worse by the destructive arrival of an interplanetary vagrant.

Ries Basin is a forcible and timely reminder that our sky is not a closed door. Change the energy output of the Sun and life on Earth will notice the change. Put the wreckage of a newly exploded star in our path and radioactive elements will come through to the ground. We do not live inside a sealed container that is isolated from the environment of space. We live on a planet that is traveling through space and time, naked—and so vulnerable.

University of Chicago paleobiologist Jack Sepkoski has compiled an exhaustive list of animals, ranging from protozoans to pachyderms, that have gone extinct during the 225 million years since the late Permian glacial period. His data reveal a pattern of mass extinction that has repeated itself like clockwork, every 26 million years, with eight "hits" and two possible "misses."

Two of these post-Permian extinctions (at the Traissic-Jurassic and the Eocene-Oligocene boundaries) coincide with glacial advances. Almost all are associated with falling sea levels and evidence of worldwide climatic deterioration. No known cycle from within the Earth would appear to account for the 26-million-year period.

Sepkoski suspects (as Jesse Stoff and I suggested in *Darwin's Universe*) that the extinctions might be tied to cyclic changes in our Sun or to some galactic property. While it is true that astronomers can still practice their craft without having to know paleontology, we seem to be approaching a time when the paleontologist can no longer practice without at least some knowledge of astronomy.

12 Vault
of the Ages

If ever there was a fragile-appearing piece of blue in
space, it's the Earth right now.

Eugene Cernan
(as *Apollo 17* neared Earth)

The general temperature of the universe has risen to 2.84 degrees
Kelvin. Ice ages have come and gone. We have watched human
evolution in reverse until at least we can no longer recognize ourselves among the fossils. And yet stepping back to 33,552,444
B.C., Split Rock has not budged an inch. It's the same shape with the
same cracks in the same places. The surrounding hills have remained unchanged for almost 34 million years. Could that be true?

Up there in the sky, the Greater and Lesser Antilles were
racing into darkness, rolling into the line of shadow that had come
sweeping across the Atlantic and now bisected Haiti and the Dominican Republic. A lake caught the last rays of the setting Sun and cast
them back into the rising night. At its surface, a tiny creature
appeared, floating there, gulping and swallowing until finally its skin
burst and a new animal emerged from within. On shimmering wings
it rose from the water and took the air.

It found others in the sky—more and more of them—rising like
summoned spirits from the nether world that dwells beneath the skin

of a lake. Along the shore they became a mighty cloud, a dancing, swirling symphony of moving bodies. Clearly the mayflies held dominion over the night, but theirs was only a transitory reign. Within hours, their dying, spent bodies would begin to cover the ground. One of them, a male, encountered something sticky and was caught fast. His left wing twisted and folded and did not move again.

Millions of years later, miners in the damp, northern highlands of the Dominican Republic would find him encased in a transparent coffin of amber. During the Oligocene epoch, he had become mired in the fresh-flowing sap of a tree and, while he lay in state in his golden tomb, the lake that had once given him sustenance disappeared, entire mountain ranges fell, the very continents shifted on the terrestrial globe and, almost unbelievably, a little insect came through with every facet of his eyes, every vein in his wings, every fine detail of his external anatomy intact.

The mayflies belong to one of the most ancient insect groups, having preserved their present shapes for 300 million years or more. The specimen recovered from the Dominican highlands represents the first known fossil occurrence of a "small mayfly" (family Baetidae). That the Baetids have not been discovered in older rocks, particularly in 40-million-year-old fossil resins from the Baltic coast, is somewhat of a mystery. Their modern descendents flourish not

Taurus-Littrow in the year 33,552,444 B.C. Photo courtesy of NASA's Johnson Space Center, Houston, Texas. Photomosaic by C.R. Pellegrino.

170

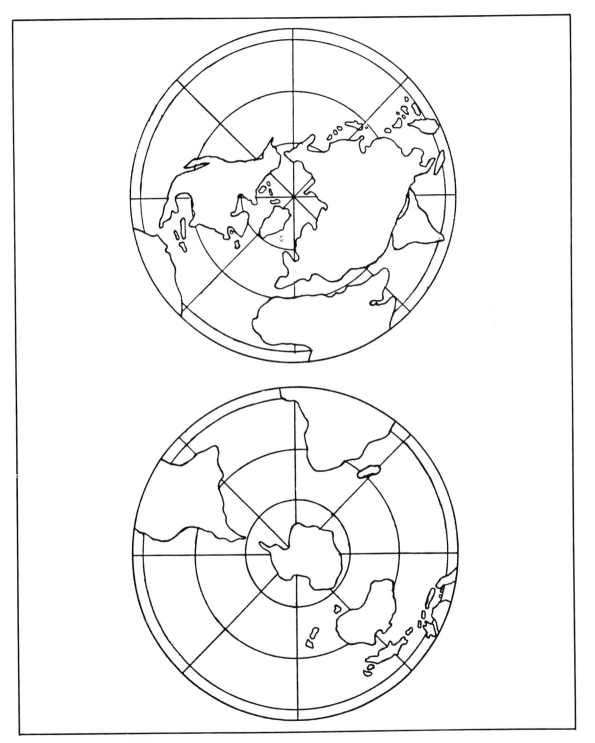

The continents in 33,552,444 B.C.

only in the Baltic and Dominion territories, but also can be found living in a variety of aquatic habitats ranging from as far north as Alaska southward to New Zealand and Patagonia, Argentina.

Either the Baetids did not exist by the time the Baltic amber deposits had formed or they did not yet range widely over the world. While mayflies are not unknown from *Baltic* resins, the "small mayflies" are entirely missing. This implies that both the Baetid family and Dominican amber are younger than Baltic amber. This finding is in agreement with Smithsonian paleobotanist Francis Nveber's recent studies of pollen spores and plant debris in amber. He concludes that most of the Dominican samples are concentrated somewhere between 30 and 35 million years ago, and thus date from Lower Oligocene times. The youngest pieces of Baltic amber are at least 5 million years older and date from the very end of the Eocene epoch.

Amber, a hardened resin exuded by plants occupying scattered positions within the botanical system, is found almost all over the world. Deposits of the "organic gem" have been laid down by the lives and deaths of forests ranging from the dawn of insects through the rise of dinosaurs and right up to the present. Now it occurs in the form of such raw materials as pine sap, kauri gum, and maple syrup.

The fossilization of these sticky secretions is not at all like the fossilization of wood or bone. We do not find in amber a mineralized cast of once-living matter. Instead, we view the original sap transformed by *polymerization* reactions, in which smaller molecules have been snapped together piece by piece to form larger molecules. Oxygen, water, oils, and other volatile substances can pass easily through the resin-polymer, but amber is a closed door to minerals.

For instance, if water laced with calcium were to percolate down through layers of sediment and encounter a piece of amber, the water might pass through the resin, but none of the calcium could enter with it. Because of this, organisms encased in amber cannot be dissolved and replaced by minerals (as in the formation of petrified wood).

When we view a mayfly in amber, we are not viewing a mineralized cast or shadow of an ancient animal; we are viewing the actual animal. Granted, a cross section through the head or thorax or any portion of his body would reveal its great age. The internal organs, cells, and the chemical machinery that propelled them have oxidized and deteriorated in spite of their amber casing.

What survives, in essence, is a mummy of the original mayfly. It is a tarry, carbonized body held together by the surrounding resin. Nonetheless, it *is* the original mayfly, and a marvel of preservation found nowhere else in the fossil record (at least nowhere else outside of ice).

The resins themselves are divided into two classes. Those originating from the Baltic are called succinites because they contain succinic acid. Dominican amber contains formic acid, and is therefore

classified as a nonsuccinite or retinite.

Detailed chemical analyses suggest that Baltic amber originated from a species of *Agathis* similar to the coniferous (cone-bearing) giant, *Agathis australis*, now restricted to 22,500 acres of New Zealand's Waipoua Forest. *A. australis*, also known as the kauri tree, is protected by an act of Parliament. Until 1905, kauri trees were bled by gum collectors; some still bear the V-shaped wounds. Older, harder "kauri gum" was mined from the forest floor. Whole boat loads of it were shipped to England and made into varnish for floors.

Deposits of kauri resin are generally regarded as being no older than a few hundred years—a few thousand at most—but the oldest kauri trees are more than a thousand years old, and the kauri forests have been around a lot longer. I have seen fist-sized pieces of New Zealand resin recovered from accumulations of soil 50 meters (163 feet) deep, and grape-sized ones embedded in lumps of 55-million-year-old coal. It is possible that the longest and most complete amber record in the world is buried under New Zealand (capped by the still-living amber forest), though much of it has already been mined.

Curiously, insects are comparatively rare in kauri gum. You need only search a teacup full of Dominican amber and you'll be guaranteed a find. To locate an insect in Baltic amber, you'd have to search a little harder—perhaps 10 teacups. Kauri gum is next to impossible.

The resin secreting Kauri (Agathis australis) is now protected by an act of Parliament. On 24 December 1835, during the Beagle's visit to New Zealand, Charles Darwin wrote: "I measured one of these noble trees, and found it 31 feet in circumference above the roots . . . and I heard of one no less than 40 feet. The forest here was almost composed of the Kauri; and the largest trees, from the parallelism of their sides, stood up like gigantic columns of wood. The timber of the Kauri is the most valuable production of the land . . . some of the New Zealand forests must be impenetrable to an extraordinary degree. Mr. Matthews informed me that one forest only 34 miles in width, and separating two inhabited districts, had only lately, for the first time, been crossed." Today, all that remains of the Kauri forest is a 35 square mile stand of widely scattered trees. Photo by C.R. Pellegrino.

I have picked my way through whole buckets and failed to discover a single fly. There are two good reasons for this. The first is that the floor of the kauri forest does not support a great deal of insect life. You can actually picnic there without being bothered. The second is that, as the tree grows, its lower branches decay from within and are shed.

But before being shed, the branches bleed thick ooze into their decaying hollows so that most kauri gum seems to occur as hardened, internal seepage in dying branches rather than an external flytrap. The internal bleeding makes life a little tougher for infective agents and wood-loving insects. A dying branch would otherwise provide a good beachhead for penetration into the trunk.

The resin permits the tree to conserve energy and building materials (protein) by enabling it to safely discard branches as they fall under the crown's shadow. The tree then diverts its resources (where they are needed most) to the construction and maintenance of the uppermost branches that eventually emerge above the forest into direct sunlight, supported by a 36-meter-high (120-foot) leafless and branchless trunk that might be as old as 1500 years. The outcome of all this is that, in the present-day kauri forest, most resin secretions are found inside fallen branches and kauri fossils are limited almost exclusively to rotting wood.

Trees belonging to the genus *Agathis* live only in warm and humid climates. This fact alone suggests that 40 million years ago, Denmark, Germany, Poland, and the Baltic states were subtropical. The suggestion has gained support in the guise of amberized March flies (family Bibionidae) and fungus gnats (family Mycetophilidae), that thrive in warm, wet places.

Near the Eocene-Oligocene boundary, the weather changed and the Baltic gum trees fell. In more equatorial reaches, amber production continued for millions of years, secreted in Dominica by leguminous (pod-bearing) trees of the *Hymenaea* genus.

Despite its great age, amber is a fragile and easily degraded substance. Lying in the ground—shielded from sunlight and warm, dry air—a granular surface layer forms that protects deeper layers from the same fate. The worst thing that can happen to a piece of amber is to be plucked from the ground, to have its protective surface layer shaved off, to be polished and placed in an open box in a warm, dry cabinet that is not airtight, and then to be left there for 40 years or so.

Almost immediately, volatile compounds begin to leak off from the surface. Scorched by direct exposure to oxygen and moving air, the exterior dries and shrinks, creating stresses that carry through to the temporarily protected interior. Within a decade, a spreading network of cracks appears on the surface and granulation begins anew. This worst-case scenario is exactly what happens to amber once it enters most museums because, until very recently, only about three or four people in the world seriously paid attention to the stuff (the number has now risen to about 10).

Insects in amber were traditionally regarded as freaks of nature, refugees from a twilight zone between zoology and geology (and those of us who studied them were often viewed in a similar light). At one world-famous museum, the paleontologists tried to pawn their amber collection off on the entomologists. The exchange went something like this: "Nobody in our department is working full time on insects," the paleontologists said.

"So what?" the entomologists said. "We don't work with fossils. You keep them."

"We don't want them. They're just taking up space."

"Well, ask the botanists if they'll have them. They are plant fossils, aren't they?"

"Good thought."

Meanwhile, the hundred-year-old collection was turning into garbage. Nobody seemed to notice.

One way of forestalling the "death" of amber is to wear it as jewelry or to handle it frequently. Contact with oils on the skin restores volatiles evaporated at and near the surface, and also provides a temporary shield against further drying. Proper care of amber should include occasional rubbing against the forehead and bridge of the nose because these are sites of copious oil production.

The best way to preserve amber is to refrigerate it between 2 and 5° C (35 to 40° F). No special equipment is needed. You can actually store it right next to the fruit and vegetables. Additional protection is gained by storage in airtight containers. I began refrigerating amber, in 1981, after accumulating a photographic record showing the growth of microscopic surface fractures in five pieces of amber over a three-year period. Under refrigeration the cracks stopped dead. Even oils from the skin failed to evaporate from the surface.*

Polished pieces of amber often exhibit a subtle, laminated internal structure in which it is possible to discern the buildup of successive layers as the product of numerous resin flows. Sven G. Larsson, of the Zoological Museum in Copenhagen, proposes a diurnal rhythm of deposition whereby the resin, warmed during the day, became fluid and ran freely down the tree trunk. This was followed by an inhibition of the flow by cooling during the night (and possibly on

---

* Refrigeration of amber nuggets measuring fist sized or larger requires very gradual cooling and warming in thermos like containers. You cannot just take large pieces of amber out of the refrigerator into warm air (and especially not into direct sunlight). Expansion of near-surface layers will *instantly* create deep fractures. This is especially true of Pliocene and Pleistocene resins from Africa, New Zealand, and the Philippines.

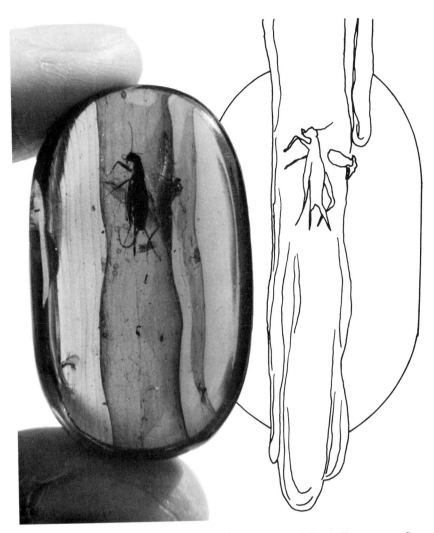

This 30-million-year-old amber stalagtite formed from successive layers of down-dripping tree sap, trapping small insects as it grew. Illustration and Photo by C.R. Pellegrino.

overcast days) so that the surface partly solidified. Then a new flow was driven down, over that of the previous day, without dissolving away completely the hardened skin already formed. As testimony to the fluid nature of many such flows, portions of spiders' webs can be seen that have been engulfed by the resin without the threads having broken.

Almost all amber contains fields of drop- or pearl-shaped bubbles varying from microscopic in size up to several millimeters across. Typically, they are air bubbles stirred into the sap as it advanced toward the ground. Some, like the microscopic variety that occur in large numbers and resemble decks of clouds, can be attributed, perhaps, to direct heating by the Sun and to the subsequent release, as vapors, of some of the resin's more volatile constituents.

Other bubbles can be linked to the death throes—exhalations

177

and regurgatations—of the creatures entombed within. Another group, prized by both collectors and researchers but seldom encountered by either, contains tantalizing liquid inclusions. When present, "water bubbles" or "bladders" will generally be seen throughout the entire piece of amber. Fluid deposits reside in identical proportion inside bubbles of all sizes, and even inside the bodies of preserved insects. Previous amber investigators have described liquid inclusions as traces of plant juices from the original amber forest or as trapped rain water. Sadly the evidence seems to favor a less spectacular origin.

The dried state of the insects is the clearest indicator that amber is not impermeable to the passage of fluids. Several years ago I tested the penetration of liquids by placing three marble-sized nuggets of Dominican amber, each containing scores of "water-filled" bubbles, in a desiccator. Within a year, much of the liquid had percolated out of the amber. Conversely, a fourth nugget containing only air bubbles was immersed in vegetable oil over the same period. The result was that the bubbles became partly filled with oil. These experiments would seem to indicate that the occasional presence of liquids in amber should be viewed, not as the remnants of an ancient afternoon shower, but as the action of recent seepage.

Looking through hundreds of amber blocks, one begins to recognize subtle, repeated traits in successive resin flows. Within a single block, some layers will appear to have run more fluid than others and, if you slice through the resin, it is within these layers that the best-preserved fossils will be found: Pieces of wood in which the individual cells have been saturated with sap; Noctuid moths with muscles and internal organs turned black with age, yet preserved in microscopic detail.

They might just as well have been immersed in Canadian balsam and made into microscope slides. In a sense, this is exactly what has occurred. If the conditions were just right, if a resin flow were warmed under direct sunlight until it acquired a consistency like oil, it then gained the ability to penetrate the tissues of anything it touched.

In late 1979, when I started speaking cautiously about the remarkable preservative qualities of Dominican amber, colleagues began to ask whether or not the muscle structures I had found were the product of a mean trick. Entomologist P. Wygodzinsky, of the American Museum of Natural History in New York, said, "I think you should consider the possibility that somebody slipped you phony amber stuffed with modern insects."

He made a good point. In science you do not accept preliminary evidence as truth, especially if that preliminary evidence seems to support one of your pet theories. Instead, you go back to your room and ask new questions. You try to disprove your hypothesis. Then, following Sherlock Holmes' advice, you eliminate *all* the most likely possibilities until what you have left, no matter how impossible, is the truth.

So, I went back to my fossils, and a few weeks later I found muscle fibers in still another insect. My entomologist friends conceded that *this* creature could not possibly be fake.

Elementary: it's a whole new creature, something that has undoubtedly been extinct for more than 26 million years.

The next year Berkeley insect pathologist George O. Poinar, Jr. began pulling amberized insects apart and examining their tissues under an electron microscope. In one fungus gnat, he found preserved nuclei, ribosomes, endoplasmic reticulum, and other cell elements—including chromosomes. In 1982, he attempted to extract the insect's DNA, hopeful that the genetic code of a 40-million-year-old creature might be studied for the first time. "It is possible that some units of the fly's DNA might still be capable of replication," Poinar said.

The discovery of variable DNA would indicate, not necessarily that the ancient fly could be resurrected, but perhaps more important, that other, more protected forms of life, such as bacterial spores, may be able to survive such catastrophic events as glaciation or even interplanetary travel—a process that some scientists have recently invoked to explain the origins of life on Earth.

Sadly, the attempt to recover and "read" the DNA has failed. The proper equipment simply does not exist yet. But give us time. In any case, Poinar's effort did produce rewards:

We've learned that the internal anatomy of these creatures is remarkably similar to what you find in flies today. The wings and legs and head, and even the cells inside are very modern-looking. It raises some questions about the change and the rate of change.

Within the depths of fossil resins, if one looks closely enough, will be seen the substance of great mystery stories. Every piece is a clue, a fragment, a part of some larger tale told only by scattered, almost random snapshots of the parade of life that has marched across the Earth's surface.

A caravan of Dominican leafcutter ants (genus *Atta*), having its fixed routes up and down the tree trunk, one day found its path blocked by a flow of resin. One after the other, the unfortunate creatures ventured into the sticky liquid, each following the trail of pheromones laid down by the insect before her.

Elsewhere, probably under a different generation of trees, a

resin flow is known to have ravaged an entire jungle, a world in miniature that carpeted the trunk and branches and cracks and crannies of the bark, and provided accommodation for a rich fauna of small animals. Sliding groundward, the rivulets of sap invaded tufts of moss and other ephiphytes, chasing mites and springtails and their predators before them. In a single piece of amber, strewn among fragmented mosses, can be viewed the bodies of a minute fly and springtail and, over there, in the corner, a spider and a beetle still clinging to a twig.

As a rule, fossil resins seem to have interred the littlest creatures in the forest. Animals greater than 10 millimeters (3/8 inches) or so across—moths, bats and lizards, by nature of the sheer power of their bodies—are hardly ever preserved in amber. Apart from numerous forgeries, only a single tree frog has been documented in amber. Discovered in the Dominican Republic in 1978, it measures about 20 millimeters (3/4 inches) long.

During life, the high and erect trees of the amber forest provided for the animal's every need. There were sunlit places where flies and beetles gathered. There were darker places where large, spreading branches emerged from the trunk—places that remained cool and moist on the hottest summer day, and were frequented by ants, tree hoppers, katydids and other sources of food.

Lying only 40 millimeters from the frog are what appear to be the partly eaten remains of a crane fly (family Tipulidae). This hints that the frog impacted on the resin after an aerial leap at the insect, perhaps remaining perched in the ooze until alarmed by his increasingly apparent inability to move. During the ensuing struggle, he discarded his catch, and the tree that had sustained him became his tomb.

Birds and mammals have left only traces of themselves in amber, obscure signatures that betray their presence in ancient forest communities. For example, innumerable insects appear to have been pecked by birds while fighting to free themselves from the resin. Clambering around the tree trunks in their search for small prey, some birds unwittingly contributed specimens of down to the fossil record. Occasionally, preserved feathers can be traced back to their owners by examination of their microscopic construction. On the basis of such studies, species of small woodpeckers and titmice are known to have inhabited northern European forests some 40 million years ago.

In several pieces of amber can be seen small hairs that were lost by mammals roving on the resin-secreting trees. Many hairs exhibit structural designs that could only have come from bats; others have been tentatively identified as belonging to squirrel-like and mouse-like animals.

A beetle and a stingless honey bee are seen in Dominican amber. 30 million years, and more, have passed. Entire mountain ranges have fallen, the very continents have shifted on the terrestrial globe, and yet two insects have endured with the facets of their eyes, every hair on their legs, and even some of their DNA intact. Photos by C.R. Pellegrino.

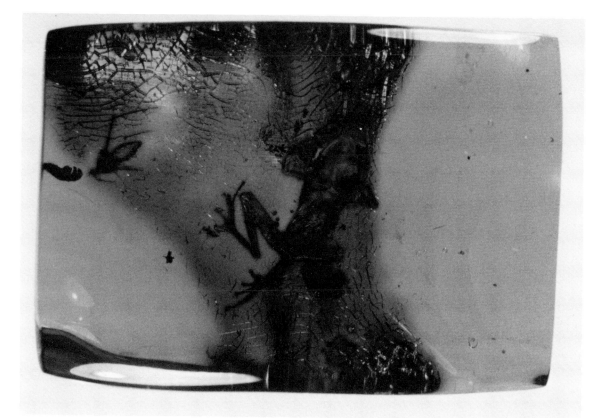

One particularly famous find on the Baltic coast contains the footprint of a small mammal. It consists of four closely placed balls of the second, third, fourth and fifth toes, behind and between which lies an elongated ball of the foot. Because no impressions of claws are visible, those familiar with the fossil tend to agree that it was made by the front paw of a small climbing carnivore landing after a spring.

There are no published traces of our own ancestors (monkey hairs or palm prints) in amber. We do know, however—from broken teeth and splinters of bone—that by 34 million B.C. arboreal and ground-dwelling monkeys proliferated in North Africa, Eurasia, and South America.

The world turned faster than it does today. Each month was shorter by almost a full minute. And the Atlantic Ocean was narrower by almost a quarter. In Egypt, the microscopic skeletons of single-celled animals called foraminifera were accumulating on a seabed where now flows the Nile River. The little shells had been piling up for millions of years, forming layers of limey mud that were in several places tens of meters deep. In time, the mud would harden into stone; and descendents of the spidery primates that roamed Africa's shores would one day cut the stone into huge blocks, carry them away on barges, and build from them the Great Pyramid of KhuFu (or Cheops) at Giza.

Between 37.5 and 40 million B.C., average winter temperatures all over Earth dropped by almost 10° C (34° F). The extinction of many plant and animal species, among them the Baltic gum trees, is known as the "terminal Eocene event."

Near 34 million B.C., another event marked the transition from early to middle Oligocene time. The distribution of forests and animals changed and, in the sea, five major Radiolarian species disappeared. Radiolaria are minute marine protozoans belonging to one of the oldest animal groups known. They have amoebalike bodies with filamentous "tentacles" radiating from elaborate and often beautiful exoskeletons.

Simultaneously, microtectites carpeted the sea floor around Cuba and the Dominican Republic and, at the same horizon in the ocean sediments, there appeared unusually high concentrations of iridium and other platinum-group elements. These elements are scarce in the Earth's crust, but are abundant in cosmic dust and stony meteorites. The tectites, taken together with the iridium anomaly and the Radiolarian extinctions, appear to be the signature of yet another giant meteroite impact.*

No one is certain where it came down or exactly what it did when it got here. The only clear point of agreement is that the effects must have been large. Dust clouds covered the Earth, and lingered for weeks or perhaps months. Here and there dark shadows were cast and weather patterns changed accordingly. During the long twilight, photosynthesis could have slowed or even come to a stop in some parts of the world (especially in higher latitudes), rocking terrestrial and oceanic ecosystems from the bottom up. Some species died (Radiolarians among them), clearing the way for new life.

The Earth seemed to welcome the darkness.

---

*In August 1981, with iridium anomales and mass extinctions making headlines in the popular press, I suggested in a letter to Luis Alvarez at Berkeley that it was time to look at iridium near the Eocene-Oligocene boundary and in other transitional layers (including the Triassic-Jurassic boundary) to determine whether an iridium spike seen 65 million years ago (more on this in Chapter 13) did actually come from an asteroid or whether we were simply witnessing a distortion of the normal, worldwide influx of cosmic dust. In other words, was it an artifact of global breaks in marine sedimentation or similar jokes of nature. "Look to the Caribean microtectites, which suggest an asteroid impact near the Eocene-Oligocene boundary, and see if you don't find an iridium spike." Indeed they did (see the 21 May 1982 issue of *Science*). The Caribbean record suggests *two* separate impacts associated with a possible increase in the cosmic dust background.

13 Dinosaur Daydreams

There are creatures which do not appear to be mentioned in the Bible. Why were they created? Were they represented in the ark? Why are they now extinct? It is possible that they are mentioned in Genesis 1:21 as great sea monsters. Though this would seem to include only the amphibians . . . they might have been herbivorous before he curse, or they might have been sent as a punishment for man's sin of violence. There may have been young dinosaurs aboard the ark, and these may have been killed off by the post-alluvial climate. That they were once contemporary with man is suggested by the ancient and widespread belief in dragons.

From a 1982 proposal for teaching "creation science" in American schools

When I was a child, something about dinosaurs troubled me. I remember asking a nun if there really had been an ark, and if there really was a God—and I was eventually hounded clear out of school. Some years later, as a graduate student, I would "question Darwin"—and be forced to leave the country I loved.

anonymous

185

*If species lived forever, we would have no science of
paleontology, and I might have become a fireman after
all.*

Stephen Jay Gould

Oh, stop living in the past.

Dad

67,106,876 B.C.

We have just stepped back across 33.6 million years, during
which time the Earth has changed more than in all previous time
jumps combined.

The general temperature of the universe was, at that time, up
to 2.89° K, and the space between the galaxies contained at least
one atom per cubic meter. The Moon was some 3890 kilometers
(2418 miles) closer to the Earth, and our days were shorter by at
least five seconds.

We do not know if true primates existed anywhere on Earth.

At the South Pole, Australia and Antarctica were joined solidly
into a single supercontinent.

The oldest mammalian fossils from South America date from
about 70 million years ago. They were all ratlike in appearance, and
they were all marsupials. Placental mammals, whose young develop
in wombs, were apparently absent in South America.

In 1982, the bones of a South American marsupial were found in
40-million-year-old strata on Seymour Island, in the northern
Antarctic Peninsula. The bones speak of warm South Polar climates
capable of supporting the South American marsupial and the plants
upon which it fed. They speak also of a proposed but never-before-
confirmed connection between South America and Antarctica (believed to date back at least 70 million years), and their presence
raises the question of origins. Did marsupials originate in Antarctica
and disperse into Australia and South America? Or did Australian
marsupials originate from South American species crossing through
Antarctica? Or was it the other way around?

To the north, paleontologist Gerard R. Case has identified
almost 15 species of 70-million-year-old sharks, each of which has
left traces of itself (mostly teeth) in both North Africa and eastern
North America. This makes sense, in light of the fact that the
Atlantic Ocean was then only half its present width, and Greenland
was joined across its continental shelf to Scandinavia and the British
Isles (Iceland did not exist yet). If the ancestors of today's eels and
bluefin tuna had left fossils behind, we might find a pattern similar to
that seen in Case's sharks.

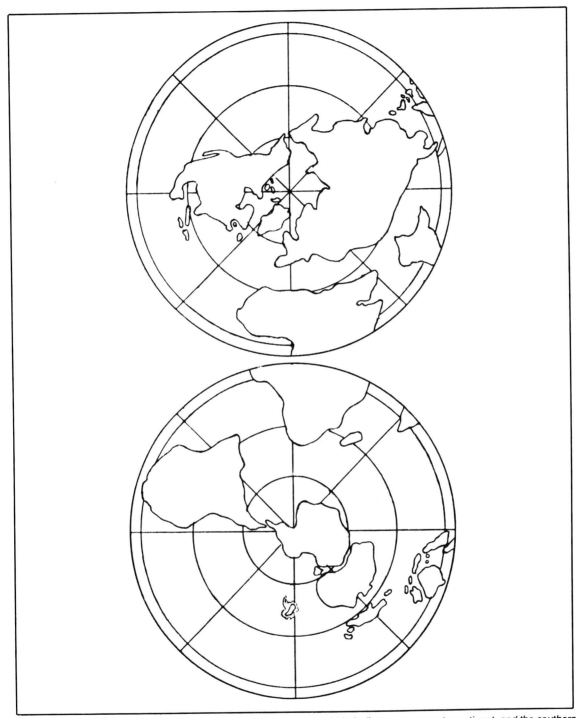

In the year 67,106,876 B.C., the Atlantic Ocean was half its present width, India was a separate continent, and the southern continents were huddled together at the South Pole.

Near Manhattan, sediments from the eroding Appalachian highlands had been piling up for some 20 million years, forming the Raritan and Magothy layers of sand, silt, and clay that are the foundation of Long Island. Parts of Manhattan, Kings, Queens, and Nassau Counties were being uplifted above sea level to become a patchwork of growing offshore islands. They would eventually expand their boundaries into each other and right into the continent. This caused streams to merge into a major river, between Long Island and Connecticut, to carve a valley that is now Long Island Sound.

This was the end of the Upper Cretaceous period; it was the age of the last dinosaurs. In eastern Montana, flowering plants were being slowly replaced by conifers more tolerant of cold winters. By approximately 67 million B.C., North America's horned dinosaurs (the rhinolike triceratops) had declined from 16 known genera to only seven. Their decline runs in parallel with a cooling of the Earth's oceans and a slow withdrawal of shallow seas from the area of the continents that began about 70 million years ago. Armored dinosaurs experienced a similar pruning of their family tree, from 19 genera to six, and the duck-billed genera withered from 29 to seven.

In Alberta, grapevines and roses still climbed up the trunks of newly evolved pines, sycamores, and willows. Not far from a stand of tall pines, two duck-billed dinosaurs bogged down in a muddy shallow and starved to death. They remained there, totally undisturbed, while the Atlantic doubled its width.

In A.D. 1916, Charles and Levi Sternberg dug them up, wrapped their skulls in plaster, and packed them off on a London-bound steamer, which was promptly torpedoed by a German submarine.

Now, immersed in deep-sea ooze, two duck-bills are entering the fossil record side-by-side with creatures they had never lived to see. Pity anyone who brings them up a million years down the line. Science fiction writers have been telling us all along that nature delights in mischief; we are powerless to prevent such roguery.

All told, there are approximately 600 dinosaur species known from fossils. These can only represent a small fraction of the species that actually lived. Dinosaur footprints and bones and other traces come almost exclusively from lowland marsh environments. In the very least, we are missing all of the upland fauna.

To get an idea of just how much information has been lost, consider that some 3500 mammal species are alive today. *At any one time*, there might have been just as many dinosaurs, and those known from fossils are spread across *all* of dinosaur time. This amounts to somewhere over 50,000 dinosaur species that nobody know about.

Many of the species already on record were smaller than reindeer. The smallest reasonably adult dinosaur, *Compsognathus,* was about the size of a pigeon. We know this to be its adult size because the tips of its leg bones lack hints of soft cartilage. The tips of human bones also become depleted of cartilage once an adult size is reached. Some large mammals—elephants and whales among them—never reach a terminal size; they simply keep on growing. Certain of their bones retain cartilaginous tips throughout life. The same appears to hold true for the largest dinosaurs.

The widespread view of dinosaurs as giants (as suggested even by the name "dinosaur," which is derived from Latin for "thunder lizard") comes in part from the hard facts of preservation. Big, thick bones are more likely to become fossils than are small bones. Go to Florida's Ice-Age phosphate pits and poke around for a few hours. What will you see? Elephant bones, horse teeth, a giant pig's teeth, and an occasional whale vertebra.

You might conclude from these that camels must have been the

A Tyrannosaurus skeleton. Photo by Brown Brothers.

smallest things around. Yet surely there were squirrels and mice and shrews. Their bones just fall apart more easily. Hence there are fewer of them, and you have to look a little bit harder to find one. Bear in mind when you look at the remains of dinosaurs that many, if not most, were smaller than you or I.

Among the smaller dinosaurs was *Deinonychus,* a 1.2-meter-high (4-foot), 68-kilogram (150-pound) cousin of the infamous *Tyrannosaurus rex* ("tyrant lizard"). In 1964, Yale University curator John H. Ostrom found a Montana "grave" containing the skeletons of three *Deinonychus* ("terrible claw"). The form and function of the legs told him of hunting creatures who ran down their prey and slashed it to death with swift precision. "Imagine that," he said. "Slashing and dodging maneuvers requiring rapid, unerring foot-eye coordination, a keen sense of balance and . . . and, just maybe, endothermy" (warm blood).

That three of these creatures were found together raised another possibility: Did they hunt in packs like wolves? Judging from the 408-kilogram (900-pound) herbivore interred with them, its bones widely scattered, Ostrom concludes that they did. "The much larger size of the prey animal also explains the dead predators at the site," he wrote in a 1978 report.

They appear to be victims of the struggle. We normally associate pack hunting with warm-blooded animals, but, in addition to *Deinonychus,* some other dinosaurs appear to have moved in packs. At Connecticut's Dinosaur State Park, thousands of dinosaur footprints have been uncovered. Some of them are parallel, suggesting herd movement. Another site, in Holyoke, Massachusetts, preserves the trackways of 28 bipedal dinosaurs, 19 of which led in a near-parallel westerly direction—clear evidence of group behavior. A third site, in Texas, records the passage of a herd of brontosaurlike animals, huge herbivores. First recognized by Roland Bird of the American Museum of Natural History as evidence of herding behavior, those trackways have been interpreted by Dr. Robert Bakker of Johns Hopkins University as resulting from a "structured" herd, with the young in the center surrounded and protected by the adults.

As a rule, dinosaurs have been more maligned than the Neanderthals. The traditional view holds that they were saurian brutes that lumbered mindlessly through life, following their noses and almost deserving of extinction. This view is changing.

Almost everywhere you look you see stamps of behavioral complexity. In the Cretaceous sediments of Peace River Canyon in British Columbia, a herd of elephant-sized hadrosaurs made trails across a broad front, walking side-by-side, with the young following literally in their footsteps. Eleven of the tyrannosaur-shaped herbivores made a sudden left turn. One of them cut off three other members of the herd who had to veer quickly to avoid a four-hadrosaur pileup. Nearby, man-sized carnivores circled in packs. Larger hunters—5.2-meter-tall (17-foot) tyrannosaurs—seemed to travel alone or at most in pairs.

Using a formula developed by R. McNeil Alexander of the University of Leeds, the walking speed of dinosaurs can be estimated by the size and spacing of their footprints. At Peace River, man-sized carnivores ran close to the highest speeds attained by men, clocking in at 16.5 kilometers (10.3 miles) per hour.

In 1982, James Farlow of Hope College found several tracks in Kimble County, Texas, belonging to a 3.2-meter-tall (12-foot) cousin of *Tyrannosaurus rex*. The animals appear to have been "in the fast track," running at the prodigious speed of 40 kilometers (25 miles) per hour.

"They could have been chasing something," Farlow suggests. "Or they might have been just horsing around. Or they could have been running away from something."

Running away from something? What would a 3.6-meter-tall, flesh-eating dinosaur be running away from?

You probably don't want to know.

In any case, there is an ever-growing body of evidence to support the belief that some dinosaurs lived in herds, like today's herbivorous mammals, and hunted in packs like lions and wolves. It seems that saurians have been gaining respectability of late, and are being viewed now as energetic, competent creatures that were neither slow of mind nor of muscle. This must be so. How else could they have held sway over the Earth for 140 million years?

The rise of mammals begins to look more and more like a filtering out and subsequent replacement of niches left vacant, by what German geologist Johannes Walther called "the great death," rather than a story of displacement by faster, wittier mammals. Some paleobiologists have taken the new dinosaurian respectability so far as to say that we must remove them from the class Reptilia altogether and place them alongside the warm-blooded birds and mammals.

Again, nature is not that simple. The brontosaur's mouth was too small to take in enough vegetation to support a warm-blooded metabolism comparable to that of an elephant's. This is not to say that dinosaurs were not warm blooded. Remember the "either/or" paradox? When all the evidence is in, we will almost certainly learn that some were, others were not, and in between these two absolutes existed a gradient of systems for regulating body temperature.

For the moment, we know of two saurian branches that were truly warm-blooded, and both of them could be found in trees. One branch, the featherless, batlike pterosaurs, were not dinosaurs proper. The second branch apparently was, and we call it Avies (the birds).

The best known intermediate or "missing link" between dinosaurs and birds, *Archaeopteryx,* might not be a link at all but merely a random limb on a freely branching tree of feathered dinosaurs.

In 1979, hollow, matchstick-sized bones that might date back as far as *Archaeopteryx* (about 140 million years ago) began turning up in Colorado's Dry Mesa quarry. A final verdict on the bones must await the discovery of more bones; but *Archaeopteryx* probably lived among contemporaries both more and less birdlike than itself. This should not surprise us. After all, orangutans share a planet with creatures both more and less manlike than themselves. We have already seen plenty of ancestors surviving alongside descendents during successive backsteps through our own branching history.

The most important thing about *Archaeopteryx* is that it had feathers. That some of its closest relatives (branches) exploited

Stegosaurus. Photo by Brown Brothers.

Many flying reptiles (Pterosaurs) were as small as sparrows, though at least one species is known to have grown as large as a jet fighter. It is said that their numbers once darkened the sky. Why are they and their saurian cousins no longer around? Bad luck it seems, nothing more. It begins to look as if there was a lot of bad luck floating around at the end of the Cretaceous. Photo by C.R. Pellegrino.

193

feathers to their next logical advantage can easily blind us to their previous "use" as a method of insulation. Only warm-blooded creatures need this kind of insulation. Dig back far enough, study the bones carefully enough, and sooner or later you are going to find feathers belonging to a wingless, warm-blooded dinosaur.

Pterosaurs were not related to birds, but—like birds—their bodies apparently required insulation. Recent fossils show that they possessed hair (again suggesting warm blood). Being flying animals, they needed to take in and process a lot of new information from their surroundings, and to make immediate in-flight course corrections if they were to avoid soaring headfirst into trees and cliffs.

Living like birds, they had to develop birdlike brains. The cerebral hemispheres, which process information coming in through the eyes and skin and ears, were gigantic in pterosaurus (compared against their saurian compatriots). The optic lobes also ballooned and the cradle of bone that housed them swelled accordingly. Birdlike or batlike brains coordinated birdlike or batlike muscles, and these must have been powered by nonreptilian respiratory and circulatory systems.

A three-chambered heart—in which oxygen-rich arterial blood arriving fresh from the lungs is permitted to slosh around with and to be partially diluted by oxygen-poor venous blood—will not support powered flight. They had four-chambered hearts (like birds and mammals). There can be little doubt about this. Given these anatomical details, at least one saurian group's classification as Reptilia now appears a little strange.

The Sun is about 30,000 light years from the center of the Galaxy, and we make a complete circuit around the galactic center about every 400 million years. Hence, between 67 million B.C. and A.D. 1984, the Solar System moved almost a quarter of the way around the Galaxy.

The spiral arms of the Galaxy are curdled with gas and dust; some of it is packed densely into huge clouds called nebulae. Given enough time, our Sun must inevitably pass through one of these clouds. It undoubtedly has in the past. When this happens, dust transforms the night sky. Through a telescope, Mars becomes dimmer than it is at present. Jupiter, Saturn, and Uranus grow successively darker through the intervening dust. Beyond them no stars appear in the sky. Nothing but the faint glow of backscattered sunlight and excited electrons. The Earth's shadow up there in the night becomes a backdrop for the meteors. Lots of meteors.

Sunward our days are made undetectably darker. As it moves, the Sun burns a hole through the cloud. Gases stream instantly away like the tails of comets. Chips of ice, which make up the bulk of the cloud's solids, flare briefly—scratching vapor across the sky.

Dust-sized and marble-sized flecks of stone are not so easily moved by the solar wind. Because sunlight gives off energy whenever it strikes matter, as much as 1 or 2 percent of the Sun's output might be scattered and absorbed by such particles and lost between the orbits or Venus and Earth. On Earth there is a slight, ominous chill in the air.

Your average, garden-variety nebula measures about 80 to 100 light years across. The Solar System is traveling through space at a velocity of 6.8 light hours per year. It could pass through the diameter of a stationary nebula in as few as 100,000 years.

Near the end of the Cretaceous, the Earth's climate cooled over a period of about 5 million to 7 million years. Right you are. That's too long, so we can't blame a nebula (totally) for the cooling.

Suffice to say that these were bad biological times. If counts of craters on different provinces of the Moon where ages are known from rock samples are any indication, they got worse. There are about 14 major spikes in the Moon's 4.5-billion-year cratering history, and—you guessed it—the most recent of these spikes falls somewhere near the Upper Cretaceous. The spikes mark periods of unusually intense bombardment of the Moon's surface, possibly as a result of new material entering the Solar System. *

Aha! As above, so below . . . .

In 1980, a Berkeley team headed by Luis and Walter Alvarez discovered the granddaddy of all iridium anomalies. From Spain to New Zealand, a thin line of sediment was found to contain concentrations of iridium at least 20 times higher than in younger Tertiary sediments immediately above and in older Cretaceous sediments immediately below.

The accumulation of iridium at the Cretaceous-Teritary boundary appeared to have occurred instantaneously. This led the Alvarez group to conclude that indeed it had occurred instantaneously, and that the extra iridium arrived all in one day aboard a giant meteorite. But from the beginning, the asteroid impact scenario suffered from too much of a good thing: A worldwide iridium spike, at least 20 times above normal everywhere you looked. Could one asteroid do all that?

"Sure could," Luis said. "And more: it threw up a canopy of dust, turned off the lights for 10 years or so. Killed all the plants.

---

* Little or none of this material has survived in the Solar System, unless it came to rest on the surfaces of asteroids. Tests show that almost all meteorites observed to fall to Earth have been exposed to cosmic rays in space for no more than 4 million years. This suggests that they were released from inside one or more asteroid-sized bodies some 4 million years ago, presumably during a collision. No stony meteorite has a cosmic-ray exposure age of more than 100 million years. Computer modeling of Earth-crossing meteoroid orbits implies that such objects have an average life expectancy of only a few tens of millions of years before they are either captured by a planet or pitched out of the Solar System by Jupiter.

Starved off the giant herbivores and the creatures that fed on them."

Now wait a minute! Most of the dinosaurs were already gone by the time the iridium spike appeared. And the spike itself? How did one little mountain of rock, having diluted some of its powdery ruin with pulverized, airborne terrestrial rock . . . ? Nope, there was simply too much iridium in New Zealand, and in the central North Pacific, and in Denmark, and half a dozen other places to be accounted for. I sometimes have a weakness for jumping to conclusions. In September 1980 I jumped to one that, at best, provided only a partial explanation and, at worst, was misleading. Luis Alvarez replied:

> If the dilution factors are as large as quoted—10,000 according to Ahrens, and 1,000 according to Grieve, then the asteroid probably landed in the sea, as you suggest . . . . If one uses up some reasonable fraction of the incoming asteroid's kinetic energy in evaporating seawater, then the energy remaining to excavate rock from the ocean floor is diminished, and the amount of diluting *rock* is decreased—most of which diluting matter is then water, rather than rock. The excess water is dumped back into the ocean (where it can't be detected), along with the mixture of asteroidal and crystal dust, to form the (iridium-rich) layer we see, with its rock dilution of the asteroidal material of about ten times. In fact, the suddenly vaporized water may be the transporting agent we've needed to spread the asteroidal material worldwide.

But still . . . there's too much iridium out there.* To which Stephen Jay Gould answered:

> I care rather little for the specifics of the Alvarez's scenario. Indeed, much of it does not make sense—particularly his desire to get plants through the catastrophe via the dormancy of their seeds, and then to get mammals through by eating those very seeds. You can't have it both ways. Thus, what excites me about the Alvarez's work is not the asteroidal

---

*The water impact scenario still stands strong (though it should not be taken as *the* answer, because it leaves some important questions unanswered). After all, the Earth's surface is, and was in the Upper Cretaceous, mostly water. But there is a better reason for suspecting that the asteroid came down at sea. In 1972, E.J.H. David demonstrated that, if an asteroid large enough to excavate a crater 20 kilometers or wider impacted on as little as 10 meters of water or ice, so much of its kinetic energy would be dissipated through the water that near-surface tectite formation would be impossible. We find no tectites from the Upper Cretaceous.

scenario, but the fact that, in his iridium anomalies, he has provided the first plausible type of evidence implicating some kind of extraterrestrial event in major extinctions—a position that has long been reasonable in theory, but could not be exploited because we didn't even know what kind of evidence to look for.

Now we know. But what does the evidence say? Too much iridium, that's what. Too much iridium to have come from a single impact. Let's look at it from a different angle. What happens if we pass the Solar System through a nebula? We see an influx of iridium-rich dust that could last for 100,000 years or so. Iridium accumulation rates 20 times higher than normal (as seen in New Zealand and the central North Pacific) would not be unreasonable, and in geological terms the accumulation would appear instantaneous.* This is exactly what we see.

Not all of the particles within the nebula are going to be dust sized. If we drop an asteroid or comet into the picture (an event with increased probability in a dust cloud), we should expect to find a secondary, more localized iridium anomaly superimposed on top of a global one.

Indeed we do, in Spain, Italy, Denmark, and down the Equatorial Current into New Mexico, iridium levels at the Cretaceous-Tertiary boundary rise as high as 160 times above normal. In Spain, the iridium enriched layer is studded with sandanine (K Al Si_3 O_8, a type of feldspar) spherules measuring about 0.5mm (1/50th of an inch) in diameter.

Polished cross sections of the spheres reveal dendrites and fan-shaped crystals radiating down from the surface, suggesting that the sandanine solidified rapidly from a molten state. The sandanine itself is believed to have formed in part from stony meteorite material. Some particles range up to and beyond diameters of 1.0mm. Particles in this size range are heavy in air and fall quickly to the ground. They must lie within a few hundred kilometers of where they formed.

All of this effectively removes the problem of too much iridium all over the world, and raises the possibility that the asteroid impact was merely a symptom of an overall abundance of cosmic debris. None of this permits us to regard meteorites (mammoth or miniscule) as the be-all and end-all of dinosaur existence.

A gradual but profound draining of the continental shelves,

---

*The Earth is at this moment sweeping up cosmic dust at an accumulation rate amounting to some 100,000 kilograms (220,000 pounds) per day. New Zealand's Upper Cretaceous iridium spike suggests that the Earth once gained weight on the order of 2 million kilograms daily, or 20 times higher than "normal."

coupled with a deterioration of the climate, began about 70 million years ago. The dinosaurs, along with many animals totally unrelated to them, declined accordingly.*

About 65 million years ago, certain types of marine plankton vanished suddenly, and with them almost all of the few dinosaur species that remained. In the rocks immediately above their last appearance, we see an iridium spike. On our side of the spike lie a few new species of plankton, the rise of birds and mammals, and the Cenozoic Era.

For the dinosaurs, that spike could not have come at a worse time. It was probably the final blow to an already-dying-and-once-prominent lineage. It begins to look as if there was a lot of bad luck floating around at the end of the Cretaceous.

The most unfortunate aspect of saurian life is that we have only bones and tracks to read from. This might not remain a permanent condition. From Cretaceous marls in Sayreville, New Jersey have come some of the oldest known samples of fossil-bearing amber. The resins date to somewhere between 95 and 100 million years ago. Insects recovered from this deposit once flew among the dinosaurs, and one of these was a blood-feeding fly belonging to the family Ceratopongonidae (biting gnats). A second fly belongs to an unidentified family, but also appears to have been a blood-feeder. Two others have been identified as Chironomidae (nonbiting midges), and that concludes a census of flies from the lower part of the Upper Cretaceous.

We are not likely to see any new additions. In 1979, somebody decided that the amber locality would be a dandy place to put condos, office blocks, parking lots, and the like. Which leaves us with two potential blood feeders. Only two. But if—and, oh, what a beautiful if—the resin upon which either of the blood-feeders landed had been sufficiently heated by sunlight to penetrate quickly into the insect's gut, and if the gut contents included a fresh meal, we might one day be able to extract white blood cells belonging to dinosaurs and actually read their genetic code.

As Poinar has learned, the equipment needed to properly extract and read amberized genes does not exist as yet. We might have to wait two decades or so before it does. In the meantime, I have put one of the flies under refrigeration, and the other will be

---

*A census of insects in Cretaceous and Tertiary amber reveals that the insect class changed almost as radically as the reptilian class. By middle to late Cretaceous time, although the living insect orders had already been established, many modern families did not yet exist and none of the insects belonged to known genera or species. In contrast, practically all insects known from Baltic and Dominican amber can be referred to existing families, about half to existing genera, and even a few to existing species.

This 95-million-year-old, blood-feeding fly (family Ceratopongonidae), discovered by paleontologist Gerard R. Case in one of the world's oldest deposits of fossil-bearing amber, might hold the key to the eventual resurrection of dinosaurs. Photo by C.R. Pellegrino.

similarly stored at Princeton's Geological Sciences Building. It might be worth the wait.

If we are lucky, if we are so very lucky as to have in amber a complete set of dinosaur genes (or even a partial set, *please*) . . . well, already we can "print out" DNA at the tedious rate of about one nucleotide per hour (you'd need millions just to make a mosquito).

Given another 20 years, there is always the hope that, if we can eventually read dinosaur DNA, we might also be able to write it and publish it. If parts of the code are missing, we might conceivably figure out what belongs in the gaps and edit in the missing paragraphs," borrowing, perhaps, from present-day animals to provide a complete set of proteins necessary for the survival of the original dinosaur. Then everything that goes into building a dinosaur could be printed in the form of true chromosomes. We could equip these with a nucleus and the appropriate cellular machinery, including a yolk and a protective shell. It would be like old times.

134,215,740, B.C.

We have retreated deep within the Mesozoic Era—to the early part of the Lower Cretaceous, to be precise. The first birds appeared about 15 million years ahead of us. Protomammals (the cynodonts) have been around for some 60 million years. Most or all of them were, at this time, egg-laying carnivores. All were small and ratlike. None were particularly common. From these humble beginnings would rise two major branches: the marsupials and the insectivores; the latter branch leading to such diverse creatures as bats, whales, gophers, and apes.

Here, near the Jurassic-Cretaceous boundary, the diversity of oceanic plankton was in decline. This suggests another episode of climatic cooling. At almost every part of the phyletic spectrum, the tempo of extinction picked up. Most of the dinosaurs came through. The stegosaurs did not.

Stegosaurus, a bull-sized herbivore, is well-known for a formidable array of plates and spikes that ran the length of its spine and its "pea brain." At the end of that massive body was a skull no bigger than a dog's, and a brain no bigger than a walnut.

Whatever qualities stegosaurs possessed, behavioral complexity was not one of them. But we can, and have, carried this point too far. The beast is popularly trumpeted as the epitome of saurian stupidity, requiring a second brain in the pelvis merely to pass the word around to all the posterior provinces. Without a spare brain (so the story goes), the animal could never keep its back half in pace with its front half. *Not so.*

While it is true that you will notice an enlargement of the spinal column near the pelvis, and while it is also true that the resulting cavity is about the size of a dog's brain, this does not permit us to conclude that the spine did in fact house a second brain. More likely, it contained a nerve-triggered, glycogen-filled gland. This makes sense for two reasons. The first is that two brains double the complexity of getting around (and if there is anything nature abhors as much as a vacuum, it is unnecessary complications). The second reason is that we find similar cavities in the spines of other dinosaurs and in the spines of present-day ostritches.

In ostritches, the cavity huses a glycogen gland wrapped in nerves. Glycogen, or animal starch, is used in muscular actions. A sac full of glycogen, located over the hind legs, could have provided *Stegosaurus* with an extra, energetic kick during emergencies. That the gland appears to have carried through to ostritches is perhaps an additional reminder of Avian ancestry.

On North America's southwest edge, almost as the last stegosaurs roamed across Montana, a slice of ocean crust plowed headlong into California, carrying with it pockets of gold that would become the focus of much excitement to cynodont-descendents.

Other bits of land piled up behind it. Seamounts, ocean plateaus, and splinters from as far away as China moved east on convective slabs as though riding a conveyor belt. Being lighter than the rocks on which they rode, they were too buoyant to slide underneath the Americas, and instead got plastered up against them. The result is a strange mosaic of rocks that do not quite match up with each other. One field contains fossils that are distinctly Chinese, but another field, right across the nearest fault line, is strewn with fossils from the Arctic. In the last 150 million years, as many as 200 pieces have been added to North America, swelling its land area by nearly 30 percent.

South America, in 134 million B.C., was welded solidly to Africa. Europe and North America were joined at Maine, and Spain (and the rain fell mainly on . . . oh, never mind). If you had a ship, you could sail east from North Africa straight into Pacific waters. Tides swept

The continents in 134 million B.C.

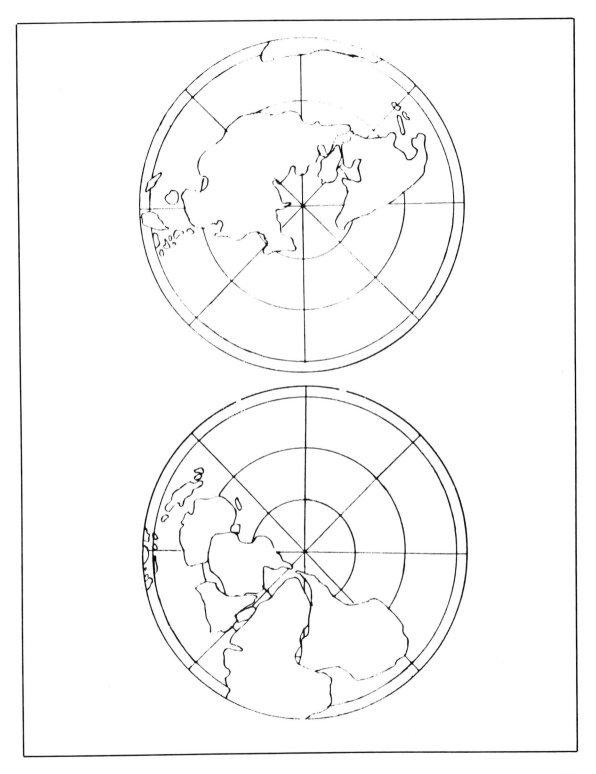

201

across vast, shallow seas, decelerating the Earth more rapidly than they do today. The day was shorter by at least one minute, and possibly by as long as a half hour. The Moon was 7700 kilometers (4785 miles) closer.

Somewhere in the sky, in a dense cloud of in-falling gas and dust, Mizar, Alcor, and Mergrez were about to be born. The general temperature of the universe was $2.97°$ K, and every cubic meter contained at least two atoms of hydrogen.

The numbers roll easily off the tongue. But let's take a pause and think about them for a moment. The whole universe has warmed $0.17°C$ since we took our first step backward in time, the whole thing. Its density has increased five-fold, and—in our next step backward—we will find space and time compressed twice again. It is hard to imagine it ever stopping.

14 Time and Tide

Astronomy is the only science that is more irrelevant than paleontology.

paleontologist Donald Baird
(commenting on this book)

In the shallows between South America and South Africa, the little Permian reptile, *Mesosaurus*, hunted bivalved crustaceans called branchiopods. While other vertebrates were creeping up onto land, *Mesosaurus'* ancestors had already been there, and at least one branch was on its way back to sea.

It was 268,433,468 B.C. South America, South Africa, Madagascar, India, Australia, Antarctica, New Zealand, and a few other vagrant bits of land were huddled together near the South Pole. In time, they would coalesce to form the supercontinent Pangea. Outside their boundaries, almost a whole hemisphere of the Earth was unbroken ocean.

Only 100 million years earlier, plants had moved onto the land and become horsetails, ferns, and leafless shrubs. They carpeted the Earth with Coal-Age forests. The first insects took wing. Beneath them, amphibians sniffed the air, and from these branched more efficient terrestrial beasts: the Reptilia.

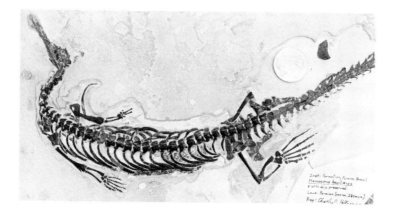

The landward movement of the Amphibia was thwarted by what amounted literally to poor waterproofing. Without scales, hair, or other external coverings, water evaporated easily, right through the skin. This might have been good for keeping cool on summer days, but it was certainly bad news for long walks into the forest.

Reptiles, with their coats of scales, were in less danger of drying out. Their eggs were hard and, like the creatures themselves, were more protected against desiccation. Unlike the amphibian egg, which must be laid in water, reptilian eggs can be laid anywhere *except* in water. The reptiles were therefore free to radiate and diversify away from lakes and rivers and seas. And they did.

Of course, when you look at the evolutionary timetable, all roads lead back to water. One way out of the sea is through rivers; tributaries are guaranteed to dry out from time to time. That fish and other creatures are bound to make their way from the ocean into these tributaries flows from the fact that near-shore species are exposed to influxes of fresh water from landward downpours. Tolerance to such influxes is probably an important adaptation that might later become an *exaptation* (an exploited "preadaptation") for living in fresh-water streams. Subsequent adaptations for surviving river dry-outs might in turn become exaptations for venturing beyond the tributaries altogether.

A second way out of the sea is directly at its edge. At the shores of seas, plants and animals are variously adapted (depending how high on the beach they live) to periodic exposure on land. Knowing this, it becomes tempting to ask what life on Earth would be like today if our planet were more "normal." What if, like the other inner, rocky worlds—Mercury, Venus, and Mars—we did not possess a sister planet massive enough and close enough to create tides?

The question of routes then takes on new and immediate significance. If the ancestors of stem reptiles lending to mammals flapped up onto the shore (rather than climbed out of a river tribu-

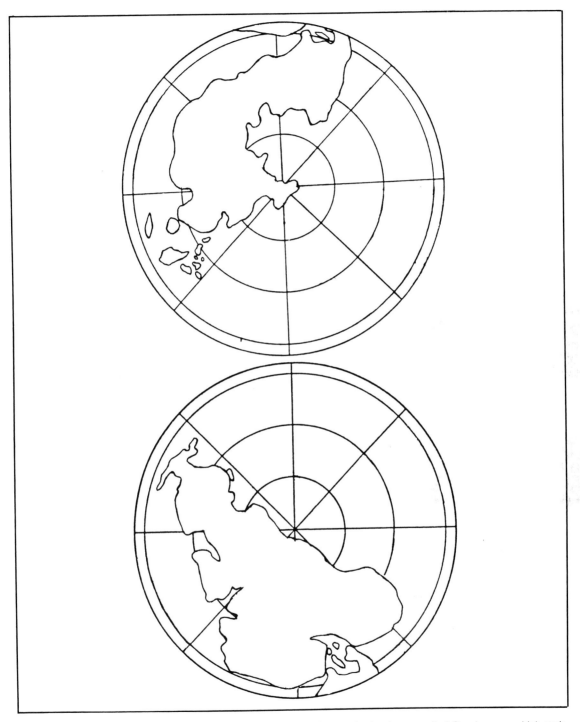

In 268,433,468 B.C., the southern continents embraced to form an impressive land mass called Gondwanna, which probably linked with the northern continents to form the supercontinent Pangea.

tary), the result is not the same. For lack of a Moon, you might now be a mindless fish.

What if exposure during low tides was the *major* impetus for getting life out of the water? This is, after all, a reasonable possibility. Plants and animals on the intertidal zone are exposed twice daily to the air, whereas the drying out of a tributary is a relatively infrequent event.

On bare continents, where grazing and preying animals did not yet exist, the first multicellular organisms to breach the intertidal barrier (presumably plants) would have been fostered by the environment—*very quickly*. But they would first have to solve the problems of breathing and staying wet and nourishing themselves away from water. These problems might not have been solved as early as they were if not for the tides. With only the drying out of rivers to nudge life out of the sea, could the invasion of land have been postponed for perhaps another quarter of a billion years? And where would that leave us?

As all the world knows, the lure of the Moon did not cease with the drawing of life onto empty beaches. Hundreds of millions of years later, it summoned sapience out of its natal sphere—the Earth.

If planet formation is a normal by-product of star formation, how common are binary worlds like the Earth and the Moon? Not very common if our own Solar System is any indication. Perhaps we should thank our lucky stars that we live on one member of a double planet. It begins to look as if we owe much of our existence to the Moon's size and proximity. If Tranquility and Taurus-Littrow were not so close at hand—and even if we had still managed to come out of the sea on schedule, to achieve consciousness, and to create and control the lightning—would V-2 rockets and *Sputnik* have led to *Apollo*? Lacking the Moon, would men have gone directly to Mars, or would our grasp instead be limited, to near-Earth orbit?

It is possible that the first hesitant steps on a world that was not our own might never have been taken if not for the Moon (which serves also as a handy package of minerals for future space industry). Our sister planet is the perfect stepping stone; it is a nice place to perform dress rehearsals for exploring Mars and Titan. Having seen the opening act, it becomes a matter of absorbing interest to ask whether or not extrasolar civilizations, if they lacked such a close planetary neighbor, would be even a tenth as likely to make the leap into deep space.

15 Floor Show

I was very careful in the selection of my ancestors.

Ernst Mayr

Do you see this egg? With it you can overthrow all the schools of theology, all the churches of the Earth.

Denis Diderot

A hen is only an egg's way of making another egg.

Samuel Butler

*Complicating, circulating
new life, new life.
Operating, generating
new life, new life.*

Depeche Mode

In the year 536,868,914 B.C., the universe was about 0.5×10^{-29} times as dense as water. Every square meter of space should have contained at least 10 atoms. These were heated to at least $3.43°$ K.

Put another way, "cold, empty space" was 100 times as dense as it is today and 50 percent warmer.

The Moon loomed 22,136 kilometers closer to the Earth, and the day was shorter by at least three minutes—perhaps by as much as an hour.

Although its massifs were still in the same places and its hills were essentially the same shape, the Taurus-Littrow Valley looked different. Craters that appeared old and impact softened in 1972 photographs were noticeably deeper and more clear cut. Missing from the valley floor were Split Rock and at least one crater large enough to accommodate an office block.

On Earth, these were middle Cambrian times. Antarctica and Canada were located on the equator, North Africa and Brazil poked into the South Pole, topsy-turvy. Save for a few wind-blown knots of DNA (virus particles, if such existed), dried bacteria, algae, and protozoans, the continents were probably without life. As near as anyone can tell, no splashes of green challenged erosive forces, and the valleys ran full with mud.

Siltstones in Australia had already preserved creatures from the Ediacaran Period (about 670 million to 550 million years ago).* They were ocean dwellers, and clearly related to modern sea pens

The Taurus-Littrow Valley in the year 536,868,914 B.C. Split Rock rests atop the hill at right. Craters appear more clear cut than they will in A.D. 1984. Photomosaic inserts courtesy of NASA's Johnson Space Center, Houston, Texas. Painting by C.R. Pellegrino.

For 536,868,914 B.C., a projection of the continents is uncertain. Based on paleomagnetic data, Antarctica was then near the equator. Australia was in the northern hemisphere, and New Guinea projected almost into the margin of North Polar Climate. Eastern Asia lie west of Antarctica, topsy-turvy. To Antarctica's east, on the equator, North America, Greenland, and Eastern Europe embraced each other.

---

*The newly named Ediacaran Period has been added before the Cambrian Period and extends from the first appearance of jellyfish, sea pens, and segmented worms—about 670 million years ago. I used to keep the old periods straight in my head with the following mnemonic iad: Campbell's Onion Soup Does Make People Purpose (Cambrian, Ordovician, Silurian, Devonian, Mississippian, Pennsylvanian, Permian). Now, with Campbell's Onion Soup tossed overboard, we could try this one: Every Class of Students Detests Memorizing Pointless Periods.

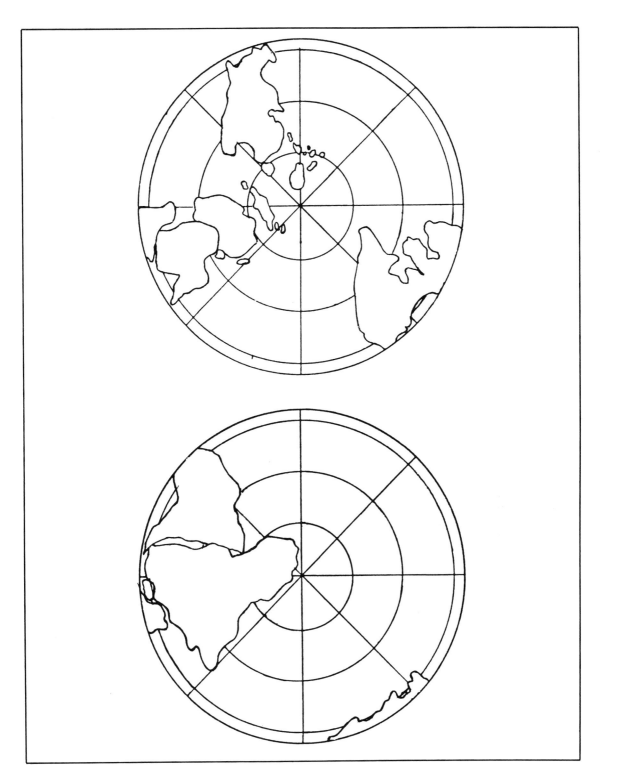

209

(soft corals), jellyfish, and segmented worms. The oldest known specimens mark the base of the Ediacaran record, which appears to have commenced in 670 million year old rocks located immediately above an episode of glacial sedimentation in south Australia. Once again, a major revolution in the history of life—in this case the first record of megacellular animal life (metazoa)—is found to coincide with the spread of ice.

About 80 million years later, at the beginning of the Cambrian Period, there occurred another brief Ice Age. By 537 million B.C., metazoans had diversified into almost all known phyla (with a few unknowns into the bargain). So dramatic was this series of branching events that paleobiologists have nicknamed it the *Cambrian explosion.*

The world's most complete record of the explosion's immediate aftermath protrudes from under western Canada. Where today stand the Rocky Mountains of British Columbia, near the Burgess Pass, once grew an algae-secreted reef that rose vertically more than 100 meters (333 feet) from the sea floor and formed a front many kilometers across.

At the base of the reef, fine silts were gathering. The steady buildup of mud triggered frequent avalanches that often spilled from the reef crest as gigantic, rolling clouds, carrying with them any creatures that lived in their path and burying them in deeper waters beyond the reach of both oxygen and scavengers. As the mud gradually compacted and consolidated into shale, the buried animals were flattened and their soft parts became thin stains of feldspar (calcium aluminosilicate). This happened about 530 million years ago.

The fossils of the earlier period, the Ediacarian, show signs of horny, organic cuticles (chitin), minor spicular strengthening, and tubes cemented together from a mixture of mucus and sand. None possessed true calcium carbonate shells (like today's clams) or exoskeletons (like today's crabs). Part of the early Cambrian diversification, as seen in the Burgess shale, included the onset of shell formation—especially through the uptake of calcium. Nobody knows why.

Many of the Burgess Pass fossils are familiar. We find among them jellyfish, sponges, worms, trilobites, brachiopods (which looked like clams), and mollusklike worms (perhaps the ancestors of clams). Other fossils, though they seem to be related to segmented worms, are rather more complex and less familiar. They are actually bizarre.

Judging from its large eyes, streamlined body, and prominent dorsal and ventral fins—each stiffened by more than 100 fin rays— *Nectocaris* was probably an efficient swimmer. It looked like a fish and it lived like a fish; nevertheless it was a worm.

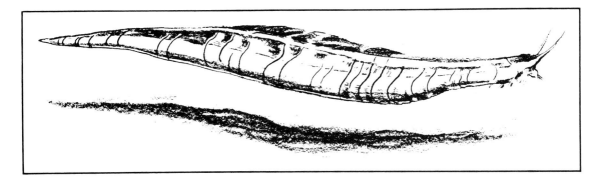

Paikia: *the closest thing we know to a 537 million-year-old ancestor. Many animals from this period are familiar. We find among them jelly fish, sponges, worms, and trilobites. Other of* Paikia's *contemporaries, though they seem to be related to segmented worms, are grotesque and strange.* Illustration by C.R. Pellegrino.

Opabinia had five eyes arranged across its head: two pointed forward, like headlamps; two pointed to the sides; the fifth pointed up. Evidently it swam close to the sea floor while watchful of both predators and prey, steering itself with a vertical tail fin, and feeding with a grasping organ located at the end of an elephantlike trunk.

Another Burgess resident was so strange that its discoverer, equating it with something out of a peyote nightmare, named it *Hallucigenia.* It drove along the seafloor on seven pairs of sharply pointed, stiltlike legs. Seven tentacles ran the length of its back, each ending, apparently, with a mouth.

Ordinary by comparison was a creature that looked like a worm but was not. We call it *Pikaia.* It was a swimming animal that lacked eyes. Instead it had a pair of small, sensory antennules at the tip of its head. A rodlike column of cells, stiffened by cartilage, was embedded in the animal's back. The rod looks like it must have been a notochord, the chief axial supporting structure in the bodies of lower chordates and in the embryos of higher ones. It thus belonged to the Phylum chordata, which has diversified since Cambrian times to beget the fishes and all other vertebrates, including dinosaurs and us.

This does not mean that *Pikaia* was *the* common ancestor of sharks and humming birds. While it is located near the trunk of the chordate tree, the trunk is likely to have had many branches even in its birth stages. *Pikaia* might represent a limb that led only to extinction. Though the animal provides a reasonable picture of what some of our remotest ancestors looked like, we might never learn which branch led to us.

In the waters near Burgess Pass, and in the world outside it, there were varieties of life that we will never know from fossils. In one little corner of the Earth, conditions were just right to preserve a large number of soft-bodied animals, but even here we can have only the most fleeting glimpse of what must have actually existed.

It is a sad fact, but a fact nonetheless, that as we accelerate away from time present the world becomes more alien, more interesting, and far less knowable.

16 The Blood of Mars

Temperature changes are sudden and most uncomfortable, as are the transitions from brilliant daylight to darkness . . .. In this deep valley, surrounded by lofty cliffs, the atmosphere was considerably denser than upon the surface of the planet above . . .. At a distance up the river rose mighty perpendicular bluffs, from the very base of which the great river seemed to rise . . .. The scattered boulders that had fallen from above and lay upon or partly buried in the turf, were the only indication that any disintegration of the massive, towering pile of rocks ever had taken place . . ..

Edgar Rice Burroughs

Up to this point in the project, the flight Lander and Orbiter were never physically or electrically in direct contact with each other, having been assembled over 1000 miles apart. Viking Orbiter 1 and Viking Lander 1 were mated for the first time on March 8 and, in testimony to the close coordination maintained since inception, everything fit perfectly. More than two weeks of intercourse and systems testing proved that the two systems would indeed "play together" during the mission.

Viking Mission Operations
Status Bulletin No. 3.
Spacecraft Prelaunch Operations
Issued April 25, 1975

In 1.07 billion years B.C., the place where Manhattan would one day stand was under water. The seas were dominated by very simple organisms, and many of them were unicellular. Some used energy from the Sun to process carbon from the environment. Others, crowding around submarine vents, used hydrogen sulfide (H_2S). Others devoured their neighbors, and still others belonged to enormous colonies resembling filaments, balls, and medusae. It is possible that several lineages of wormlike creatures had evolved by this time. If so, they swam under a Moon that was some 31,000 kilometers (19,266 miles) closer to an Earth where days contained as few as 21.5 hours.

Bearing in mind that only a handful of rocks are known from this period, the drawing of maps becomes an intractable problem. Suffice to say that the continents must have been shuffled as much during the interval between 1.07 billion B.C. and middle Cambrian time as during the last 537 million years. If 1 billion years ago you stood on the floor of Taurus-Littrow and looked down on the Earth, you would be hard-pressed to believe it was your own planet. Even the Moon looked different. Some of the familiar craters seen today did not exist as yet, and the projectiles that would excavate them still wandered aimlessly—out there—where every cubic meter of space contained at least 20 atoms heated to 4.06° K.

On Mars, a volcano so tall that Mount Everest is by comparison a foothill was building up and up and up—until it poked clear through the planet's troposphere. The caldera—hundreds of square kilometers of it—was alive with faulting and lava floods, gases and commotion. Tubes in the volcano's flanks bled vapor and basaltic lava. The discharge streamed down through cloud decks into an atmosphere that, at its deepest reaches, was 50 to 100 times thinner than the air you are breathing.

Today, Olympus Mons is truly gigantic, a shield of lava outflows big enough to cover the state of Nebraska, or New Zealand's North Island, or Greece. Though it towers 27 kilometers (17 miles) above the Martian surface, its slopes are inclined only 4° to the horizon. Standing there, you would think yourself to be on an almost level plain, rather than on the side of the biggest mountain known anywhere in the Solar System.

A Viking's-eye-view of Olympus Mons' caldera shows volcanic craters with depths of 3 kilometers (2 miles). Faulting and lava floods are visible. The scarcity of meteorite impact craters on the summit indicates that, geologically speaking, it is relatively young. Photos courtesy of NASA/JPL.

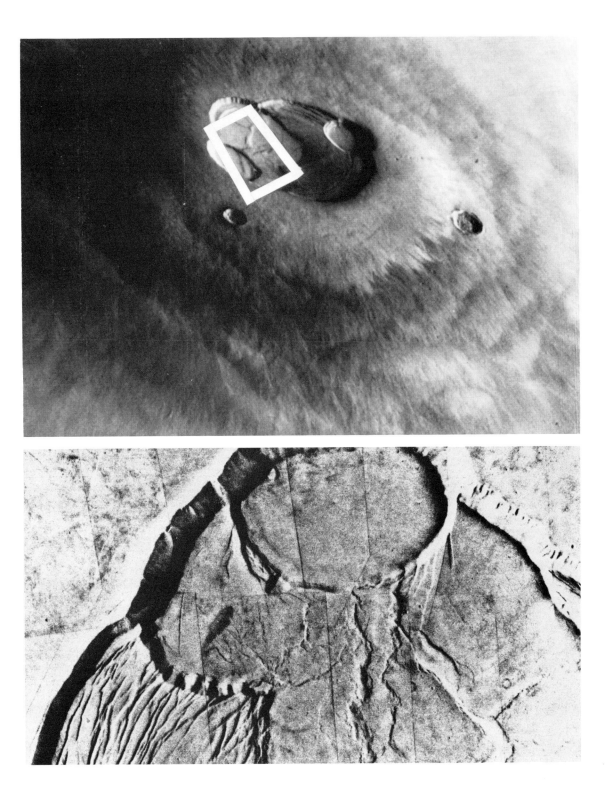

215

Mars is only about one-half as wide as Earth and has only one-sixth its volume. Being smaller, it cooled faster and developed a thicker, less pliable crust. As one might expect, on Mars there are no movable continental plates as there are on Earth. Instead of forming a chain of progressively older volcanos, like the Hawaiian Emperor chain, Olympus Mons has been sitting over the same plume of ascending lava for almost 2 billion years—growing almost forever.

As today, much of the Martian water supply was, near 1 billion B.C., tied up as ice and ground water ranging generally between a few tens of meters and 2 kilometers below the surface. At noontide, temperatures climbed from a midnight low of more than 100° C below zero to the melting point of water-ice. The atmospheric pressure was so faint that water in air would boil. An ice cube, if warmed, would sublime slowly from a solid to a gas (experiencing no intermediate liquid phase) until it evaporated out of existence.

Soils that "breathed in" the Martian air must therefore have been dry to depths of 10 meters (33 feet) or more. This would be especially true in lower, warmer latitudes.

Several planetary geologists have suggested that a large aquifer once connected (and still does connect) ice at the polar caps with subsurface "swamps" near the equator. On occasion, briny water accumulating in low areas apparently broke out across the surface to carve outwash plains hauntingly reminiscent of Washington State's channeled scablands. Under lower gravity, we would expect boulders and soil to be more easily swept away by running water. This is actually what we see.

Multikilometer craters and other obstacles were cut into streamlined shapes as if torn up by a liquid hurricane. Glutted with sediments, boiling as they ran, the Martian outfloods could not possibly endure. They became a vapor in the sky—vanishing almost in midstride—leaving channels that appear to rise from nowhere and go nowhere. In their wake, the vapor pressure rose; but this too was only transistory. Some of the volatiles must have condensed near the poles to form Martian snow. Others were eroded out of the stratosphere by solar wind.

The Sun, pouring its mass out into space in the form of energy, was approximately 1.2 percent more massive than it is today. An equal or perhaps even a greater quantity of our star's hydrogen has been rafted away on the solar wind during the last billion years. Under the stronger crush of gravity, hydrogen atoms at the Sun's core smashed together more violently than they do today, and the Sun burned a little brighter. In the outer reaches of Mars' atmosphere, hydrogen and other light gases were nudged gently toward Pluto and Charon.

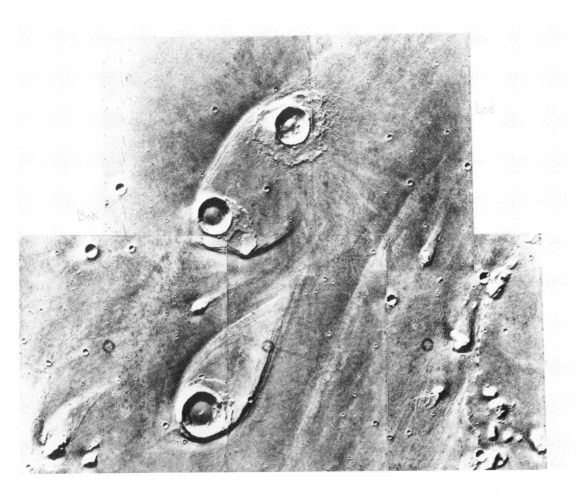

In June 1976, Viking Orbiter 1 eyed streamlined islands. Near the mouth of Mars' Ares Valley, at 20°N, 31°W, braided channels betray a past Martian flood. The islands are eroded remnants of ancient craters around which the water, flowing from the lower left, diverged. The uppermost of the three large craters (each measuring about 15 kilometers across) was formed after the flood. Scores of smaller, post-outwash impact scars suggest that this region of Mars has been dry for at least a billion years. Photo courtesy of NASA/JPL.

Deep below, outcroppings of volcanic rubble glistened in the sunlight. No one and nothing moved. A desert was sleeping.

A.D. 1979: Scattered boulders, sheets of shifting sand, air so cold that ice sublimes.

No, this is not Mars. This is Antarctica's dry valley region on the southern edge of the Ross Sea. Into this range of peaks and valleys flows the ice, carrying with it an assortment of pebbles from space—the meteorites. Near Ross Island, ice piles up against the Olympus, Asgard, and Royal Society Mountains—stagnating there, and evaporating in the wind. The pebbles do not evaporate. They stay on the surface, and accumulate to form the world's richest lode of meteorites. From this lode has come one of the most beautiful surprises of our time: More than a piece of the sky, one rock appears to be a piece of Mars.

Grayish-red in color, isotopic tests show that the rock solidified from molten lava between 1.1 and 1.3 billion years ago. All

217

well and fine, but you might be tempted to ask about tectites and the fact that there are, after all, billion-year-old volcanic rocks on Earth. How do we know it didn't come from Earth?

That's a good question. It's the same question the rock's discoverers came up with after they answered the obvious, "How old are you?" A new answer leading to lots of new questions would have to be found before anyone could point to a corner of the sky and say, "I think you came from there."

Mars did not emerge as a beforehand answer needing only a carefully thought out series of proofs. Science does not work that way. Our answers do not blossom like the products of perfect seeds. Almost always, the path to the elusive eureka is paved with nonanswers and surprising results.

If you are smart, pay attention, and do not let the wish to be right trick you into ignoring or, even worse, changing your results "just a little" (for which you'd deserve to have your teeth drilled in a country where they haven't discovered novacaine or N_2O yet), you double back and check the reality of your results, admit that some previous answers might be wrong, and start asking new questions.

All right, first answer: a 1.1 to 1.3 billion-year-old rock.

That's pretty old, but it's more than 3 billion years younger than any asteroid debris we know of. So how do we know if it really came from out there? That one's easy.

Anything that spends even a few years out in space, exposed to the bombardment of cosmic rays, will form certain easily identifed radioactive isotopes. The rays also leave signatures in the form of distinctive tracks through crystals. A search for signs of cosmic-ray exposure has revealed that the rock spent no less than 2 million years on the other side of the sky.

How do we know that a piece of the Earth wasn't pitched into orbit, eventually to fall back again? And if not from Earth, how many bodies do we know that have been volcanically active within the last 1.3 billion years? Venus, Mars, Io . . .. How often might we expect a piece of one of them to fly aimlessly through space, eventually to find a target as pinpoint small as Earth?

How likely is that?

About as good as your chances of throwing a dart into the Grand Canyon and hitting a specific grain of sand, that's how likely.

Now wait a minute. That dart will, when it reaches the bottom, hit *someplace*. It will impact on *some* grain of sand. It only seems impossible after the fact, after we see where it has hit and say, "Gee, if I had thrown that just the slightest bit harder, or one millionth of a degree farther to the left, or if the wind had been just a tad different, I wouldn't have hit the same grain of sand, and I couldn't hit it again even if I devoted the rest of my life to the effort."

The paradox results from letting after-the-fact observers get into the act. Go to Taurus-Littrow and select any hole in the ground, trace the meteorite that dug it back across billions of kilometers of space, and then start adding up the improbabilities of it ever finding that particular spot.

Looked at in this way, we can prove that any particular crater represents a summation of so many unlikely events (a missed collision here, a "helpful" collision there, finding the Moon in the right place at the right time, etc.) that it could not possibly exist. Yet the Moon is full of craters. And the Antarctic ice cap is full of meteorites from all sorts of absurdly unlikely places.

Although it may seem impossible, in hindsight, that a specific path was followed from one place (a meteorite's point of origin) to another (an impact on Antarctica), it is not truly impossible. And if something is not truly impossible, then it will probably occur.

So where does that leave us? It leaves us with four possible parent bodies for a billion-year-old rock that spent at least 2 million years in space: Venus, Earth, Mars, and Jupiter's volcanic moon, Io. We can easily eliminate two of these.

The Venusian atmosphere is so dense—at the surface it is 1/14 as dense as water—that nothing is going to reach the hypersonic speeds necessary to get outside without burning itself to cinders (that is, microtectites). Anything ejected from Io would have been confined by the gravitational pull of nearby Jupiter. That leaves two candidates: Earth and Mars.

In late 1982, Donald Bogard, a geologist at Houston's Johnson Space Center, removed flecks of glass from the meteorite. They looked like Ries Basin glass, and for an apparently good reason. A census of potassium-argon isotopes in the glass revealed that it has solidified about 180 million years ago. It had solidified from partly re-melted blobs of lava inside a rock that had laid undisturbed for more than a billion years.

The re-melting, and re-crystalization a few minutes later, re-cords a violent event in the rock's history. This was presumably the moment of forceful ejection from the parent planet (Earth or Mars?), and Bogard reasoned that bubbles in the glass might have trapped some of the surrounding atmosphere. Happily, he found what he was looking for: Chemically inert (noble) gases—neon, argon, krypton, and xenon—elements that do not easily combine with other elements to form compounds. They remain in air in their original concentration; and concentrations inside the bubbles are more similar to the Martian atmosphere than they are to the Earth's. We know this because we have the 1976 *Viking* results for comparison.

For example, the ratio of argon-40 to argon-36 is above 2000 to 1 in the meteorite, about seven times the Earthy ratio and representing about 400 times as much argon-40 as could have been produced by the decay of potassium-40 during the last 180 million

Looking for Mars in Antarctica.

Relative Abundance

	Mars	Earth	Antarctic Meteorite
Argon 40	2700±500	296	2400
Argon 36	1.00	1.00	1.00
Neon 20	0.80	0.47	0.80
Krypton 84	0.04	0.05	0.04
Xenon 132	0.004	0.002	0.006

The relative abundances of noble gases (scaled to argon 360 in the atmosphere of Mars, the Earth, and a possible Mars rock from Antarctica named EETA 79001.

years. The ratio of argon-40 to argon-36 in the Martian atmosphere is 2700 (± 500) to 1.

Similarly, the ratio of xenon-129 to xenon-132 in the meteorite is comparable with *Viking* results (about 2 to 1), and far below the terrestrial ratio of 128 to 1.

In early 1983, Robert O. Pepin and colleagues at the University of Minnesota began looking at nitrogen isotopes in pieces of the same rock. *Viking I* and *II* showed us that nitrogen in the Martian air exists in a distinct pattern, it is mysteriously rich in the heavy nitrogen-15 isotope. On Earth, nitrogen-15 accounts for 0.38 percent of the atmospheric nitrogen content. On Mars, the concentration is 0.61 percent—almost twice as high.

In early March, 1983, laughter could be heard coming form Pepin's lab. "That's it!" he shouted. "It's from Mars. I don't think there's any doubt."

"Well," he said later. "I don't think there's *much* doubt:"

> The results are ambiguously positive. They are positive because the spectrometer detected 15 percent more nitrogen-15 than would be found in a sample from Earth's atmosphere. They are ambiguous because this is not high enough to match the *Viking* data from Mars. We need about 60 percent. The pieces of rock we recovered could have absorbed ordinary nitrogen during processing in the laboratory. Or maybe the (ejection) event left the rock with a mixture of atmospheric nitrogen and non-enriched gas from the rock's non-glassy component. Or maybe the Martian atmosphere was different 180 million years ago. But that rock—it just smells like Mars.

OK, so we have a definite maybe on our hands that leaves us

with the question: What would Martian lava be doing in Antarctica?

Again asteroids come into the picture, splashing pieces of the red wilderness clear into space. In support of this possibility, at least one Antarctic meteorite has been identified as coming from the Moon, proving that impacting asteroids can propel rocks to at least the 2.4-kilometer (1.5-mile) per-second velocity required to escape the Moon's gravity.

The idea that some meteorites might have originated on the Moon has been around for some 200 years. The first positively identified lunar meteorite, named ALHA 81005, from Antarctica, was not confirmed until early 1983. It is a lunar regolith breccia (translation: surface rock "glued" together from fragments).

Compared with rocks brought back by *Apollo* astronauts and *Luna* robots (USSR), it is consistent with an origin high in the lunar mountains. It also contains splinters of basalt characteristic of Taurus-Littrow and other lava-flooded lowlands. This leads some geologists to suspect that a lava plain existed "within throwing distance" of the spot from which ALHA 81005 came.

Mysteriously, the meteorite is almost entirely lacking KREEP, a type of lunar rock with a name that is an acronym for a specific combination of potassium (K), rare earth elements (REE), and phosphorus (P). Satellites launched overboard by the Apollo *15* and Apollo *16* crews, and still orbit around the Moon, have broadcast data suggesting that the Moon's KREEPy side faces Earth; hence, ALHA 18005 might be our first sample from the lunar far side.

We may even be able to name a specific far side crater. One hint comes from Antarctic ice. None of it dates older than 700,000 years. We know this because the same cosmic-ray bombardment that tells us how long a rock has been in space also tells us how long it has been on the ice. When a meteorite lands on Earth, isotopes produced by exposure to cosmic radiation are produced no longer, and begin to decay as a function of time. Within the ice, meteorites become "time probes." Although the Earth residence age of ALHA 81005 has not yet been tested, I've recently wagered a year's subscription to *OMNI* that it will turn out to be less than 800 years.

There is a reason for this. In 1978, J. Derral Mulholland and Odile Calame of the French Geodynamics and Astronomical Observatory called attention to laser ranging results that showed the Moon to be wobbling with a period of about 3 years and an amplitude of about 3 meters. They concluded that something big had struck the Moon within the last 1000 years or so, and that the Moon was still ringing from the strike.

The chronicles of Gervase of Canterbury record what might be taken as an eyewitness account. On the evening of June 18, 1178, "there was a bright New Moon, and as usual in that phase its horns were tilted towards the east. Suddenly, the upper horn split in two.

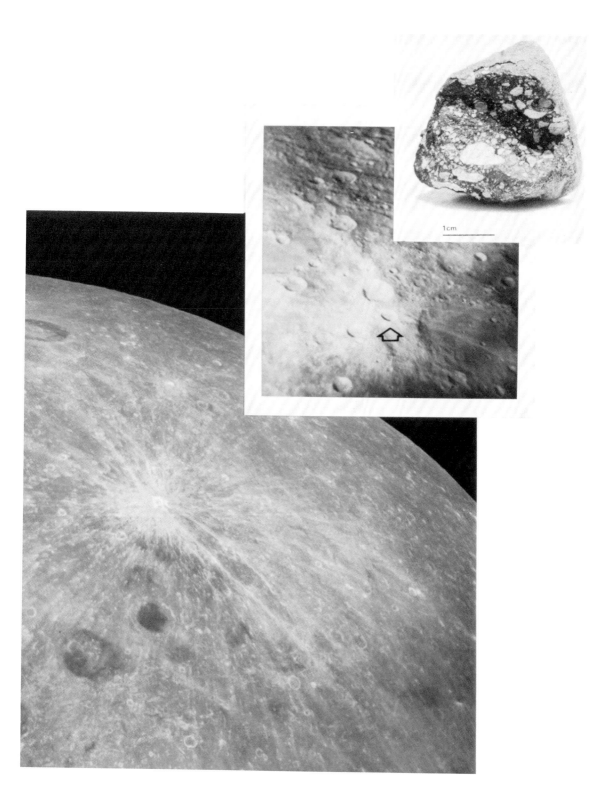

1cm

From the midpoint of the division, a flaming torch sprang up, spewing out fire, hot coals, and sparks."

Exactly in the region referred to in Gervase's report lies a very fresh-looking crater with bright rays of fine powder splashing out for hundreds of kilometers in every direction. It is called Giordano Bruno. It lies in highland terrain, where it is within 150 kilometers of lowland lava plains. It is 20 kilometers across. And we are lucky because it could just as easily have come down in the Atlantic.

Some physicists question the possibility that flying mountains could punch down with enough force to hurl projectiles away at the 5.0 kilometers (3.1 miles) per second necessary to raise them from the Martian surface to an infinite altitude. In answer, George Wetherill of the Carnegie Institution has suggested a steam catapult effect, whereby an asteroid broke through to subsurface ice and water, vaporizing it, and sending pieces of Mars aloft on jets of steam.

The emerging picture is one of planets and moons exchanging matter with each other, as if they were passing bits of gossip over a fence. This thought forces us to think about solar systems in general. If, around another star, one planet developed bacterial life, and a second planet later became suitable for life, what would happen if rocks from the former reached the latter?

Is panspermia real? Can living DNA spread outward from one planet to others?

Sure can. We've done it ourselves. The *Apollo* 12 explorers proved as much when they returned to Earth with pieces of the *Surveyor* 3 robot. Years earlier, someone had breathed on wires inside *Surveyor's* camera, and—for almost 2½ years—hitchhiking virus particles had remained dormant on the Moon, inside the camera. Brought back to Earth they began to multiply. Today, on both Soviet and American space probes, we have unwittingly spread the seeds of life to the Martian deserts. Our DNA might actually be hurtling out of the Solar System altogether, aboard *Pioneer* and *Voyager* spacecraft.

But what of Mars rocks? We might learn from the Antarctic specimen whether or not life could have existed on Mars 1.3 billion years ago. I doubt that it could. Looking back *another* 3 billion years, however, we know that Mars was certainly more hospitable than present. The air was thicker and warmer. Here and there we see hints of ancient downpours and rivers.

If shirt-sleeve surroundings did exist on Mars, and if life developed in them—even virus particles or protocells—it could have spilled over to Earth, adding foreign verse to a molecular symphony already at play in our seas. There might now be Martians on the Earth. And they might be partly us.

The rock called ALHA 81005 (top) was found in Antarctica. Giordano Bruno (center) was photographed by the Apollo 16 *crew and (bottom by Fred Haise during the* Apollo 13 *flight).* Courtesy of NASA's Johnson Space Center, Houston, Texas.

17 The Ultimate Fox Hole

We all agree that your theory is mad. The problem which divides us is this: is it sufficiently crazy to be right?

Niels Bohr

Charles: I am quite interested in your suggestion for a speculative piece about the possibilities of life on (or rather, in) the Jovian moons.

Ben Bova (20 December 1979)

Charles: It's too speculative.

Jack Wiley (1980)

Note: The Saturnian Moon Enceladus (diameter = 500 km) . . . Voyager 1 data suggest an unusually smooth surface. The Moon may have experienced gravitational flexing between Tethys and Saturn, which would have extended the life of its sub-surface seas. One or more photos and captions may be inserted (in Chapter 8), depending on what the August 25 near encounter (87,000 km) reveals . . . I am hoping for re-surfaced terrain similar to that seen on Ganymede. Possible tectonic re-working/obliteration of old crater fields.

C.R. Pellegrino (July 1981)
(in a prepublication note about *Darwin's Universe*)

There is, one knows not what sweet mystery about this sea, whose gently awful stirrings seem to speak of some hidden soul beneath.

Herman Melville

In our work on the early history of the asteroids, Jesse A. Stoff and I came across a feature in need of a name. Peering out at us from the models and the equations and the meteorites was a "crazy" prediction that asteroids once contained underground streams.

During the first half billion years or so of an average asteroid's life, heating by relatively short-lived radioactive elements must have produced temperatures as high as 2000° C (3632° F) near the center. We know this from meteorites containing both the radioactive decay products and partially remelted silicates. This is the same sort of thing that—combined with heat produced by the original packing together of rock, ice and dust from the presolar nebula—melted the Earth's interior.

Inside every asteroid, between the molten or nearly molten core and the cold, airless surface, there existed an intermediate zone where temperatures ranged between the boiling and freezing points of water (and we know from analyses of meteorites—chips of broken asteroids—that there was plenty of water).

Here were places outside the Earth where water could (and did) exist in its liquid state. But what to call them? I've a weakness for puns, and since everybody else at the time seemed to be raving about black holes, white holes, and worm holes, we elected to confuse matters further by introducing Fox Holes. We named the warm, moist zones in honor of University of Miami molecular biologist Sidney W. Fox, who demonstrated that amino acids mixed in water and cooked in certain ways will knit themselves together to form very large, spheroid molecules.

Sure enough, we find in certain crumbly, wet and carbon-rich meteorites a stunning variety of molecular ornamentation. Included are fatty acids, amino acids, purines, pyramidines, precursors to chlorophyll, and perhaps the birth stages of life itself. Unfortunately, asteroids are small—as celestial bodies go—and they quickly lost their internal heat, freezing solid within the first half billion years of their existence. Although the first steps in the direction of life had already been taken, the process was apparently cut down in midstride.

By 2,147,481,650 B.C., the asteroids were as cold and dead as old bones. The Fox Holes were gone.

On Earth, the oceans swarmed with cyanobacteria (blue-green algae), protozoans, and green multicellular threads.

You might not have guessed it from a quick look around the Solar System, but there were other oceans to be explored. One of these oceans was hidden beneath hundreds of kilometers of clouds, and hundreds more of ice, on the planet Neptune. It was a lifeless place. The planet itself was more than 17 times as massive as Earth. Thousands of kilometers deep, the ocean pressed down with such tremendous force that carbon could exist only in its crystal form. There were diamonds in the sky.

Another more hospitable ocean circled Saturn. We know from analyses of *Voyager 2* images that Enceladus' surface was being reshaped by volcanic forces. There were fractures, ridges, and valleys. Ancient crater fields were being obliterated by newer, smoother plains. Some craters had been cut in two by encroaching tides of upwelling crust. This is unusual activity in a body composed mostly of ice, and so small that it would fit comfortably inside the state of New Mexico. Stranger still, there was an ocean in that little world—yes, *in* it. Enceladus contained one of the oldest Fox Holes in the Solar System and, as such, it also contained one of the most likely sites for the synthesis of life.

But a world as small as Enceladus should have long ago frozen clear through to its very center. By 2 billion B.C., its surface—every square meter of it—should have been saturated with craters. Enceladus didn't know this and developed smooth plains anyway. Deep down something was melting the ice.

It was the tide. Enceladus was (and still is) caught in the middle of a gravitational tug-of-war. On one side was Saturn. On the other side were Tethys (a 1050 kilometer-wide satellite that sometimes swept past Enceladus at only one-sixth the distance separating Earth from the Moon) and Dione (a 1120 kilometer-wide satellite that approached within almost one-half the distance separating Earth from the Moon, and with which Enceladus shared a 2:1 resonance).

Tidal friction occurring between Saturn and its satellites dumped enormous loads of energy into Enceladus' interior—and kept it wet. Salts, hydrates of ammonia (ammonia chemically bound with water), methane clathrates (whereby molecules of methane are caged within a latticework of ice or other crystals, and the properties of the crystals are essentially those of the enclosed methane) and other non water substances were probably also at work. Together they induced melting by lowering the freezing temperature of the water (just as salt spread on New York's highways melts snow and ice).

The topography of Enceladus' few surviving craters, as seen

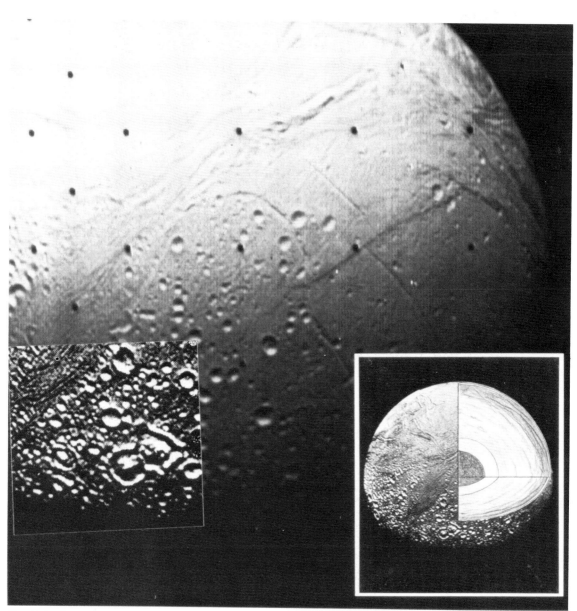

Enceladus is an ice world small enough to be accommodated by the state of New Mexico. Yet it apparently contains an ocean of liquid water overlaying a rocky core only 155 kilometers (97 miles) across. Pressures on the seafloor are equivalent to those encountered at a depth of 1.38 kilometers (0.62 miles) in Earth's oceans. Several tens of kilometers above the rock base, the ocean becomes ice. The ice apparently has a "plastic" consistency, getting progressively harder and cooler and less dense as you approach the surface. The underlying ocean is protected by the planet's outer skin. If an asteroid splashes down on Enceladus, "plastic" ice flows up like tooth paste through the puncture, then freezes solid, forming a dome-shaped crater floor. Two such craters, each more then 30 kilometers (19 miles) in diameter, can be seen at the bottom left. We can see, in these two largest craters, that the once "plastic" ice is now brittle like rock. This is a revealed by a smaller, bowl-shaped crater on top of the larger dome. Photos courtesy of NASA/JPL. Schematic based on calculations by C.R. Pellegrino.

through *Voyager* 2, allows us to peer literally into the skin of a Saturnian Moon. On the oldest, most heavily cratered fields, small craters ranging in diameter from 5 to 15 kilometers (3.1 to 9.3 miles) occur as sharply chiseled, bowl-shaped depressions up to 3 kilometers (1.9 miles) deep. The largest craters on Enceladus' old, cratered terrain are about 35 kilometers (21.8 miles) across, and the asteroids that excavated them apparently burst through to depths of 5 or 7 kilometers (3.1 or 4.4 miles).

The floors of these deepest craters are convex and domed upwards. Relaxation and upfilling have taken place. Once exposed, the deep ice squeezed up through the hole, almost like toothpaste, and then froze solid (as indicated by a crisp, 2 kilometer-wide depression on the top of one 30-kilometer crater dome). This means that the world's outer 2 to 3 kilometers of ice are rigid, like rock, but that the viscosity of ice (i.e., its resistance to forces that cause it to flow) decreases to a molasses like consistency at depths of 5 to 7 kilometers.*

Because the viscosity of ice decreases with increasing temperature, and because the viscosity of ice on Enceladus decreases with increasing depth, it seems reasonable to conclude that the inside of Enceladus is (or was) warmer with increasing depth. Dig down deep enough and you are bound to find liquid water. This means that metals, silicates, and other heavier-than-water substances have sunk to the ice world's bottom.

With a density of 1.1 (water has a density of 1.0), Enceladus must possess a rocky core measuring some 155 kilometers (97 miles) across. This core is truly a world within a world. It is a planet so small that a submarine could take you all the way around its 488-kilometer (303-mile) circumference in a single afternoon. Here, at the bottom of a Fox Hole—on this world without a sun—the ocean presses down with a force of 150 atmospheres (equivalent to pressures encountered at depths of 1.38 kilometers in Earth's oceans). Above, the ocean stretches skyward for perhaps several tens of kilometers, terminating at a self-sealing icy shell. If an asteroid punctures the shell, viscous ice flows up and clots solid, healing the wound.

Down on the sea bottom, during the first half billion years of Enceladus' history, amino acids, porphyrin molecules, and other complex organic substances were synthesized. We can be reasonably sure of this because such molecules were being manufactured inside asteroids and comets. Two billion years later, in the period we have now stepped back to, preliving chemical evolution on Earth had

---

*Viscosity also decreases as a function of closeness to young terrain. Within 30 kilometers (19 miles) of newly formed ridges, craters down to diameters of 8 kilometers (5 miles) have become domed.

matured from ropes and droplets of amino acids, and nucleic acid knots, to chromosomes tucked inside nuclei and powered by photosynthesis. A cup full of ocean water would have told you that life on Earth had really started. Hundreds of little green cells would also have told you that energy from the Sun sustained it.

In the warm, dark recesses of Enceladus, there was no sunlight. There was no photosynthesis. If, by 2 billion years ago, we are to imagine cells with genes inside one of Saturn's moons, than we are forced to ask what they were using for food.

There is an alternative to sunlight. Sulfur compounds, especially hydrogen sulfide (H_2S), can be slowly oxidized or burned by cells. The energy derived from oxidation can then be directed toward the splitting of carbon dioxide into separate carbon and oxygen atoms (this process, the opposite of oxidation, is called reduction).

An organism could then "steal" the carbon atoms, linking them together to form carbohydrates and other materials that go into building cell walls and organelles (a process called carbon fixation), and liberating oxygen as a by-product. Other organisms might capitalize on the oxygen, as animal cells do on Earth—perhaps releasing sulfides as by-products—so that a symbiosis similar to that seen between terrestrial plants (which produce oxygen used by animals) and animals (which produce some of the carbon dioxide used by plants) might develop.

An extra terrestrial ecology based upon sulfides instead of sunlight is not the mere product of abstract fantasy It is the product of careful observation right here on Earth. The process is called *chemo*synthesis rather than *photo*synthesis, and it is known to occur near sulfide-rich hot water vents located some 2.5 kilometers (1.6 miles) under the Pacific Ocean.

If there were sulfide oases inside Enceladus (and ubiquitous supplies of sulfur droplets in certain stony meteorites suggest that there were), then around them the seafloor might have supported dense communities of cells. It is fun to speculate about what might have become of them (if in fact they did exist), given another 2 billion years of evolution.

Living on a rock surface only 155 kilometers (97 miles) across, they would have lacked the opportunity to undergo the isolation and subsequent branching events that are so likely to occur on a world as big as Earth. The surface area of the Earth measures a half billion square kilometers. The seafloor of Enceladus measures about 76 thousand square kilometers. Considering also that the food supply is likely to have been small, limited to perhaps a few life-sustaining acres, life might never have gotten to the jellyfish or crab stage given even all of Enceladus to experiment with for 4 billion years. That leads us to another important question: How long did Enceladus' Fox Hole last?

At a depth of 2.6 kilometers (1.6 miles), hot water spurts from hydrothermal vents on the Galapagos Rift, on the East Pacific Rise. Protruding from the seafloor like organ pipes, the vents create oases by supplying hydrogen sulfide (H_2S) that can be slowly oxidized or burned by living cells. Inside a geologically active ice world (Jupiter's moon Europa, which has boiled most of its volatiles off into space, is one good candidate for such a world), an ecology based on sulfides instead of sunlight can develop. In this respect, the Galapagos vent tube worm, Rifta pachyptila (shown here living in dense communities around a vent), provides a dramatic view of what life could be like on (or, more correctly, in) another world. The worm's tissues posses enzymes capable of catalyzing the synthesis of the energy-storing molecule adenosine triphosphate (ATP) from adenosine diphosphate (ADP). The energy required for making ATP and ADP comes from reducing power generated by the oxidation of sulfur compounds (primarily H_2S). Other enzymes use the energy derived from sulfur oxidation to reduce and fix carbon dioxide, releasing oxygen as a by-product (which can in turn be used for further oxidation). This first example of an animal that produces its own food, like a plant, lacks both a mouth and a digestive system. It is as strange as the extraterrestrial life forms whose existence it suggests –almost like having an alien in our seas. Photos courtesy of Dudley Foster, Kathleen Crane, and the RISE Project Group, Woods Hole, Massachusetts.

231

Because truly craterless surfaces were revealed by *Voyager* 2, the process that shaped Enceladus' smooth plains and grooved terrain must have been active right into Jurassic and Cretaceous times. It is difficult to imagine this process stopping after dinosaurs appeared on Earth or that it will stop tomorrow.

It is possible that volcanoes whose lava is water are present on the surface. The water would probably be erupted in a gaseous rather than a liquid phase. Some of it would fall back as snow and the rest would escape to space. This explains, perhaps, why Enceladus' surface reflects about as much sunlight as freshly-fallen snow. In fact, it reflects almsot 100 percent of the sunlight that falls upon it. Together with the coincidence of the densest part of Saturn's E ring with Enceladus' orbit (including Enceladus as the source of the ring), this further suggests that the satellite presently contains a "live" Fox Hole.

It might not be alone. Other possible cradles of life include Europa, an icy satellite of Jupiter measuring only slightly smaller than the Earth's Moon.

Tidally flexed between two of its sister satellites and Jupiter, Europa has vented most of its volatiles into space. Like the Earth, it is composed mostly of rock. One of *Voyager* 2's last glimpses of Europa now provides a strong case for a geologically active world beneath the ice. Taken three days after the robot's 1979 encounter with Jupiter (and not studied until 3 years later), closing shots reveal a faint plume rising 120 kilometers (75 miles) above the crescent moon. Looking back over its shoulder, *Voyager* might have made us witness to an eruption of volcanic water.

The case for Europan geysers is further strengthened by *Voyager* data showing that sunlight reflected from the surface at different angles behaves as though it were illuminating a relatively fresh layer of frost. The surface of the world is virtually craterless. It is also marked by globe-circling lines resembling cracks in the ice; that is exactly what they are.

Current models suggest that the ice varies between 5 and 16 kilometers (3 to 10 miles) in thickness, and covers an ocean 32 kilometers (20 miles) deep. Pressure at the sea bottom is equivalent to water pressure at depths of 6.1 kilometers (3.8 miles) on Earth. It is conceivable (if not likely) that the Europan Fox Hole provides two of the same essential ingredients that make life possible on Earth's abyssal plains: liquid water and an energy source, in the form of sulfides ascending through subsurface volcanoes and hot water vents.

As an indulgence, let us imagine that megacellular life has evolved in such a world, and that it has led to the emergenre of sentient beings (a pre requisite for subsurface intelligence will be an ice world with a relatively large rocky core and a correspondingly

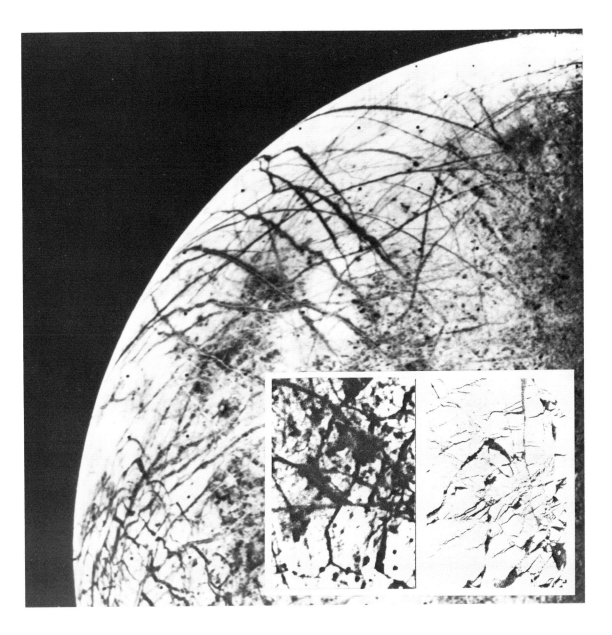

Europa's network of cracks and streaks is suggestive of rather impressive wrenchings and tearings and refreezings. The inserts show high resolution views of Europa's surface (left insert: diameter=100 km; photograph by Voyager 2) and cracked, refrozen pack ice near Alaska (photographed by Landsat). Photos courtesy of NASA/JPL.

greater surface area: Enceladus is simply "not on", but Europa— given enough time—might just do the trick).

Would they then discover space? On Earth there was no question. From the ground we could look into space directly. Even so it took many centuries for us to figure out exactly what stars were (the Spanish Inquisition didn't help matters).

From the bottom of an Europan Fox Hole, nothing of the astronomical universe—the stars, the planets, the Sun—would be

233

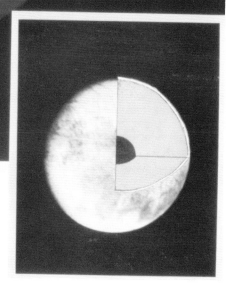

visible. If we are assuming creatures blessed with curiosity and a taste for the mysterious, then surely they will go into the sky to learn if and where it ends. And there they would find the strangest of things: the sky ends. You can go only so far, and then you bang your head on a worldwide ceiling of ice. I can almost hear the "experts" on the ground shouting, "See! What did we tell you! The universe ends there. We are at its center. And that is all there is."

No that is not all there is. Other minds would infallably look beyond the ice. If radio telescopes could be built and operated under water, our hypothetical Europans would detect Jupiter as a huge disk-shaped radio source that moved on the other side of the sky. Frequently it eclipsed a smaller, more distant and more powerful radio source—the Sun. Seismic studies might reveal that the ice had a finite thickness, and that there was indeed an "outside."

What would they do next? Start a mining operation? Would they simply start chipping away at the ice? And if one party of explorers did manage to break through to the other side, the result might be embarrassing. Stepping out of a water environment into a vacuum

Two of the Solar System's most geologically active moons, Io (left) and Europa (right), are viewed in transit against Jupiter. As seen in the sectioned sphere at the lower right, Europa has retained a thin shell of ice (perhaps 30 kilometers deep), overlaying a hidden ocean of liquid water. Most of this world's volume probably consists of silicate rock (grey), with a differentiated stony iron core (black). A census of possible abodes for life near Jupiter and Saturn (at present count, as many as four —and we haven't even looked at Uranus and Neptune or the Pluto-Charon pair yet) suggests that most life in the universe exists inside ice worlds, which makes our kind of life relatively uncommon, perhaps even freakish. Photos courtesy of NASA/JPL. Schematic based on data complied by Voyager scientist Torrence Johnson.

. . . what might be left or the expedition would be a very poor advertisement for space exploration.

Just for the sake of argument, let's assume that they anticipate the hazzard (after all, they will already know that water pressure decreases as a function of altitude). Let's permit them to break safely through the ceiling and emerge onto the surface of their planet. Clad in space suits they look up. What then? What would they think the stars were?* Would they even be able to see the stars?

Like cave-dwelling organisms on Earth, they might lack eyes. Sensing surroundings as vibrations, textures, minute changes in temperature, and smells is not very helpful to observational astronomers.

Looking outward from our Earth, and assuming our own Solar System to be typical, we can see immediately that ice worlds must be at least five times more abundant than rocky, Earth-like planets. Because rocky worlds seem to be so outnumbered by globes of rock and ice, gravitational resonances of the kind seen in Enceladus and Europa might be far more likely to produce the warm, wet environments necessry for life than are rocky planets located just the right distance from just the right kind of star and possessing just the right amount of mass to hold just the right kind of atmosphere.

In paging through the catalog of possibilities, an ice world need not be located at any specified distance from a star in order to develop a suitable Fox Hole. The orbit of Neptune will do just as well as the orbit of Jupiter. It need only be somplace cold. We don't even need the right kind of star. Those traditionally shunned white dwarfs and multiple star systems must now be considered more seriously as potential sites for the development of life.

It could happen almost anywhere.

This being the case, most life in the universe might exist inside ice worlds, and we surface dwellers have become members of a galactic minority. Still, when the question of life outside the Earth comes up, most of us think first of Sun-like stars. We look for the nearest stars and then start calculating how far away an Earth-like planet would have to orbit so as to be neither fried nor frozen, but cooked slowly at the triple point for water. We have, it seems, projected the working patterns of our own world as the standard for all worlds. With Europan and Enceladan perspectives added to our view of the universe, we might have to change our minds.

---

*Their situation is perhaps analogous to the responses of terrestrial pygmies, who—brought out of the dense forest for the first time—could not immediately comprehend the vast distances of "the outside," and thought that men near the horizon must indeed be very small.

18 Genesis and Galactic Blight

And the Earth was without form, and void, and darkness was upon the face of the deep.

Genesis

Beginnings are apt to be shadowy, and so it is with the beginning of that great mother of life, the sea.

Rachael Carson

It has taken the planet Earth four and a half billion years to discover that it is four and a half billion years old.

George Wald

No one can even begin to grasp what four and a half billion years means in terms of waiting time at the airport, but it is clearly longer than next Thursday at 4:15 P.M.

Harlan Ellison

It was hot.

The Earth was practically new in 4,294,965,298 B.C. It was still steaming from the heat of accretion, and from the decay of short-lived radioactive elements injected into the Solar System almost at the moment of its formation (about 4.6 billion years B.C.).

The crust, floating like slag in a steel blast furnace, was considerably thinner and far more pliable than it is today. Scores of continental plates were present everywhere. From a world-spanning network of tears and ruptures flowed streams of basaltic lava. There was steam and dust and radioactivity in the air. And torrential rains. Where lava contacted water, the sea drew back with stolen heat—leaping and hissing and turning white.

This was the protocell era; from it simple organic molecules emerged as the phenomena we call life. By 4 billion B.C., and probably many millions of years earlier, microscopic bags of polymer had appeared in our seas. Some were probably capable of using certain molecules (the flattened, ring-shaped porphyrins, for example) for storing and releasing energy. Others clumped together and exchanged "useful" molecules with each other. Still others, resembling naked threads and wheels of RNA, formed symbiotic linkages with amino acid sacs (and/or originated as useful by-products inside the sacs). These were not life; but they were getting close to it.

Despite widespread belief, butterflies, buffaloes, apples, and snakes are not descended from a single protocell ancestor. Instead, one protocell type—resembling the mitochondrian "powerhouse" of animal cells—became incorporated inside other protocells, which began separately and were probably already on their way to becoming such diverse creatures as spirochaetes and paramecia. Prophyrin-loaded protocells resembling the chloroplasts of green plants were probably among the earliest recognizable life forms seen on Earth. From that time—from the very beginning—plants and animals were divided kingdoms.

The idea that trees and men have a common ancestor is merely that: an idea. The development of both, it seems, was running along separate tracks at the start. Each had its own identity. Only in the geological sense is our ancestry linked with the kauri. In this sense, our shared parent is the Earth itself, in whose exhalations and regurgitations the crucial molecules were assembled (with a little input from comets and meteorites).

It is hardly conceivable that a first forbear arose in one rocky pool, spread its progeny throughout the world's oceans, and then diversified to become worms, sponges, and seaweed. We know as much from laboratory studies. If we expose amino acids in water to an energy source (heat, shock waves and/or electrical discharges will do nicely), we see them accreting to form microspheroids and hollow tubes of different shapes and sizes.

We see in the products of such experiments not one preliving entity—or even one kind of preliving entity—but millions of individual entities in an area the size of your fist. The same thing was probably seen on Earth as conditions became just right for the building of preliving bags of polymer and free-floating knots of RNA. Once protocells had appeared they flourished everywhere.

On Mars, life might have gotten a start near 4.3 billion B.C. Water runoff channels are common on terrain dating back past 3.9 billion B.C. There are even hints of rain on the Martian surface—indicating an atmosphere considerably thicker than the present one—but the endless winter was fast approaching.

Even small, asteroid-sized bodies were warmer and wetter than they are today. Heated by relatively short-lived radioactive elements, temperatures near their cores soared high enough to melt glass and iron. Spectroscopic studies have shown that basaltic lava once erupted onto the surface of Vesta (diameter equals 530 kilometers), suggesting rather spectacular heating in at least one asteroid.

Somewhere between the seething cores and the frozen surfaces of these bodies there existed zones of thickness, measured in kilometers, where temperatures ranged between the freezing and boiling points of water: Fox Holes. As described in Chapter 17, meteorites believed to have come from such zones contain amino acids and other molecules essential for building cells. But asteroids, being small, lose heat quickly. By 4 billion B.C., most had cooled enough to shut down their Fox Holes, and the life-building process came to a screeching halt.

On the moon, Taurus-Littrow did not exist as yet. Near the center of its Earth-facing side, huge impacting bodies had excavated KREEP from deep within and sprayed it almost to the far side. Extrusions of liquid magma welled up to fill the wounds, forming dark lava seas called maria. The Moon was some 55,000 miles closer to the Earth, and almost within the Roche limit. Perhaps that explains why the Moon's center of mass is displaced in an Earthward direction and why its maria are clustered near the middle of its Earthward face.

The terrestrial day was as few as 10 hours long.

The Earth and the Moon and the Galaxy beyond were bathed in a background glow that heated every corner of the universe to a minimum temperature of 10.4° K. Space was 50 times denser than it is today. Every cubic meter contained no less than 100 atoms and, compared against the present composition of the universe, a greater proportion of those atoms were hydrogen and helium.

All of the atoms on this planet that are not hydrogen, helium, and lithium were generated during the lives and deaths of stars. According to the best available evidence, the embryonic universe did not remain hot enough and dense enough long enough to permit the assembly, from protons and neutrons, of atomic nuclei heavier than lithium.

An abbreviated history of elemental genesis goes something like this: About 10 billion years ago, and possibly as long as 15 billion years ago, the average density of the universe was about 1 atom per cubic centimeter. This tells us that there was a crucial period for galaxy formation.

Galaxies did not exist in their present state at a time earlier than the 1-atom-per-cubic-centimeter boundary (at which time Andromeda and the Milky Way and some of our closest neighbors were nuzzled shoulder to shoulder). They were not born much later because gas spread between clusters of galaxies quickly (within a billion years or so, give or take 300 million) becomes too thin to form new ones.

Next, perturbations in the infant galaxies pulled atoms together into the first solar systems.* But they were not like our Solar System. Although you would have found giant, gassy worlds like Jupiter circling at the appropriate distances from their stars, you would have seen no rings, no icy satellites, no rocky inner planets. You could have scoured every cubic centimeter of a Jupiter-like world, and anything within 50 light years of it for all the elements heavier than lithium and you would have been unable to make a single rock.

Once the stars got started, however, things really (if you'll pardon just one more pun) began to heat up. Within the biggest and hottest stars, hydrogen atoms were fused together to make more helium, releasing energy as they did so. Helium was fused to form the first nuclei of carbon and oxygen, and these begat such heavy elements as magnesium, silicon and iron—the stuff from which trees, Taurus-Littrow and the towers of Manhattan are made.

The most massive stars in the Galaxy began coughing up heavy elements almost as soon as they were born. This is because the life of a star is determined by its mass. If our Sun—a rather medium-sized star— is destined to consume most of its hydrogen content during a lifetime of 10 billion years or so, a giant like Alkaid, which shines with the power of 630 suns, will, under the stronger crush of gravity, quicken the tempo of fusion. Alkaid will burn, collapse, erupt, and spew its contents after less than a million years of life.

A million years after the first stars appeared in our galaxy, supernovas began pumping carbon, oxygen, silicon, and metals into

Nucleosynthesis pathways of helium and carbon, showing the genesis of isotopes of oxygen, magnesium and aluminum (the term isotope defines any of two or more forms of the same element having the same number of protons in the nucleus, or the same atomic number, but different atomic weights). All elements in the universe heavier than lithium (element number 3) were generated during the lives and deaths of stars. Uranium and gold and other particularly heavy elements are created only during supernova explosions (or, in the case of lead, by the decay of heavy elements ejected by supernovae). Atomic weights given for each atom shown here represent the number of protons and neutrons. For example, helium-4 (element number 2) is formed by the fusion of four protons –that is, hydrogen nuclei –to produce one helium nucleus containing two each of protons and neutrons. One helium nucleus is lighter than the sum of the four protons from which it is made. The missing mass is shed as energy; it keeps the star burning.

---

*As described in Chapter 1, gas clouds today can and often are pressed together to form new stars by shockwaves from supernovae. Supernova-induced star formation appears to be widespread in our galaxy. This process does not explain how gas clouds collapsed to form the very first stars when there weren't other stars to provide the needed kick. Making stars then becomes a little harder; but that is someone else's problem.

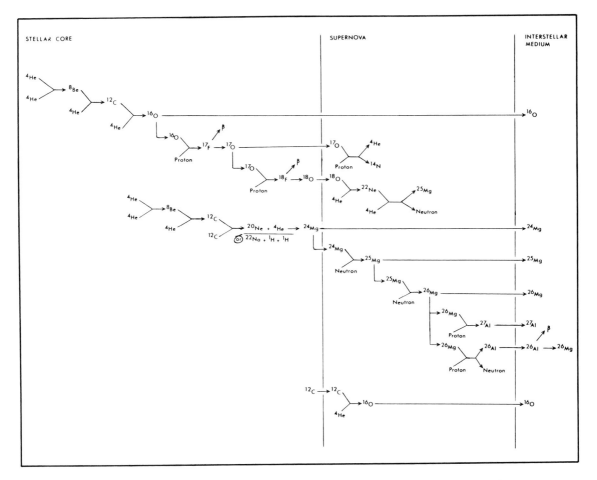

the interstellar medium. Present observational evidence suggests that, on average, a new star forms in our galaxy every year and a supernova occurs every 15 to 60 years. Given these birth and death rates, stars should far outnumber supernova remnants. And they do, just look around. When the galaxy was a billion years old, heavy elements began to disperse through interstellar space. In almost no time at all they became wrapped up in new solar systems.

At last, the Galaxy could begin to make rocks. How soon the Galaxy was able to make Earth-sized rocks capable of sprouting life depends on many things, including wishful thinking. According to the most optimistic estimates, heavy-element abundance in the spiral arms of the Galaxy increased from zero to between 33 and 50 percent of the Solar System's present value within the first 2 billion years. Astronomers refer to this as Prompt Initial Enrichment (or PIE in the sky), whereafter stars continued to manufacture and expel heavy elements at an exponentially decaying rate. This model predicts that, given a 15-billion-year-old galaxy, the interstellar medium contained between 91 and 96 percent of its present heavy-element abundance when our Solar System formed (80 to 92 percent if the galaxy is only 10 billion years old).

Less optimistic estimates of heavy-element accumulation rates suggest that production has remained roughly constant throughout time. Heavy-element enrichment was about 30 to 45 percent below present levels when the Sun and planets formed. A census of the contents of our Solar System (whose Sun is not yet generating any elements heavier than helium), and a comparison with the contents of the interstellar medium does not suggest significant enrichment of extra-solar space after the Earth came into existence.

We must be cautious of acceptinl this conclusion as fact. In the universe things are never as simple as they appear on paper. The Solar System and the space around it are not contained in a corked bottle. We can be polluted by new ejecta and diluted by new hydrogen.

Recent observations suggest that high-velocity clouds of hydrogen and helium (presumably in primordial proportions of 93/7) might presently be falling down into the galactic plane. This hydrogen "snow" could increase the density of interstellar space by 1 or 2 percent per billion years, keeping the ratio of hydrogen to heavier elements roughly constant during the last 4 billion years.

Some astronomers have argued that there is no strong case for viewing the clouds as in-falling clouds (rather than viewing them as extensions of the Galaxy), except for their usefulness in making certain theories come out right.

Comparison of Elemental Abundances.

	Solar System	Orion Nebula	Planetary Nebula
Hydrogen	12.00	12.00	12.00
Helium	10.90	11.04	11.23
Carbon	8.60	3.37	8.70
Nitrogen	8.00	7.63	8.10
Oxygen	8.80	8.79	8.90
Flourine	4.60		4.90
Neon	7.60	7.86	7.90
Sodium	6.30		6.60
Sulfur	7.20	7.47	7.90
Chlorine	5.50	4.94	6.90
Argon	6.00	5.95	7.00
Potassium	5.50		5.70
Calcium	6.40		6.40

A comparison of elemental abundances in the Solar System, in the Orion Nebula (presumably representative of present heavy-element enrichment in the interstellar medium), and the average of several planetary nebulae (the elliptical, off-thrown outer atmospheres of dying starts). The abundances are normalized to hydrogen. Data for fresh supernova ejecta (for example, the Crab Nebula) are absent

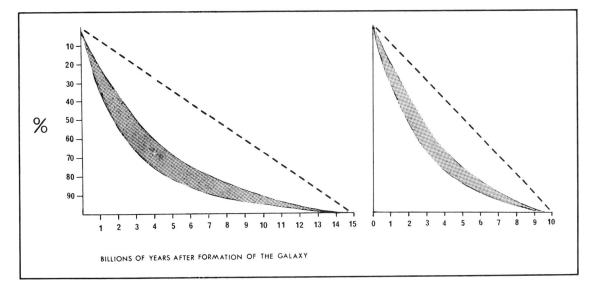

%

BILLIONS OF YEARS AFTER FORMATION OF THE GALAXY

Heavy element accumulation rates are shown as a function of time (for a galaxy aged 15 and 10 billion years), demonstrating that there was a specific "instant" during which life could begin in the universe (on the surfaces of Earth-like planets). The dashed lines represent constant heavy element accumulation rates (apparently not the case). Actual rates probably lie within the bounds of shaded curves, based on calculations of Tinsley (in NATO, 1974) and Pellegrino (1983). Clearer resolution of the accumulation curve, which depends (among other things) on a more precise fix on the age of the galaxy, will permit the setting of statistical limits on the possibility of finding electronic civilizations like our own (that is, on the surfaces of Earth-like worlds). In other words, the possibility of extraterrestrial civilizations can actually be measured as a function of time.

because of such formidable observational difficulties as separation of supernova remnants into small, outracing fliaments that differ in density, velocity, and perhaps in composition as well. *Data compiled by Virginia Trimble.*

Adding to the confusion, the Dutch-American astronomer Bart Bok announced on 20 January, 1983 that the Galaxy, due mostly to free hydrogen "out there," might extend three times farther and be 10 times more massive than was previously thought. If so, he has probably found the invisible (gravitational) "glue" that holds clusters of galaxies together. In the same stroke, he might have found enough gravity to close the universe into a *finite and unbounded* sphere (see Chapter 3), and one can only love him for it.

So, very cautiously, we will accept exponential heavy-element production as being more likely than linear production. Doing this, we are saying that the abundance of heavy elements in the Galaxy was probably no more than 20 percent below present levels—and perhaps as little as 4 percent—in the year 4.6 billion B.C.

Let's look a little closer at this idea. We will assume a 15-billion-year-old galaxy and work with the basement figure of 4 percent enrichment over the last 4.6 billion years (given a 10-billion-year-old galaxy, the minimum change during the same interval of time is 8 percent). If the Solar System were forming today—instead of 4.6 billion years ago—a 4-percent greater abundance of heavy elements would add a worldwide layer of rock that extended 92 kilometers (57 miles) over our heads. Our planet's surface area would be increased by 15.2 million square kilometers (2.7 percent) and its volume by 27.9 billion cubic kilometers (4.0 percent).

Planets shed primordial heat (generated over their entire volumes by the kinetic energy of accretion and the decay of radioactive elements) at the surface. In addition, as objects of the same shape increase in size, volumes increase faster than surface areas. An additional 92 kilometers of rock spread over the Earth would reduce by 1.3 percent the relative surface area through which the heat, generated over an *added* volume equivalent to 1.6 times that of our Moon, could be radiated into space.

The outcome of all this is that 4.6 billion years down the road, the Earth's interior would be more than 5.2 percent hotter than it is today. The crust would have formed both thinner and later, and the origin of life might have been delayed for a quarter billion years or more. Convection cells, on which the continents float, would be smaller, more numerous, and more active—terrifyingly active. It is possible that civilized life could not have any stable existence on land.

Looking down the arrow of time, if we push the formation of the Earth *back* 4.6 billion years beyond the date indicated by the Solar System's oldest rocks (that is, back to 9.2 billion years ago), then we find *at least* 15 percent fewer heavy elements available for building planets. There would now be over 300 fewer kilometers (187 miles) of rock beneath your feet. The Earth's volume would be decreased by 91 billion cubic kilometers (15 percent), enough to contain 6.6 moons. Its surface area would be smaller by 24 million square kilometers (5 percent), enough to cover half the Moon.

As a result, the 9.2-billion-B.C. Earth would have much less internal heat to radiate through almost the same surface area. The crust would solidify more than twice as fast, and to substantially greater depths. Continental drift would, within 2 billion years or so, become retarded or nonexistent. The pull of gravity would be some 15 percent weaker, and life-sustaining gases would erode away under the solar wind. Water in the upper atmosphere would dissociate into hydrogen and oxygen—just as it does today. The difference is that more of the hydrogen would be blown off from a 15 percent less massive Earth. The heavier oxygen atoms would remain behind to combine with surface rocks and carbon—lots of carbon.

Carbon dioxide is soluble in water and, once dissolved, can be chemically bound to form line ($CaCO_3$) and other minerals (the process of CO_2 absorption is assisted on Earth today by clams and other shell-secreting organisms, not to mention plants).

If a 15 percent less massive Earth began losing hydrogen (and thus water), then it would from the very first be finished. More and more of the carbon dioxide vented into the air by Olympus Mons-like volcanoes would stay there because the shrinking oceans could not remove it fast enough. It is worth noting that if all the CO_2 on Earth were liberated from limestone and dolomites and oceans, and if all the carbon in living things were bound with oxygen, we would have more than 100 atmospheres of CO_2, like Venus).

CO_2 gas absorbs strongly in the infrared and releases the absorbed light as heat energy. We call this the *greenhouse effect* (glass warms a greenhouse by converting wavelengths of infrared light into wavelengths of heat). Fill the air with CO_2 and the temperature soars—causing more water to evaporate.

The process can easily reach a flash point and become self-sustaining. Water vapor also absorbs in the infrared. The less water the Earth has pooled on its surface the more rapidly CO_2 levels rise. This evaporates more water, which adds more CO_2 to the air and brings more hydrogen into the upepr atmosphere —where it escapes into space—and so on, and so on, until at last some 100 atmospheres of CO_2 have been liberated and the Earth has become a lifeless furnace like Venus—and for the same reasons.

There might be a place beyond our present orbit where we could insert a 15 percent less-massive Earth and hope for life to get started, but it is difficult to imagine a smaller Earth being close enough to the Sun to hold water in its liquid state and still maintain a grip on stratospheric hydrogen. The size limitations on planets capable of developing and sustaining surface life might be far narrower than we used to think (in which case Fox Holes might have got a head start on the rest of the Galaxy).

Now we know the meaning of 15 percent. It is likely that, 9.2 billion years ago, the heavy element deficiency was as high as 28 percent, and possible that it ran up to 60 percent. In either case, the formation of Earth-like worlds with just the right mass in just the right orbits becomes statistically less probable as we increase our distance from 4.6 billion B.C. Moving both forward and backward in time, we eventually cross points where the emergence of surface-dwelling life is precluded by the "wrong" elemental abundances.

Maybe you are wondering why I've raked up all these tedious numbers and chemicals. There is a good reason. They have important implications for Francis Crick's *directed panspermia* theory, a proposal for the origin of life (put forward by the codescriber of DNA itself) so fraught with controversy and alluring possibilities that one discussion of the topic, by grown men with Ph.Ds., quickly deteriorated from name-calling to food throwing.

Stated briefly, the theory goes like this: The origin of life requires so many conditions (and their probability goes down with their multiplication) as to be a "miracle" that happened only once in our whole island of stars. Because our space probes have already contaminated the Moon and Mars with hitchhiking virus particles, and because two *Pioneer* and two *Voyager* probes, viruses and all, have been pitched to the stars, what's to say that DNA—life itself—did not come from the other direction, arriving on rockets sent by creatures like ourselves?*

What you have just read is *what*. Just for a start, there is no reason on Earth why our planet, which happened to be warm and wet and able to stay that way, could not have cooked up its own life. Second, if we are to assume, as Crick suggests, that a previous civilization seeded life on Earth some 4.3 billion years ago, then, even by our most optimistic estimates, we must also assume 4.5 billion years of previous evolution on a planet that formed almost 9 billion years ago. That brings us back to the meaning of 15 percent.

As all the tedious chemistry and numbers have shown, sufficient time probably has not elasped (since the Big Bang) for creatures like ourselves to evolve twice. An electronic civilization capable of interstellar travel could not have come into existence by the time the Sun and Earth arrived on the scene.*

Even if Crick turns out to be wrong about directed panspermia, the idea has raised new and important questions about elemental abundances throughout time. That is the value of any good theory: the questions it raises, not whether it is right, or partly right, or entirely wrong. In answer to the new questions, Crick writes:

> Charles, you do indeed raise a valid point: how long after the Big Bang could planetary systems be formed that were not too dissimilar from the earth? Obviously this depends, at least in part, on the composition of interstellar dust . . . I now realize that (this) should be looked into more closely. The argument you give rather implies that the density of appropriate elements rose steadily with time and therefore may not have been high enough 9 billion years ago. However, this is not necessarily the case, for two reasons. The first is that the bigger stars burn up very fast, and so there are likely to have been many more supernovae explosions in the early stages of the universe than later on. The second is that star formation (with planets) will remove dust, so that possibly some rough equilibrium may be set up.

It is precisely that *removal* of dust, by planets, that we really have to think about. Statistically, planets forming today should be sopping up more heavy elements and, in the process, growing fatter

---

*Responding to the proposal, Stephen Jay Gould once said, "One dollar will get you five that he's wrong this time. But it will only get you five, because he's been right about too many other creepy things."

*Unless we consider ice worlds, there is not sufficient time. But could a civilization capable of developing space technology develop in a Fox Hole? Here, the questions raised are so new that I cannot furnish even criteria for how we might go about answering them. How do you smelt metal under water? Are there alternatives for metal? Can civilization progress without the invention of fire? The questions go on.

than those forming 4.6 or 9.2 billion years ago. Their associated suns should also be richer in these elements.

As the galactic supply of hydrogen and helium is fused, in the absence of any apparent source of replenishment, the relative abundance of more massive, rock-building elements should increase steadily. As Crick suggests, there might exist a saturation point (analogous to the upper limit of crater formation on the Moon, at which point the formation of new craters must eventually be balanced by the obliteration of old ones), at which the rate of heavy-element injection into the interstellar medium (by supernovae) equals the rate of removal (by star and planet formation).

Even so, we are looking at a hypothetical balance only between the production and uptake of interstellar dust—*all* dust: hydrogen, gold and the whole periodic table. Enrichment of the dust with heavy elements, as hydrogen is cycled through stars, expelled via supernovae, and cycled again, is progressive. In essence, then, carbon, silicon, and iron must keep piling up in space—forever.

If we imagine a progression toward an increasingly matter-dominated universe (as hydrogen is used up and fusion burning gradually slows), with the rate of removal *exceeding* the rate of injection (as it does now, with as many as 60 stars forming for every one that explodes), then the history of the universe leads ultimately to growing populations of black holes, neutron stars, cooling white dwarfs, and worlds of rock and rock-ice so gigantic as to be incapable of supporting life. The future begins to look like "hell freezing over."

This is the Era of Galactic Blight. Before it, to the opposite extreme, lies a universe containing no elements from which planets and living things can be made. Between these two extremes lies the Genesis Era, wherein a few very rare Earth-sized worlds begin to form, then more and more of them, and finally fewer and fewer. It occupies the last 5 to 9 billion years (depending on the age of the universe), and probably extends several billion years into futurity.

If there was, as seems to be the case, a specific "instant" during which the universe could begin to produce habitable planets, then the Earth seems to have accreted almost as soon as heavy elements necessary for the building of such worlds had accumulated in quantities that made their appearance likely. It is possible that almost all the planets that will ever evolve electronic civilizations are doing so about now (give or take a few hundred million years). In that case things might be getting a little crowded out here. It is also possible that ours is one of the first life-building planets to have formed. That would rank us among the oldest and smartest of creation's achievements.

The trick is to resolve a clear image of heavy element accumulation rates throughout time. Neither Crick, nor I, nor anyone else has progressed very far in this direction. The problem is complicated by the fact that no one really knows how old the universe is, and by the fact that we have almost no empirical information on the formation of stars and none on galaxies. We know nothing observationally about when the galaxies formed, what changes took place in them after they formed, and we do not know the size of our own galaxy within a factor of 10. As University of Maryland astronomer Virginia Trimble once put it:

> Several of the vital stages in the evolutionary scenario are accomplished only by saying "let there be galaxies," "let there be stars," and so forth . . . There does not seem to be any immediate danger of running out of unsolved problems.

Crick has added a note of urgency to the need for understanding some of the problems—particularly finding the beginning of my so-called Genesis Era—and from this to learn whether or not we are in fact one of the galaxy' first electronic civilizations. He warns that it might be dangerous for us not to know.

Dangerous?

"Yes, dangerous," he says. "There's always the possibility that we will be invaded."

19 Deja Vu

History never repeats
I tell myself before I go to sleep

Split Enz

Never look back. Something might be gaining on you.

Leroy "Satchel" Page

The only place to run from the future is into the past.

Stephen King

Time present and time past
Are both perhaps present in time Future,
And time Future contained in time past.

T.S. Eliot

Past, present and future are only an illusion, even
though a stubborn one.

Albert Einstein

Here we are, all together in the year 8,589,932,594 B.C.
The Earth and the Moon and most of the stars in our sky do not

exist yet. And somewhere between here and 17,179,867,186 B.C. there is almost no telling what will and will not exist. What *can* be told is that, in our next step backward, we will cross a point in which the universe is about 1 million times denser than it will be in A.D. 1984: 1 atom per cubic centimeter. At this point, the universe is only 10 million years old. The temperature is high enough to sustain life: 280° K (7° C, 44° F). But there is no life—anywhere. Nothing except light atoms, empty space, radiation, forces, and tomorrow.

If we stepped backward from 8.6 billion B.C. and watched very carefully, we would notice that the oceans of space-time between and within the galaxies were in a state of contraction. As space-time contracted, it carried with it the galaxies.

If we take the A.D. 1984 rates at which galaxies both near and far appear to be receding from the Earth and clock them backward as far as we can, we find that they all come crashing in on our heads between 10 and 15 billion B.C. Almost nothing is known of this strange, cosmic crunch period. It is made stranger by Cambridge physicist Stephen Hawking's proposal that the universe was then speckled with mini black holes and other unusual flotsam and jetsam of the Big Bang, including embryonic galaxies—swollen and without stars.

Stepping back farther yet, to a time when the universe was only 1 million years old, every cubic centimeter contained 100 atoms heated to more than 700° C.

At half this age, we find ourselves immersed in a universe that is white hot. Electrons are stripped from atomic nuclei and become part of the surroundings. Brilliant yellow light emanates from every direction. We are entering the Decoupling Era; hydrogen atoms, now separated into free protons and electrons, are scattering in odd directions.

Pushing back another 490,000 years, we emerge from the Decoupling Era into the Epoch of Equal Densities (also called the lower limit of the Matter Era). It's sort of like stepping from the frying pan into hell. The universe is 10,000 years old. A teaspoonful of matter weighs as much as a teaspoonful of radiation (compared with a 1984 cosmic background radiation that is less than 1/1000th as dense as matter). On the other side of the Epoch of Equal densities, which lasts only a few hours, lies a universe dominated more by radiation than by matter. It is appropriately named the Radiation Era.

Nothing very important happens to the universe during the next 10,000 years of our backward journey. Of course, temperatures and pressures continue to increase exponentially. The next major event in the history of the universe does not occur until we are within a few minutes of the Big Bang. The universe at this stage has become like the core of a hydrogen bomb, fusing protons and neutrons into heavier nuclei.

In theory, everything should have wound up in tightly bound iron nuclei. Luckily for carbon-based life, space-time was expanding at a psychopathic rate, and fusion rates failed to keep up with the expansion. The process stopped at lithium.

Probing back to Time Zero plus 14 seconds, we encounter 3-billion-degree temperatures. A second earlier it is hotter yet. It is so hot that electrons, positrons (the positively charged antimatter counterparts of electrons), and photons of light are blasted to scattered wave fronts almost as soon as they appear.

Time Zero plus one second.

Temperature: 10,000,000,000° C.

Density: 100,000 times that of water.

We enter the ghostly Lepton Era. Here the cauldron of creation is hot enough to produce electron pairs (electrons and positrons) that immediately annihilate each other. Other very light particles appear and disappear in the celestial din.

We pass from here into the Hadron Era, and yet another episode of warring matter and antimatter: the emergence and immediate disappearance of proton-antiprotron pairs. As we first contact this era, the universe is 1/10,000 of a second old. The temperature has risen to degrees measured only in the unimaginable realm of trillions (the American-French trillion, referred to here, is one followed by 12 zeros). The space occupied by a virus is denser than a million planets.

During this first chip of time, all the universe observable through the most powerful of today's telescopes—Europa, Alkaid, Andromeda and the farthest quasars—would fit inside the diameter of your thumbnail. And this, it now appears, was embedded in an expanse of space-time 100,000,000,000,000,000,000 times larger. Because of this, if two points are more than, say, 13 billion light years apart, the space between them is presently separating (expanding) so rapidly that a light beam starting out from one point will never reach the other. That is why we cannot and might never be able to observe anything of the universe beyond a distance of 13 billion light years.[*]

Looking beyond the Hadron Era, we fall through to the Quark Era. Ordinary particles such as protons cannot possibly exist here because all the universe observable today is crushed into a space *smaller* than a proton. The universe is at this point a *jiffy* old. A jiffy is the travel time of light across the diameter of a proton, that is, 10^{-23} or 1 billion-trillionths of a second. (Hence the phrase, "Be back in a

---

[*] The two points are not actually traveling faster than the speed of light. Rather, they are at rest in space that is expanding, and the rate of expansion between two objects increases as a function of the distance between them. This is why objects more than 13 billion light years from us can appear to be racing away from us faster than light, and why the whole universe beyond that distance is totally unobservable from Earth.

jiffy.") The jiffy temperature is 10^{22} degrees, and its density is one followed by 55 zeros times the density of water (by comparison, the density of a neutron star is smaller by 40 powers of 10). At this point, the tiniest fluctuations in space and time race clear across the universe.

What the universe is 10^{-43} of a second old—when its density is 10^{94} times that of water—we smash into a rather nasty thing called the Planck Barrier. It is the cosmologist's equivalent of the old map makers "Here Be Monsters." Beyond the Planck Barrier lies chaos and the inevitable breakdown of known physical laws. Princeton's John Wheeler can be credited (or blamed) for inventing the Planck Barrier; it translates literally into the other side of time. He visualized Planck space-time as being hopelessly knotted up in a turbulent foam. Temperature and density soar to the infinite, pulling the "here" and "now" and "then" apart until we can push back no farther. Time is no longer understandable in terms of orderly, sequential events. If you've ever wondered what life is like in a black hole, drop in at the Planck Barrier and look around.

All right, so it looks like the universe rose from infinitely curved, infinitely dense, and infinitely hot space-time.

And where did that come from?

Good question.

The most interesting guess (while highly speculative) is that it came from the recollapse of a previous, ordered phase—perhaps another universe. In support of this guess, and in reference to an early chapter of *Darwin's Universe,* Carl Sagan suggested that the Big Bang might be "merely the most recent cusp in an infinite series of cosmic expansions and contractions."

If this is true, could an infinite series of rebounding universes be connected, somewhere, like a snake head to tail? Could our present rebound, expansion, and eventual collapse be identical to one that has gone before it, and to another that will come after? Every molecule might ultimately wind up in the same place all over again. Untold billions of years ago, and untold billions of years from now, you might have sat in this same place—and you might sit in this same place—reading this same book.

Perhaps you remember—a ways back, in Chapter 1—I said it was only fair to tell you before you read on . . . Yea, didn't I warn you that this is a story with no ending?

Bibliography

Readers interested in further explanations of the topics covered in this book will find the following lists of publications helpful.

Thoughts for a Countdown
Carr, A., and P.J. Coleman, "Sea Floor Spreading Theory and the Odyssey of the Green Turtle," *Nature*, Vol. 249, page 128; 1974.
Morowitz, H. "Two Views of Life," *Science 83*, Vol. 4, page 21; January 1983.
NASA, *Planetary Science: A Lunar Perspective*. Lunar and Planetary Institute, Houston, Texas, 1982.
Sadler, P.M., "Is the Present Long Enough to Measure the Past," *Nature*, Vol. 302, page 752; April 28, 1983.

Down from Space
Burke, J., *Connections*. Little Brown and Company, 1978.
Irving, D., *The German Atomic Bomb*. Simon and Schuster, 1967.
Jastrow, R., "The New Soviet Arms Build Up in Space," *New York Times Magazine*, October 3, 1982.
Keyworth, G.A., "The Role of Science in a New Era of Competition," *Science*, Vol. 217, page 606; August 13, 1982.
Pellegrino, C.R. and J. Stoff, *Chariots for Apollo: the Making of the Lunar Module*. Atheneum, 1985.

Shrinking Horizons

Asimov, I., *Exploring Earth and Cosmos*. Crown, 1982.

Borges, J.L., *Labyrinths*. New Directions, New York, 1962.

Bronowski, J., *The Ascent of Man*. Little, Brown and Co., 1974.

Callahan, J.J., "The Curvature of Space in a Finite Universe," *Scientific American*, Vol. 235, page 90; August 1976.

Carson, R., *The Sea Around Us*. Signet, 1950.

Darwin, C., *The Descent of Man*. John Murray, London; first printing 1871.

Harrison, E.R., *Cosmology: the Science of the Universe*. Cambridge University Press, 1981.

Henahan, J., *The Ascent of Man: Sources and Interpretation*. Little, Brown and Co., 1974.

Rucker, R., *Infinity and the Mind*. Birkhauser, 1982.

Islands

Baker, V.R. and D. Nummedal, *The Channeled Scabland*. NASA (Washington), Planetary Geology Program, 1975.

Birchfield, G.E. and J. Wertman, "Topography, Albedo, Temperature Feedback and Climate Sensitivity," *Science*, Vol. 219, page 284; January 21, 1983.

Budyko, M.I., *The Earth's Climate: Past and Future*. Academic, 1982.

Canby, T.Y., "Search for the First Americans," *National Geographic*, Vol. 156, page 330; September 1979.

Doumas, C.G., *Thera: Pompeii of the Ancient Agean*. Thames and Hudson, 1983.

Druffel, E.M., "Banded Corals: Changes in Ocean Carbon-14 During the Little Ice Age," *Science*, Vol. 218, page 73; October 1, 1982.

Eddy, J.A., "How Constant is the Sun?" *National History*, Vol. 88, page 80, December 1979.

Eddy, J.A., "The Maunder Minimum," *Science*, June 18, 1976.

Eddy, J.A., R.L. Gilliland and D.V. Hoyt, "Changes in the Solar Constant and Climatic Effects," *Nature*, Vol. 300; December 1982.

Emiliani, C., "Ice Sheets and Ice Melts," *Natural History*, Vol. 89, page 82; November 1980.

Fued Wendorf, et. al., "An Ancient Harvest on the Nile," *Science 82*, Vol. 3, page 68; November 1982.

Gough, D., "A Bridge in a Gap in Solar Oscillations," *Nature*, Vol. 302, page 18; March 3, 1983.

Gould, S.J., *The Panda's Thumb* (chapter 19), W.W. Norton and Co., 1980.

Gregory, J., "Solar Terrestrial Influences on Weather and Climate,"

Nature, Vol. 299, page 401; September 30, 1982.

Hammond, N., "The Earliest Maya," *Scientific American*, Vol. 236, page 116; March 1977.

Hammond, N., "Unearthing the Oldest Known Maya," *National Geographic*, Vol. 162, page 126; July 1982.

Hammond, N., D. Pring, et al., "Radiocarbon Chronology for Early Maya Occupation at Cuello, Belize," *Nature*, Vol. 260, page 579; April 15, 1976.

Imbrie, J. and J.Z. Imbrie, "Holding the Climatic Response to Orbital Variations," *Science*, Vol. 207, page 943; February 29, 1980.

Isbell, W.H., "The Prehistoric Ground Drawings of Peru," *Scientific American*, Vol. 259, page 140; October, 1978.

Isbell, W.H. and K.J. Schreiber, "Was Huari a State?" *American Antiquity*, Vol. 43, page 372; 1978.

Kerr, R.A., "Sun, Weather and Climate: A Connection?" *Science*, Vol. 217, page 917; September 3, 1982.

Kerr, R.A., "Orbital Variation—Ice Age Link Strengthened," *Science*, Vol. 219, page 272; January 21, 1983.

Kukla, G. et al., "Orbital Signature of Interglacials," *Nature*, Vol. 290, page 295; March 26, 1981.

Lewen, R., "What killed the Giant Mammals," *Science*, Vol. 221, page 1036; September 9, 1983.

"Nazca Balloonists," *Time*, December 15, 1975, p. 50.

Pellegrino C.R. and J.A. Stoff, *Darwin's Universe: Origins and Crises in the History of Life* (Chapters 10, 11, 12). Van Nostrand Reinhold, 1983.

Philander, S.G.H., "El Nino Southern Oscillation Phenomena," *Nature*, Vol. 302, page 18; March 3, 1983.

Robock, A., "The Little Ice Age" *Science*, Vol. 206, page 1402; 1980.

Smith, P.E.L., "Stone-Age Man on the Nile," *Scientific American*, Vol. 235, page 30; August 1976.

Solheim, W.G., "Southeast Asia: New Light on a Forgotten Past," *National Geographic*, Vol. 218, page 73; October 1, 1982.

Stuiver, M. and P.D. Quay, "Changes in Atmospheric Carbon-14 Attributed to a Variable Sun," *Science*, Vol. 207, page 11; January 4, 1980.

Suetonius, G., *"The Twelve Caesars"* (originally published approximately A.D. 60) Fascimile edition translated by Robert Graves, Penguin Books, 1957.

Sullivan, W., "Rio Artifacts May Indicate Roman Visit," *New York Times*; October 10, 1982.

Thunell, R.C., "Cenozoic Paleotemperature Changes and Planktonic Foraminiferal Speciation," *Nature*, Vol. 289, page 670; February 19, 1981.

You're Looking Very Neanderthal Today

Eldredge, N., "Alternative Approaches to Evolutionary Theory," *Bulletin of the Carnegie Museum of Natural History*, Vol. 13, page 7; 1979.

Eldredge, N., and S.J. Gould, 1972. Punctuated Equilibria an Alternative to Phyletic Gradualism. (In) *Models in Paleobiology*, ed. T.J.M. Schopf, page 82; Freeman, Cooper and Co., 1972.

Gould, S.J., *Ontogeny and Phylogeny*, Belknap Press of Harvard University Press, 1977.

Gould, S.J., "Is a New and General Theory of Evolution Emerging?" *Paleobiology*, Vol. 6, page 119; 1980.

Gould, S.J., "Opus 100," *Natural History*, Vol. 92, page 10; April 1983.

Gould, S.J., and N. Eldredge, "Punctuated Equilibria: The Tempo and Mode of Evolution Reconsidered," *Paleobiology*, Vol. 3, page 115; 1977.

Haldane, J.B.S., "Can a Species Concept Be Justified?" (In) *The Species Concept in Paleontology*, ed. P.C. Sylvester-Bradley, page 95, Systematics Association, Publication no. 2, London 1956.

Howells, W.W., "Neanderthal Man: Facts and Figures" (In) *Paleoanthropology: Morphology and Paleoecology*, edited by Russell H. Tuttle. Mouton, 1975.

Howgate, M., "Cladistics Evolving Gradually," *Nature*, Vol. 302, page 108; March 10, 1983.

Hull, D.L., "Are Species Really Individuals?" *Systematic Zoology*, Vol. 25, page 174; 1976.

Lewin, R., "No Gap Here in the Fossil Record," *Science*, Vol. 214, page 645; November 6, 1981.

Lewin, R., "Molecules Come to Darwin's Aid," *Science*, Vol. 216, page 1091; June 4, 1982.

Lewin, R., "Molecular Drive: How Real, How Important?" *Science*, Vol. 218, page 552; November 5, 1982.

Malmgren, B.A., and J.P. Kennett, "Phyletic Gradualism in a Late Cenozoic Planktonic Foraminiferal Lineage," *Paleobiology*, Vol. 7, page 156, 1981.

Mayr, E., et al., "Punctuationism and Darwinism Reconciled?" *Nature*, Vol. 296, page 608; April 15, 1982.

Natural History (Special Hawaii Issue), Vol. 91; December 1982.

O'brien, S.J. and W.G. Nash, "Genetic Mapping in Mammals: Chromosome Map of Domestic Cat," *Science,* Vol. 216, page 257; April 16, 1982.

Pellegrino, C.R., "Fossils and Their Environments: a Tale of Pleistocene Crabs," *Earth Science,* Vol. 33, page 7; Winter 1979.

Pellegrino, C.R., "Morphologic Excursions in Canterbury Crabs (*Tumidocarcinus sp.,* New Zealand) During a Late Miocene

Episode of Climatic Cooling and Extinction," *Paleobiology* (reviewed by N. Eldredge: in preparation).

Raup, D.M. and R.E. Crick, "Kosmoceras: Evolutionary Jumps and Sedimentary Breaks," *Paleobiology,* Vol. 8, page 90; Spring 1982.

Rensberger, B., "The Emergence of *Homo Sapiens," Mosaic,* November 1980.

Rensberger, B., "A New Face for the Neanderthals," *Science 81,* Vol. 2, page 40; October 1981.

Rensberger, B., "Facing the Past," *Science 81,* Vol. 2, page 40; October 1981.

Rhodes, F.H.T., "Gradualism, Punctuated Equilibrium and the *Origin of Species," Nature,* Vol. 305, page 269; September 22, 1983.

Schopf, T.J.M., "Punctuated Equilibrium and Evolutionary Stasis," *Paleobiology,* Vol. 7, page 156; 1981.

Schopf, T.J.M. and A. Hoffman, "Punctuated Equilibrium and the Fossil Record," *Science,* Vol. 219, page 438; February 4, 1983.

Stanley, S.M., *Macroevolution.* W.H. Freeman and Co., 1979.

Stanley, S.M., *The New Evolutionary Timetable.* Basic Books Inc., New York, 1981.

Trinkaus, E. and W.W. Howells, "The Neanderthals," *Scientific American,* Vol. 241, page 118; December 1979.

Williamson, P.G., "Morphological Stasis and Developmental Constraint: Real Problems for Neo-Darwinism," *Nature,* Vol. 294, page 214; November 19, 1981.

Wolpoff, M.H., *Paleoanthropology.* Knopf, 1980.

The Naming of Names

Cherfas, J. and J. Cribbin, "Updating Man's Ancestry," *New York Times Magazine,* page 22; August 29, 1982.

Cracraft, J. and N. Eldredge, *Phylogenetic Analysis and Paleontology.* Columbia University Press, 1979.

Eldredge, N. and J. Cracraft, *Phylogenetic Patterns and the Evolutionary Process: Method and Theory in Comparative Biology.* Columbia University Press, 1980.

Eldredge, N. and I. Tattersall, *The Myths of Human Evolution.* Columbia University Press, 1982.

Fleischer, R.C. and R.F. Johnson, "Natural Selection on Body Size and Proportions in House Sparrows," *Nature,* Vol. 298, page 747; August 19, 1982.

Gould, S.J., *Ever Since Darwin,* (Chapter 5). W.W. Norton and Co., 1977.

Gould, S.J., Of Wasps and WASPS," *Natural History,* Vol. 91, page 8; December, 1982.

King, M.C. and A.C. Wilson, "Evolution at Two Levels in Humans and Chimpanzees," *Science,* Vol. 188, page 107; April 11, 1975.

Lewin, R., "Evolutionary History Written on Globin Genes," *Science,* Vol. 214, page 26; October 1981.

Mayr, E., *The Growth of Biological Thought.* Harvard University Press, 1982.

Mayr, E., "Biology Is Not Postage Stamp Collecting," *Science,* Vol. 216, page 718; May 14, 1982.

Petry, D., "The Pattern of Phyletic Speciation," *Paleobiology,* Vol. 8, page 56; Winter 1982.

Rukang, W. and L. Shenglong, "Peking Man," *Scientific American,* Vol. 248, page 86; June 1983.

On the Origin of the Fittest

Cronin, N.T., Boaz, et al., "Tempo and Mode in Human Evolution," *Nature,* Vol. 292, page 113.

Delson, E., "Paleoanthropology: Pliocene and Pleistocene Human Evolution," *Paleobiology,* Vol. 7, page 298; Summer 1981.

Gould, S.J., "Darwinism and the Expansion of Evolutionary Theory," *Science,* Vol. 216, page 380; April 23, 1982.

Levinton, J.S. and G.P. Rightmire, "Evolutionary Stasis in *Homo erectus,*" *Paleobiology,* Vol. 8, page 307; Summer 1982.

Rightmire, G.P., "Patterns in the Evolution of *Homo erectus,*" *Paleobiology,* Vol. 7, page 241; 1981.

Thorne, A.G. and M.H. Wolpoff, "Regional Continuity in Australasian Pleistocene Human Evolution," *American Journal of Physical Anthropology,* Vol. 55, page 337; 1981.

Wu, x-z., "A Well-Preserved Cranium of an Archaic Type of Early *Homo Sapiens* from Dali, China," *Scientia Sinica,* Vol. 24, page 530; 1981.

Habits from the Good Old, Old, Old Days

Coppens, Yves, F.C. Howell, G. Isaac, R. Leakey, *Earliest Man and Environments in the Lake Rudolf Basin: Stratigraphy, Paleocology and Evolution.* University of Chicago Press, 1976.

Falk, D., "Cerebral Cortices of East African Early Hominids," *Science,* Vol. 221, page 1072; September 9, 1983.

Herbert, W., "*Homo* Homeless: No Early Food Sharing," *Science News,* Vol. 122, page 390; December 18, 1982.

Isaac, G., "The Food-Sharing Behavior of Protohuman Hominids," *Scientific American,* Vol. 238, page 90; April 1978.

Isaac, G. and E.R. McCown (eds), *Human Origins; Louis Leakey and the Earliest East African Evidence.* W.A. Bengamin Inc., 1976.

Kyte, F.T., Z. Zhou and J.T. Wasson, "High Noble Metal Concentrations in a Late Pliocene Sediment," *Nature,* Vol. 292, page

417, July 30, 1981.

Lewin, R., "How Did Humans Evolve Big Brains?" *Science,* Vol. 840; May 21, 1982.

McNab, B.K., "Food Habits, Energetics and Population Biology of Mammals," *American Naturalist,* Vol. 116, page 106; 1980.

Martin, R.D., "Relative Brain Size and Basal Metabolic Rate," *Nature,* Vol. 293, page 57, 1981.

Susman, R.L. and J.T. Stern, "Functional Morphology of *Homo habilis,*" *Science,* Vol. 217, page 931; September 3, 1982.

Lucy in the Sand with Foot Notes

Benveniste, R.E. and G.J. Todaro, "Evolution of C-Type Viral Genes," *Nature,* Vol. 252, page 456; 1974.

Boaz, N.T., F.C. Howell and M.L. McCrossin, "Faunal Age of the Usno, Shungura B and Hadar Formations, Ethiopia," *Nature,* Vol. 300, page 633; December 16, 1982.

Brown, F.H., "Tulu Bor Tuffat Koobi Fora Correlated with the Sidi Hakoma Tuffat Hadar," *Nature,* Vol. 300, page 631; December 16, 1982.

Chilton, M.D., "A Vector for Introducing New Genes into Plants," *Scientific American,* Vol. 248, page 50; June 1983.

Dawkins, R., *The Selfish Gene.* Oxford University Press, 1976.

Fox, T.D., "Mitochondrial Genes in the Nucleus," *Nature,* Vol. 301, page 371; February 3, 1983.

Gould, S.J., "The Ultimate Parasite: What Happens to Bodies if Genes Act for Themselves," *Natural History.* Vol. 90, page 7, November 1981.

Gould, S.J., *Hen's Teeth and Horses Toes.* W.W. Norton, 1983.

Herbert, W., "Lucy; The Trouble with Dating an Older Woman," *Science News,* Vol. 123, page 5; January 1, 1983.

Herbert, W., "Lucy's Uncommon Forebear," *Science News,* Vol. 123, page 88; February 5, 1983.

Hollowang, R.L., "Cerebral Brain Endocast Pattern of *Australopithecus afarensis* Hominid," *Nature,* Vol. 303, page 420; June 2, 1983.

Johnason, D.C., et al, "A New Species of the genus *Australopithecus* (Primate: Hominidae) from the Pliocene of Eastern Africa," *Kirtlandia,* No. 28; 1978.

Johnason, D.C. and M. Edey, *Lucy: The Beginning of Humankind,* Simon and Schuster, 1981.

Johnason, D.C. and T.D. White, "A Systematic Assessment of Early African Hominids," *Science,* Vol. 203, page 321; January 29, 1979.

Johnason, D.C. and T.D. White, "On the Status of *Australopithecus* afarensis," *Science,* Vol. 207, page 1104; March 1980.

Keller, E.F., "McClintock's Maise," *Science 81,* Vol. 2, page 54; October 1981.

Leakey, M.D. and Hay, R.C., "Pliocene Footprints in the Laetoli Beds at Laetoli Northern Tanzania," *Nature*, Vol. 278, page 317; 1979.

Leakey, R., Interview, *OMNI,* Vol. 5. page 94; March 1983.

Ledoux, L., et al., "DNA Mediated Correction of Thiamineless *Arabidopsis thalina*," *Nature*, Vol. 249, page 17; 1974.

Lewin, R., "Do Jumping Genes Make Evolutionary Leaps?" *Science*, Vol. 213, page 634, August 7, 1981.

Lewin, R., "Were Lucy's Feet Made for Walking?" *Science,* Vol. 220, page 700; May 13, 1983.

McClintock, B., "The Control of Gene Action in Maise," *Brookhaven Symposia in Biology no. 18,* 1965.

Miller, J.A., "Giant Mice Grow from Rat Hormone Gene Transplant," *Science News,* Vol. 122, page 389; December 18, 1982 (*see also* December 16).

Nevers, P. and H. Saedler, "Transposable Genetic Elements as Agents of Gene Instability and Chromosomal Rearrangements," *Nature*, July 14, 1977.

Palmiter, R.D., et al.,: Dramatic Growth of Mice that Develop from Eggs Microinjected with Metallothionein-Growth Hormone Fusion Genes," *Nature*, Vol. 300, page 611; December 16, 1982.

Roberston, M., "Gene Families, Hopeful Monsters, and the Selfish Genetics of DNA," *Nature*, Vol. 293, page 333; October 1, 1981.

Stroun, M., et al., "Natural Release of Nucleic Acids from Bacteria into Plant Cells," *Nature,* Vol. 227, page 607; 1970.

Thomas, L., *The Lives of a Cell,* Viking Press, 1974.

A Geography Lesson

Attenborough, D., *Life on Earth*. William Collins Sons Co. Ltd., 1979.

Colbert, E.H., "Fossils and the Drifting Continents,"*Fossils,* Vol. 1, page 5; 1978.

Gould, S.J., "Free to be Extinct" *Natural History,* Vol. 91, page 12; August 1982.

Hsü, K.J., "When the Black Sea Was Drained," *Scientific American,* Vol. 238, page 53; May 1978.

Lambeck, K., "Where Has That Moon Been?" *Nature*, Vol. 703; August 19, 1982.

Marshal, L.G., et al., "Mammalian Evolution and the Great American Interchange," *Science*, Vol. 215, page 135; March 12, 1982.

Molnar, P. and P. Tapponnier, "The Collision Between India and Eurasia," *Scientific American,* Vol. 236, page 30; April 1977.

Motz, L., (ed.) *Rediscovery of the Earth*. Van Nostrand Reinhold, 1975.

Mudie, P.J. and J. Helgason, "Palynological Evidence for Miocene Climatic Cooling in Eastern Iceland About 9.8 Myr Ago," *Nature,* Vol. 303, page 689; June 1983.

Sclater, J.G. and C. Tapscott, "The History of the Atlantic," *Scientific American,* Vol. 240, page 156; June 1979.

The Face of Siva

Ferris, S.D., A.C. Wilson and W.M. Brown, "Evolutionary Tree for Apes and Humans Based on Cleavage Maps of Mitochondrial DNA," *Evolution,* April, 1981.

Ganapathy, R., "The Tunguska Explosion of 1908: Discovery of Meteoritic Debris Near the Explosion Site and at the South Pole, *Science,* Vol. 220, page 1158; June 10, 1983.

Pal, D.K., et al., Beryllium-10 in Australasian Tectites: Evidence for a Sedimentary Precursor," *Science,* Vol. 218, page 787; November 19, 1982.

Raeburn, P., "An Uncommon Chimp," *Science 83,* Vol 4, page 40; June 1983.

Raup, D.M., "Large Body Impacts and Terrestrial Evolution Meeting," *Paleobiology,* Vol. 8, page 1; Winter 1982.

Rubin, A.E., "Glass Menagerie," *Griffith Observer,* page 2; April 1979.

Shaw and Wasserburg, "A Detailed Study of the World's Tectites Using 5m-Nd and Rb-Sr Systematics," *Earth and Planetary Science Letters,* Vol. 60, no. 155; 1982.

Simons, E.L., "Ramapithecus," *Scientific American,* Vol 236, page 28; May 1977.

Smith, P.J., "The Origin of Tectites - Settled at Last?" *Nature,* Vol. 300, page 217; November 18, 1982.

Whitten, P., et al., "Our Forebears' Forebears," *The Sciences,* Vol. 20; February 1983.

Woodruff, F., S.M. Savin and R.G. Douglas, "Miocene Stable Isotope Record: A Detailed Deep Pacific Ocean Study and Its Paleoclimatic Implications," *Science,* Vol. 212; May 1981.

Vault of the Ages

Alvarez, W., et al., "Iridium Anomaly Approximately Synchronous with Terminal Eocene Extinctions," *Science,* Vol. 216, page 886; May 21, 1982.

Ganapathy, R., "Evidence for a Major Meteorite Impact on the Earth 34 Million Years Ago: Implications for Eocene Extinctions," *Science,* Vol. 216, page 885; May 21, 1982.

Larsson, S.G., "Baltic Amber: a Paleobiological Study," *Entomonograph,* Vol. 1, (Scandanavian Science Press Ltd., Klampenborg, Denmark); February 1, 1978.

Pellegrino, C.R., "Fossils in Amber," *Smithsonian,* IN PRESS.

Pellegrino, C.R., (IN) G.R. Case, *"A Pictorial Guide to Fossils"* (Chapter 16). Van Nostrand Reinhold, 1982.

Poinar, G.O., "Sealed in Amber," *Natural History*, Vol. 91, page 26; June 6, 1982.

Poinar, G.O. and R. Hess, "Ultrastructure of 40 Million Year Old Insect Tissue," *Science,* Vol., 215, page 1241; March 5, 1982.

Rice, P.C., *Amber: the Golden Gem of the Ages.* Van Nostrand Reinhold, 1980.

Dinosaur Daydreams

Alvarez, L., et al., "Extraterrestrial Cause for the Cretaceous-Terticery Extinction: Experiments and Theoretical Interpretation," *Science*, Vol. 208, page 1095; June 6, 1980.

Alvarez, L., et al., *Geological Implications of Impacts of Large Asteroids and Comets on the Earth.* Special Paper 190, Geological Society of America, Boulder, Colorado, 1983.

Archibald, J.D., "The Earliest Known Paleocene Mammal Fauna and Its Implications for the Cretaceous-Tertiary Transition," *Nature*, Vol, 291, page 650; June 25, 1981.

Bakker, R.T., "Ecology of the Brontosaurus," *Nature*, Vol, 229, page 172; January 15, 1971.

Bakker, R.T., "Dinosaur Renaissance," *Scientific American,* page 58; April 1975.

Bakker, R.T. and P.M. Galton, "Dinosaur Morphology and a New Class of Vertebrates," *Nature,* Vol. 248, page 168; 1974.

Benton, M.J., "Large Scale Replacements in the History of Life," *Nature,* Vol. 302, page 16; March 3, 1983.

Brain, C.K., *The Hunters or the Hunted? An Introduction to African Cave Taphonomy.* University of Chicago Press, 1981.

Clenens, W.A., J.D. Archibald, L.J. Hickey, "Out With a Whimper Not a Bang," *Paleobiology,* Vol. 7, page 293; Summer 1981.

Colbert, E.H., *Wandering Lands and Animals.* Hutchinson, London, 1974.

Coney, P., et al., "Cordilleran Suspect Terranes," *Nature,* November 1980.

Gilmore, J. and J. Knight, "Nonmarine Iridium Anomaly Linked to Extinctions," *Science,* Vol. 212, page 1376; June 19, 1981.

Gould S.J., *The Panda's Thumb.* (Chapter 25), W.W. Norton and Co., 1980.

Halstead, L.B., *The Evolution and Ecology of Dinosaurs.* Eurobook, London, 1975.

Herbert, W., "Fossil Raises Question About Earliest Primates," *Science News,* Vol. 121, page 372; June 5, 1982.

Hickey, L.J., "Land Plant Evidence Compatible with Gradual, Not Catastrophic, Change at the End of the Cretaceous," *Nature,* Vol. 292, page 529; August 6, 1981.

Higgins, A., "The Conodont Animal," *Nature,* Vol. 302, page 107; March 10, 1983.

Hopson, J.A., "Relative Brain Size and Behavior in Archosaurian Reptiles," *Annual Review of Ecology and Systematics,* Vol. 8, page 429; 1977.

Jones, D.L., et al., "The Growth of Western North America," *Scientific American,* Vol. 247, page 70; November 1982.

Kerr, R.A., "Impact Looks Real, the Catastrophe Smaller," *Science,* Vol. 214, page 896; November 20, 1981.

Kerr, R., "The Bits and Pieces of Plate Tectonics," *Science;* March 7, 1980.

Man, J., *The Day of the Dinosaur.* Galahad Books, 1978.

Mossman, D.J. and W.A.S. Sargeant, "The Footprints of Extinct Animals," *Scientific American,* Vol. 248, page 74; January 1983.

Orth, C.J., et al., "An Iridium Abundance Anomaly at the Palynological Cretaceous-Tertiary Boundary in Northern New Mexico," *Science,* Vol. 214; December 18, 1981.

Ostrom, J.H., "A New Look at Dinosaurs," *National Geographic,* Vol. 154, page 152; August 1978.

Ostrom, J., "Bird Flight: How Did it Begin?" *American Scientist,* Vol. 67, page 46; 1979.

Pellegrino, C.R., "The Fallen Sky," *Astronomy,* Vol. 9, page 66; April 1981.

Pellegrino, C.R. "Dinosaur Capsule," *OMNI* (IN PRESS).

Pellegrino, C.R., R.A. Muller, et al., exchange of letters on "Periodic Extinctions and Unseen Solar Companions," *Nature* and *OMNI* (IN PRESS).

Pollack, J.B., et al., "Environmental Effects of Impact-Generated Dust Cloud: Implications for the Cretaceous-Tertiary Extinctions, *Science,* Vol. 219, page 87; January 21, 1983.

Rogers, G.C., "Oceanic Plateau as Meteorite Impact Signatures," *Nature,* Vol. 299, page 341; September 23, 1982.

Smit, J. and G. Klaver, "Sandinine Spherules at the Cretaceous-Tertiary Boundary Indicate a Large Impact Event," *Nature,* Vol. 292, page 47; July 2, 1981.

West, S., "A Patchwork Earth," *Science 82,* Vol. 3, page 46; June 1982.

Woodburn, M.O. and W.J. Zinsmeister, "Fossil Land Mammal from Antarctica," *Science,* Vol. 218, page 284; October 15, 1982.

Time and Tide

Brosche, P. and J. Sundermann, *Tidal Friction and the Earth's Rotation II.* (Proceedings of a workshop, Bielefeld, Germany, Sept., 1981). Springer-Verlang, 1982.

Gould, S.J., *The Panda's Thumb.* (Chapter 31). W.W. Norton and Co., 1980.

Gould, S.J. and E.S. Urba, "Exaptation—A missing Term in the Science of Form," *Paleobiology*, Vol. 8, page 4; Winter 1982.

Kahn, P.G.K. and S.M. Pompea, "Nautiloid Growth Rhythms and Dynamical Evolution of the Earth-Moon System," *Nature*, Vol. 275, page 606; 1978.

Kemp, T.S., *Mammal-like Reptiles and the Origin of Mammals*. Academic Press, New York, 1982.

Pellegrino, C.R., "The Role of Desiccation Pressures and Surface Area/Volume Relationships on Seasonal Zonation and Size Distribution of Four Intertidal Decapod Crustacea from New Zealand: Implications for Adaptation to Land, *Crustaceanna;* Fall 1983.

Floor Show

Cloud, P. and M.F. Glaessner, "The Ediacarian Period and System: Metazoa Inherit the Earth," *Science*, Vol. 217, page 783; August 27, 1982

Conway, M. and H.B. Whittington, "The Animals of the Burgess Shale," *Scientific American*, Vol. 241, page 122; July 1979.

Hanson, E.D., *The Origin and Early Evolution of Animals*. Wesleyan University Press, 1977.

Sepkoski, J.J., et al., "Phanerazoic (500 Myr—Present) Marine Diversity and the Fossil Record," *Nature*, Vol. 293, page 435; October 8, 1981.

Williams, G.E., "Sunspot Periods in the Late Precambrian Glacial Climate and Solar-Planetary Relations," *Nature*, Vol. 291, page 624; June 25, 1981.

The Blood of Mars

Bogard, D.D. and P. Johnson, "Martian Gases in an Antarctic Meteorite?" *Science*, Vol. 221, page 651; August 12, 1983.

Calame, O. and J.D. Mulholland, "Lunar Crater Giordano Bruno: A.D. 1178 Impact Observations Consistent With Laser Ranging Results," *Science*, Vol. 199, page 875; February 24, 1978.

Carr, M.H., *The Surface of Mars*. (includes extensive bibliography) Yale University Press, 1981.

Eberhart, J., "Moonrock Yes, Marsrock Maybe," *Science News*, Vol. 123, page 196; March 26, 1983.

Kerr, R.A., "A Lunar Meteorite and Maybe Some from Mars," *Science*, Vol. 220, page 288; April 15, 1983.

Lunar and Planetary Science Conference Session 17 March 1983 (IN PRESS).

Morrison, D. (ed.) *Satellites of Jupiter*. University of Arizona Press, 1983.

Pepin, R.O., "Martian Meteorites: Signs in the Air," *Science News*, Vol. 123, page 223; April 2, 1983.

Pieri, D., "The Ancient Rivers of Mars," *The Planetary Report,* Vol. 3, page 4; February 1983.

Wilford, J.N., "Rock Appears to Be First Known Visitor from Mars," *The New York Times,* page c1; March 15, 1983.

Wright, I.P. and C.T. Pillinger, "When is a Meteorite Not a Meteorite?" *Nature,* Vol. 303, page 384; June 2, 1983.

The Ultimate Fox Hole

Arp, A.J. and J.J. Childress, "Sulfide Binding by the Blood of the Hydrothermal Vent Tube Worm *Riftia pachyptila,*" *Science,* Vol. 219, page 295; January 21, 1983.

Cairns-Smith, A.G., *Genetic Takeover and the Mineral Origins of Life.* Cambridge University Press, 1982.

Dickerson, R.E., "Chemical Evolution and the Origin of Life," *Scientific American,* Vol. 239, page 70; September 1978.

Eberhart, J., "Europa: A Moon of Ephemeral Oases?" *Science News,* Vol. 122, page 390; December 25, 1982.

Eigen, M., et al., "The Origin of Genetic Information," *Scientific American,* Vol. 244, page 88; April 1981.

Felbeck, H., "Chemoautorophic Potential of the Hydrothermal Vent Tube Worm, *Riftia pochyptila* Jones (Vestimentifera)," *Science,* Vol. 213, page 336; July 17, 1981.

Folsome, C.E., *The Origin of Life: A Warm Little Pond.* W.H. Freeman and Co., 1979.

Gehrels, T.(Ed.), *Asteroids.* University of Arizona Press, 1979.

Hiatt, B., "Sulfides Instead of Sunlight," *Mosaic,* page 15; August 1980.

Holger, W.J., and G.Q. Wirsen, "Chemosynthetic Primary Production at East Pacific Sea Floor Spreading Centers," *Bioscience,* Vol. 29, page 592; October 1979.

Kerridge, J.F. and J.D. MacDougall, "Clues to the Origin of Sulfide Minerals in C I Chondrites," *Earth and Planetary Science Letters,* Vol. 43, No. 3, page 359; June 1977.

Kuhn, H. and J. Waser, "Evolution of Early Mechanisms of Translation of Genetic Information into Polypeptides," *Nature,* Vol. 298; August 5, 1982.

Morrison, D., *Satellites of Jupiter.* University of Arizona Press, 1982.

Okihana, Hand C. Ponnamperuma, "A Protective Function of the Coacervates Against UV Light on the Primitive Earth," *Nature,* Vol. 299, page 347; September 23, 1982.

Pellegrino, C.R., "Extraterrestrial Life: New Hope in Our Own Solar System," *OMNI* (IN PRESS: August 1984).

Pellegrino, C.R. and J.A. Stoff, *Darwin's Universe: Origins and Crises in the History of Life.* (Chapter 8). Van Nostrand Reinhold Co., 1983.

Pellegrino, C.R. and J.A. Stoff, "The Lively Meteorites," *Astronomy,* Vol. 8, page 66; September 1980.

Pellegrino, C.R. and J.A. Stoff, "Organic Clues in Carbonaceous Meteorites,"*Sky and Telescope,* Vol. 57, page 330; April 1979.

Plescia, J.B. and J.M. Boyce, "Crater Numbers and Geological Histories of Iapetus, Enceladus, Tethys and Hyperian," *Nature,* Vol. 301, page 666; February 24, 1983.

Poirier, J.P., "Rheology of Ices: Key to the Tectonics of the Ice Moons of Jupiter and Saturn," *Nature,* Vol. 299, page 683; October 21, 1982.

Ponnamperuma, C., ed. *Cosmochemistry and the Origin of Life.* Reidel, 1983.

Powell, M.A. and G.N. Somero, "Blood Components Prevent Sulfide Poisioning of Respiration of the Hydrothermal Vent Tube Worm Riftia pachyptilia,"*Science,* Vol. 219, page 297, January 21, 1983.

Simon, C., "Life Under Pressure: Vent Microbes Grow at 250° C or More," *Science News,* Vol. 302, page 327; June 11, 1983.

Squyres, S.W. et al., "Liquid Water and Active Resurfacing on Europa," *Nature,* Vol. 301, page 225; January 30, 1983.

Stoff, J.A. and C.R. Pellegrino, *A Piece of the Sky.* (in preparation).

Van Valen, L., "Energy and Evolution," *Evolutionary Theory,* Vol. 1, page 179; 1976.

Voyager 2 Special Issue, *Science,* January 29, 1982.

Walsby, A.E., "Bacteria that Grow at 250° C," *Nature,* Vol. 303, page 381; June 2, 1983. (See also letter from J.A. Baros and J.W. Deming on page 423 in same issue.)

Genesis and Galactic Blight

Blitz, L. and S. Kulkarni, "The New Milky Way,"*Science,* Vol. 220, page 1233; June 17, 1983.

Brewer, R., *Contact With the Stars: The Search for Extraterrestrial Life.* W.H. Freeman, 1982.

Chen, A., "Signs of First Intergalactic Hydrogen Cloud Spotted," *Science News,* Vol. 123, page 148; March 5, 1983.

Cordell, B.M., "Venus," *Astronomy,* Vol. 10, page 6; September 1982.

Crick, F., *Life Itself.* Simon and Schuster, 1982.

Crick, F., Interview, *OMNI,* Vol. 4; March 1982.

Eldredge, N. and I. Tattersall, "Future People," *Science 83,* Vol. 4, page 74; March 1983.

Glassgold, A.E. et al., eds., *Symposium on the Orion Nebula to Honor Henry Draper.* New York Academy of Sciences, 1982.

Gorenstein, P. and W. Tucker, "Rich Clusters of Galaxies," *Scientific American,* Vol. 239, page 110; November 1978.

Hawkins, M.R.S., "Direct Evidence for a Massive Galactic Halo," *Nature,* Vol. 303, page 406; June 2, 1983.

Herbst, W. and G.E. Assovsa, "Supernovas and Star Formation," *Scientific American,* Vol. 241, page 138; August 1979.

Lynden-Bell, D. (ed), *The Big Bang, and Element Creation.* The Royal Society of London, 1982.

Margulis, L., *Symbiosis in Cell Evolution.* W.H. Freeman and Co., 1981.

McDonough, T.R., et al., "The Search for Extraterrestrial Intelligence (SETI)" *The Planetary Report* (Special Issue), Vol. B; April 1983.

Rubin, V.C., "Dark Matter in Spiral Galaxies," *Scientific American,* Vol. 248, page 86; June 1983.

Silk, J., "Did the Tail Wag the Cosmic Dog?" *Nature,* Vol. 303, page 200; May 19, 1983.

Silk, J., "From Dwarfs to Giants - Signposts of Galaxy Formation," *Nature,* Vol. 301, page 574; February 17, 1983.

"The Search for Extraterrestrial Intelligence," *The Planetary Report* (special issue), Vol. 3, March 1983.

Thomsen, D.E., "T - Tauri's Companion May Be a Protoplanet," *Science News,* Vol. 123, page 342, May 28, 1983.

Tinsley, B.M., (in) *Astrophysics Journal,* Vol. 198, page 145; 1975.

Trimble, V., "The Origin and Abundances of the Chemical Elements," *Review of Modern Physics,* Vol. 47, page 877; October 1977.

Trimble, V., "Mapping the Universe," *Nature,* Vol. 300, page 13; November 4, 1982.

Trimble, V., "Supernovae, Part I: The Events," *Review of Modern Physics,* Vol. 54, page 1183; October 1982.

Trimble, V., "Supernovae, Part II: The Remanents, Production of Cosmic Rays and Gamma Rays, Nucleosynthesis and Galactic Evolution," *Review of Modern Physics,* IN PRESS.

Deja Vu

Calder, N., *The Key to the Universe: A Report on the New Physics.* Penguin Books, 1977.

Davies, P., *Other Worlds.* Simon and Schuster, 1981.

Ferris, T., "Physics' Newest Frontier," *New York Times Magazine,* September 26, 1982.

Frautschi, S., "Entropy in an Expanding Universe," *Science,* Vol. 219, page 593; August 13, 1982.

Hawking, S. and G. Ellis, *The Large Scale Structure of Space-Time.* Cambridge University Press, 1979.

Kron, R.G., "The Most Distant Known Galaxies," *Science,* Vol. 216, page 265; April 16, 1982.

Mac Robert, A., "Beyond the Big Bang," *Sky and Telescope,* Vol. 65, page 211; March 1983.

Petrosian, V., "Place Transitions and Dynamics of the Universe," *Nature,* Vol. 298, page 805; August 26, 1982.

Silk, J., *The Big Bang.* W.H. Freeman and Co., 1980.

Trefil, J.S., *From Atoms to Quarks.* Charles Scribner's Sons, 1980.

Waldrop, M.M., "Bubbles Upon the River of Time," *Science,* Vol. 215, page 1082; February 26, 1982.

Waldrop, M.M., "The Large Scale Structure of the Universe," *Science,* Vol. 219, page 1050; March 4, 1983.

Waldrop, M.M., "Inflation and the Arrow of Time," *Science,* Vol. 219, page 1416; March 25, 1983.

Weinberg, S., *The First Three Minutes.* Bantam Books, 1979.

Zeldovich, B.J. Einasto and S.F. Shandarin, "Giant Voids in the Universe," *Nature,* Vol. 300, page 407; December 2, 1982.

Index

Index

About the Author

Charles R. Pellegrino is an astronomer/paleontologist and Fellow of the British Interplanetary Society. He writes internationally for science magazines and journals, including *JBIS, OMNI, Smithsonian, Astronomy, Nature* and *Crustaceana*, and he frequently contributes to NASA/JPL brainstorming sessions on exobiology and long-range planning. At Brookhaven National Laboratory, he coordinates design studies for the next 70 years in space, which include the industrialization of Mercury (a world that might turn out to be the most valuable piece of real estate in the Solar System) and hydrogen-antihydrogen annihilation propulsion. He has also contributed to Senate hearings on U.S.-Soviet cooperative ventures in space (rather than competitive ones) and is currently working toward this goal with Isaac Asimov, Brookhaven physicist Jim Powell, spacecraft designer Al Munier, Carl Sagan, Arthur C. Clarke, and Senator Spark Matsunaga.

In 1979, he and Jesse Stoff proposed their Fox Holes theory: the idea that the first steps in the direction of life were taken independently in short-lived streams inside the asteroids, and that advanced life forms might now be present in oceans concealed beneath the icy surfaces of certain Jovian, Saturnian, Uranian and Neptunian moons—even inside Pluto and Charon. The theory was, at first, rejected by scientific journals as "too speculative" and by popular magazines as "too complicated." Following Dick Hoagland's 1980 report on their work in the magazine *Star and Sky*, their "crazy" idea began to gain serious attention. Arthur C. Clarke made it the cornerstore of *2010* and *20001*, and a number of astronomers (notably Robert Jastrow, Director of NASA's Goddard Institute for Space Studies and Clair E. Folsome, of University of Hawaii's Exobiology Labs) have listed Pellegrino and Stoff's publications on the subject as required reading for their students.

OTHER POPULAR TAB BOOKS OF INTEREST

TAB TAB BOOKS Inc.

Blue Ridge Summit. Pa. 17214

Send for FREE TAB Catalog describing over 750 current titles in print.

Clinical Risk Management
in Primary Care

Edited by

Keith H

Director, MPS
Leeds

and

Mal

Associ
Newc
Found
Effect
Morpeth, No

Forewor

Sir Lian

Chief Medic
England

Radcliffe
Oxford •

£35.33

Radcliffe Publishing Ltd
18 Marcham Road
Abingdon
Oxon OX14 1AA
United Kingdom

www.radcliffe-oxford.com
Electronic catalogue and worldwide online ordering facility.

_____

British Library Cataloguing in Publication Data

A catalogue record for this book is available from the British Library.

ISBN 1 85775 869 2

Typeset by Anne Joshua & Associates, Oxford
Printed and bound by TJ International Ltd, Padstow, Cornwall